Religion and Transformation
in Contemporary European Society

Studying Jihadism

Band 14

Herausgegeben von Kurt Appel, Christian Danz,
Jakob Helmut Deibl, Rüdiger Lohlker, Richard Potz
und Sieglinde Rosenberger

Die Bände dieser Reihe sind peer-reviewed.

Rüdiger Lohlker (ed.)

World Wide Warriors

How Jihadis Operate Online

With 61 figures

V&R unipress

Vienna University Press

Bibliografische Information der Deutschen Nationalbibliothek
Die Deutsche Nationalbibliothek verzeichnet diese Publikation in der Deutschen
Nationalbibliografie; detaillierte bibliografische Daten sind im Internet über
http://dnb.d-nb.de abrufbar.

**Veröffentlichungen der Vienna University Press
erscheinen im Verlag V& R unipress GmbH.**

© 2019, V& R unipress GmbH, Robert-Bosch-Breite 6, D-37079 Göttingen
Alle Rechte vorbehalten. Das Werk und seine Teile sind urheberrechtlich geschützt.
Jede Verwertung in anderen als den gesetzlich zugelassenen Fällen bedarf der vorherigen
schriftlichen Einwilligung des Verlages.

Umschlagabbildung: RaT-Logo (Gerfried Kabas, Wien).
Redaktion: Marlene Deibl
Druck und Bindung: CPI books GmbH, Birkstraße 10, D-25917 Leck
Printed in the EU.

Vandenhoeck & Ruprecht Verlage | www.vandenhoeck-ruprecht-verlage.com

ISSN 2198-5235
ISBN 978-3-8471-0938-9

Inhalt

Rüdiger Lohlker
Introduction: Confusion meets Confusion 7

Rüdiger Lohlker
Collective Organizers: Lone Wolves, Remote Control, and Virtual
Guidance 9

Ali Fisher
Interrogating the electronic ribat: Data Science in the study of the
Jihadist movement 43

Ali Fisher / Nico Prucha
A Milestone for "Islamic State" Propaganda: "The Clanging of the
Swords, part 4" 71

Clemens Holzgruber
"Now You See Me – Now You Don't": Analysing Jihadists' Online
Privacy-Enhancing and Counter-Surveillance Strategies 157

Contributors 193

Index 195

Rüdiger Lohlker

Introduction: Confusion meets Confusion

As confusing as the role of religion in jihadism[1] seems to be for those not familiar with Arab culture and Islam, almost as confusing is the role of the Internet in invigorating jihadism for many researchers. The chapters of this book will try to reduce the level of confusion, based on an understanding of theology and history of Islam and based on insights from Data Science, thereby going beyond the state of play of much Western conventional research on jihadism.

In 1991 in the aftermath of the first war of the USA (and allies) against Iraq an referring to the American Civil War Manuel De Landa stated:

> "The development of the metallic cartridge and breech-loading firearms caused a revolution in tactics that took military commanders over a hundred years to digest."[2]

Things did not change, another technology is applied today. As in former times the impact of these new technologies is still not understood.

We are living in a period of military innovations in which terrorists have weaponized the Internet[3] and Jihadi technicians demostrate their ability to adopt to new technological developments The chapters of this volume seek to bring together developments in social media, the innovations of jihadists with developments in the strategic thinking of jihadists, based mainly on evidence based research into Arabic language sources and documents from the jihadists themselves.

This volume seeks to remedy a deficiency of much Western research on jihadist terrorism, namely its disregard for religion and the Internet. We will leave aside that the surprising fact that terrorism research at least at 9/11 tends to ignore the role of thea coherent theology and religion underlying jihadism. The

---

1 Jihadism means a transnational movement with a specific Islamic theology and the use of violence as the main distinction from other contemporary Islamic movements.
2 Manuel De Landa, *War in the Age of Intelligent Machines*, New York: Swerve Editions 1991, p. 29.
3 See the remarks on the consumerization of warfare in the chapter by Lohlker.

authors rely mainly on evidence produced by the jihadis themselves, not ignoring it as much of conventional research does.⁴

Rüdiger Lohlker describes the technical aspects of recent jihadist dissemimation of operational ressources. The chapter includes further remarks on jihadists online strategies.

Ali Fisher criticizes the technical deficienties of current research on jihadism, not understanding the real operations of jihadists online.

Ali Fisher and Nico Prucha present a case study on the dissemination of jihadist videos online.

Clemens Holzgruber analyzes the jihadist discussion on secure communication online giving insides into the tools used by jihadists.

All the chapters introduce ressources that are ignored in conventional research because they are in Arabic and religiously contextualized. This makes it necessary to do a close reading of the sources to enable the research community to leave the mainstream discourses. Stressing a coherent theology of jihadism does not mean jihadism is understood by referring to Islam, the Qur'an etc. We subscribe to the idea recently written down by Ould Mohamedou:

> "In time the problem emerged thus: to understand Western terrorists of the 1970s such as the German Red Army Faction or the Italian Red Brigades, one is invited to examine the societal condition of post-war Germany Italy, the ambient malaise in these countries 25 years after Nazism and fascism, and their relationship with their rebellious youth; to make sense of al-Qaeda or IS, one is asked to read the Qur'an."⁵

The present volume tries to give insights that may remedy this approach turning to the practice of jihadists, not focussing on the speculations about what they think and what is Islam or not.⁶

We have to thank our reviewer for helping us to clarify some ideas in this volume.

---

4 By way of exception, in the case of the attackers of the WTC in 2001, the role of the "Spiritual Manual" and its religious content has been recognised (Hans G. Kippenberg/Tilmann Seidensticker (eds.), *The 9/11 Handbook*, London/Oakville, CT: Equinox 2006).
5 Mohammad-Mahmoud Ould Mohamedou, *A Theory of ISIS: Political Violence and the Transformation of the Global Order*, London: Pluto Press 2018, pp. 8–9.
6 Shahab Ahmed, *What is Islam? The Importance of Being Islamic*, Princeton/Oxford: Princeton University Press 2016.

Rüdiger Lohlker

Collective Organizers: Lone Wolves, Remote Control, and Virtual Guidance

Intro

Terrorism 'research' is dominated by media-induced vocabulary, which tries to demonize and hype the imminent threat of terrorist violence: lone wolves or remote control terrorism are two of the most prominent phenomena.[1] What is neglected, however, is an attempt to understand what is happening on the ground in jihadist practice.[2]

The chapter is organized in a rhizomatic way mirroring the swarm-like movement of jihadi online communication (see below); the chapter is not following a linear story line. It is based on a careful selection of jihadi online communication during the last years and uses Arabic language sources to close the gap of knowledge that is evident in current mainstream research on jihadism. Since the knowledge of Arabic sources in this research is negligable we feel forced to offer as much information as possible. Any attempt of synthesis would be premature and stand in the way of a thorough understanding of jihadi communition.

Discussing jihadi swarms means analyzing collective processes of self-organization evolving intentionally but also non-intentionally.

Collective Organization

Talking about collective organizers in the context of Jihadism studies is somewhat unusual. A brief remark on the concept of the collective organizer by someone who would nowadays be called an 'expert' may be helpful in order to

---

[1] For an overview on the literature on jihadi lone wolf terrorism see Sarah Teich, *Trends and Developments in Lone Wolf Terrorism in the Western World: An Analysis of Terrorist Attacks and Attempted Attacks by Islamic Extremists* (http://www.ctcitraining.org/docs/LoneWolf_SarahTeich2013.pdf) (accessed March 4, 2018).
[2] The ideas presented were inspired by discussions during Jakarta Geopolitical Forum 2017. I have to thank Ferdinand Haberl for reading a pre-final version of this chapter.

gain a better understanding of the phenomena we are talking about. Vladimir Ilyich Lenin, quoting himself in his seminal treatise titled *What is to be done?*, says:

> "A newspaper is not only a collective propagandist and a collective agitator, it is also a collective organizer. In this respect it may be compared to the scaffolding erected round a building under construction; it marks the contours of the structure and facilitates communication between the builders, permitting them to distribute the work and to view the common results achieved by their organised labour."[3]

Understanding the media as an organizing force of an underground organization is a crucial part of the argument lied out in this article. However, we will not argue that there is a fixed structure, "a scaffolding", within Jihadi online structures, but rather that there is a collective aspect to Jihadi online communication. Not Bolshevik-style organized collective, but a collective organizing itself as a swarm. Ali Fisher has used the word of 'swarmcast' in this context[4] but a longer quotation may be useful in order to clarify this concept:

> "In the Swarmcast model there is no longer a clear division between the audience and a content producer in control of the means through which to broadcast content to that audience. Instead, once content is produced and released, it is often the distributing network of media mujahideen, rather than the original producer, that ensures continuing content availability. This type of activity can be understood with the help of the concept of netwar; defined as 'lower-intensity conflict at the societal end of the spectrum' in which 'a combatant is organised along networked lines or employs networks for operational control and other communications' [...] in their most extreme incarnations, beyond that which Ronfeldt and Arquilla envisioned, the media mujahideen, and other dispersed networks, cease to depend on centralised direction, and instead adopt genuine swarming behaviours as observed in nature. This extends the understanding of netwar and requires netwar to include the importance of emergent behaviour and collective action in complex systems. [...]
> The recognition and approval of the media mujahideen, the decision to engage via social media and the increasing violence in Syria provided an opportunity for jihadist groups such as ISIS and JaN to evolve their online strategies which became increasingly aligned with the concepts of netwar. In doing so both ISIS and JaN have enabled them to disseminate content through an interconnected network that is constantly reconfiguring, akin to the way a swarm of bees or flock of birds constantly reorganises in flight. It marks a shift from the hierarchical and broadcast models of communication during conflict to a new dispersed and resilient form which embraces the strength of emergent behaviour; the user curated 'Swarmcast'. [...] Resilience against takedowns and account suspensions has become an important element of the Jihadist Swarmcast. This resilience has emerged over the last two years as jihadist groups have moved from

---

3 Vladimir I. Lenin, *What is to be done? Burning Questions of our Movement*, New York: International Publishers 1969, p. 105.
4 See his chapter on data science in this volume and the chapter of Nico Prucha and Ali Fisher.

broadcasting content via a few 'official' accounts to a dispersed network of media mujahideen who have been able to ensure that jihadist content maintains a persistent online presence. [...] this dispersed form of network structure is attuned to the information age, in which a mode of conflict based on netwar is largely about 'who knows what, when, where, and why, and about how secure a society, military, or other actor is regarding its knowledge of itself and its adversaries.' The structures imagined by Arquilla and Ronfeldt in their vision of netwar are sufficiently interconnected to reconfigure after disruption, as a flock of birds reconfigures after avoiding a predator. In other words, loss of a few important nodes cannot inhibit overall operational ability to maintain a persistent presence."[5]

The Swarmcast has been reconfigured by the emergence of *Telegram* as the main jihadi communication platform, which has been largely ignored by mainstream jihadism research, remaining clueless as to how this platform may work. We must to stress – again and again – that there is no disrupt between the communicative and the operative aspect of jihadism, which has long been known to be an important factor of jihad doctrines. Real life and virtual life go together well – including what has been aptly called 'consumerization of warfare.'[6] Indeed, there is a coherent worldview with a coherent mind-set and a consensus on the basic military concepts. As Norman Cigar wrote several years ago in his seminal book on *Al-Qa'ida's Doctrine for Insurgency*[7]:

> "In many ways, Al-Muqrin's *Guerilla War* reflects a general consensus on doctrine present within the QAP[8] leadership, arguably the product of shared experiences and discussions over the years, which he codified. [...] Al-Muqrin had apparently long pondered the issues involved in the text and had already taught the 'Practical Course' in Afghanistan. The QAP's teaching of basic military and political concepts reflects the dissemination of a collective outlook and extreme commitment to transcendental goals, which created an atmosphere where ideas ceased to be proprietary and became part of the movement's accepted canon of operative art."

Again, we may notice the collective aspect of jihadi thought, even at a relative stage of recent jihadi history. The entanglement of technical experience-based operational art combined with 'military and political concepts' and the 'com-

---

5 Ali Fisher, Swarmcast: How Jihadist Networks Maintain a Persistent Online Presence, in *Perspectives on Terrorism* 9iii (2015) (http://www.terrorismanalysts.com/pt/index.php/pot/article/view/426/html) (accessed January 8, 2018). For references see this article. Further remarks on the lack of robust data analysis in http://uscpublicdiplomacy.org/blog/interpreting-data-about-isis-online?platform=hootsuite (accessed January 8, 2018).
6 Andrea Zapparoli Manzoni/Paolo Passeri, Consumerization of Warfare, in *Hackmageddon* June 16, 2011 (http://www.hackmageddon.com/2011/06/16/consumerization-of-warfare/) (accessed January 14, 2018).
7 Norman Cigar, *Al-Qa'ida' Doctrine for Insurgency: 'Abd al-'Aziz al-Muqrin's A Practical Guide for Guerilla Warfare,* Dulles, Va: Potomac Books 2009, p. 12.
8 Al-Qa'ida on the Arab Peninsula (RL).

mitment to transcendental goals' (read: a coherent theological worldview as a basic structure of Jihadi activities) has been lost in the turmoil of short-sighted and short-termed reactions to jihadi operations. Jihadism research has indeed lost its momentum due to its loss of understanding.

It is a truism that research on jihadism is still far away from holistically understanding the phenomenon it claims to research.[9] Even worse, once the Internet enters the debate "online illiterates" join the community of researchers and claim to be competent critics.

Marc Sageman's insights with respect to the most recent developments may be characterized as 'leaderless Jihad',[10] whilst they have never been systematically integrated into reflections on terrorist phenomena.[11] The following pages are to outline a new approach towards an understanding of the combined operational jihadi efforts aimed at adapting to ever-changing circumstances. This approach is based on first-hand knowledge of Arabic language sources, which are the main linguistic resource of jihadi communication. What Malcolm W. Nance wrote several years ago still holds true: "The field of terrorism [...] is a specialized subject that requires serious study, and requires that those in the front line of defense be as knowledgeable as possible."[12] In this regard, jihadi operations – especially online but also offline – still need 'serious study'.

One of the most significant phenomena still in need to be seriously studied is the ability of jihadists to create new technical applications to be used at an operational level.

Turning Offline

Recent research has convincingly demonstrated the fashion in which ISIS blue-collar technicians[13] have been developing their manufacturing process. A good example may be Khalid Sheikh Mohammed who "received a degree in me-

---

9 For the case of lone wolf-jihadism see Raffaello Pantucci, *A Typology of Lone Wolves: Preliminary Analysis of Lone Islamist Terrorists* (https://s3.amazonaws.com/academia.edu.documents/24801864/1302002992icsrpaper_atypologyoflonewolves_pantucci.pdf?AWSAccessKeyId=AKIAIWOWYYGZ2Y53UL3A&Expires=1520163311&Signature=y8UNcwCk85FLxkIy9NwG%2BXWvTs4%3D&response-content-disposition=inline%3B%20filename%3DA_typology_of_lone_wolves_preliminary_an.pdf) (accessed March 4, 2018).
10 Marc Sageman, *Leaderless Jihad: Terror Networks in the Twenty-First Century*, Philadelphia, PA: University of Pennsylvania Press 2011.
11 The first instalment of 'leaderless terrorism' or 'lone wolves' grew out of the white supremacist movement in the US, namely by Tom Metzger and Alex Curtis in the 1990s.
12 Malcolm W. Nance, *Terrorist Recognition Handbook: A Practioner's Manual for Predicting and Identifying Terrorist Activities*, Boca Raton et al.: CRC Press 2014³, p. 1.
13 It's not only media mujahideen and fighters that should be looked at.

chanical engineering from North Carolina A&T State University, the Associated Press reported, he received permission to build a vacuum cleaner from scratch. Mindless hobbyism, according to his CIA holders, or the mark of a maker. The schematics had been downloaded from the Internet."[14]

IS cadres did something similar. When they were running out of supplies

> "they did something that no terrorist group has ever done before and that they continue to do today: design their own munitions and mass-produce them using advanced manufacturing techniques. Iraq's oil fields provided the industrial base – tool-and-die sets, high-end saws, injection-molding machines – and skilled workers who knew how to quickly fashion intricate parts to spec. Raw materials came from cannibalizing steel pipe and melting down scrap. ISIS engineers forged new fuzes, new rockets and launchers, and new bomblets to be dropped by drones, all assembled using instruction plans drawn up by ISIS officials."[15]

The next step may be the utilization of 3-D printers in order to produce the resources they need, using information readily available on the Internet. Even if this technology may be used up to now only for providing supply parts for weapons it is an innovation that may be important for jihadi operations in the future. Here we can see another aspect of merging real and virtual life. In fact, this is already happening right now – not using 3-D printer devices – but distributing jihadi knowledge online. For the moment, let's leave aside other supply chains from Eastern European Countries, China, the USA, Russia, Saudi Arabia, Libya, Sudan, etc. – ranging from battlefield captures to diverted materiel – adding to IS-produced ammunition (see above). Let us focus instead on IS widely using IEDs: "IS forces have manufactured and deployed improvised explosive devices (IEDs) across the battlefield on a quasi-industrial scale."[16] Yet again, we can see the IS blue-collar technicians at work.

The knowledge these technicians can easily be detected by following jihadi Arab-language communication.

---

14 Brian Castner, Exclusive: Tracing ISIS' Weapons Supply Chain – Back to the US, in *Wired* (https://www.wired.com/story/terror-industrial-complex-isis-munitions-supply-chain/) (accessed January 6, 2018).
15 Ibid.
16 Conflict Armament Research, *Tracing the Supply of Components Used in Islamic States IEDs. Evidence form a 20-months Investigation in Iraq and Syria*, London: Conflict Armament Research 2016, p. 7.

Turning Online Again

Since January 2016 a large amount of resources has been disseminated online under the title 'lone wolves' or *'al-dhi'āb al-munfarida'* – the Arab equivalent for lone wolves.[17] Contrary to the common perception of terrorism research the main target is not 'the West'; other targets are in fact also mentioned in a programmatic series posts in a *telegram* channel called *wilāyat sainā'* (province of Sinai), a channel which at is part of the milieu of IS-related channels on this platform.[18] The post reads (just an except):

> "Stand up! Take up any weapon and massacre the infidels and don't spare anyone [...] O lone wolves, know that this world is ephemeral and will not exist forever [...] The lone wolves are the secret weapon of the [Islamic] State. They are the unit of revenge for god, the prophet, and the believers [...] By god, by god! O you rejectionists (*rawāfid*)[19], you hypocritical Arabs (*munāfiqīn*)[20], you will not live in peace [...] You will not be able to forget that there are lone wolves who will take revenge for their brothers on the battlefield [...] You heretic (*murtadda*) organizations, you may have cut off the way of migration (*hijra*) [to the Islamic State], but you won't be able to cut off the trail of the wolves."[21]

The *telegram* channels related to IS,[22] bearing the name of "lone wolves" etc., which were used for dissemination of ideas are to some extent inactive by now.[23] The files are still available through other groups and channels on that platform regardless – demonstrating the resilience of jihadi online operations, the swarm-like movement of the jihadi online sphere.

Al-Qa'ida followed the example of IS in using *telegram* channels for the dissemination of ideas on effective military operations.[24] Since some examples of

---

17 'Lone wolves' are described as a very innovative, but often misunderstood as loners although being integrated in a virtual or real network (Marcel Serr, Einsam, innovativ & brandgefährlich. 'Lone wolf'-Terrorismus: Einführung und aktuelle Entwicklungen, in *Österreichische Militärische Zeitschrift*, 1 (2018), pp. 71–75). We are in need of an integrated concept to avoid chasing after any new operation of jihadis.
18 We are not talking about 'official' channels, a ridiculous attempt to create a state-like enemy. If we understand ISIS – and al-Qaeda – as swarm-like entities the desperate search for structures that can be identified with European-US structures is such endeavours are helpless and inefficient.
19 A derogatory term for Shiites.
20 A derogatory term going back to the early times of the Islamic community.
21 *telegram* September 22, 2016 (channel *wilāyat sainā'*).
22 Since the use of ISIS seems to be the result of ignoring the changing configuration of the *Islamic State* we stick to IS as the official designation of this entity. For the important link of (proto-)state building jihadi style and black markets see Aisha Ahmad, *Jihad & Co.: Black Markets and Islamist Power*, Oxford et al.: Oxford University Press 2017.
23 The time of writing is September 2017.
24 This study is based on material collected online and archived by the author.

the cross-over use of resources by several armed groups will be given, we shall only occasionally mention the specific Jihadi organization or group disseminating the resources.[25]

There have been earlier attempts to build an online structure supporting jihadi operations. A study on online courses in al-Qa'ida related jihadi fora concludes[26] in 2013:

> "Jihadi e-learning courses are a marginal phenomenon, yet they should not be ignored. While there are still very few active participants in such courses, they attract large interest among online jihadists. The quality of the courses has improved over the last few years, and there are dedicated people online who are interested in developing them further. As training in jihadi conflict areas has become difficult, more recruits are likely to try and obtain paramilitary skills before going abroad – or before attempting to carry out a terrorist attack at home. Some of these would-be jihadists might consider joining regular armed forces or private shooting clubs in their home country. A far less risky venture is to seek out jihadi training courses online because they allow the participants to remain anonymous while conducting their training."[27]

The turn towards the "individual jihad" in the form of lone wolf terrorism becoming famous in recent times is not new:

> "Due to the extreme pressure on Al-Qaeda's current sanctuaries abroad, Al-Qaeda leaders seem to be expanding their strategy to include so-called 'leaderless jihad.' The concept is not new. The jihadi strategist Abu Mus'ab al-Suri wrote and lectured on the idea back in the 1990s, and held several lecture series to trainees in jihadi training camps. The strategic concept developed by al- Suri became known as al-muqawama al-islamiyya al-'alamiyya, 'The Global Islamic Resistance.' He praised 'lone wolf' terrorist attacks that were conducted by individuals that had no connection to Al-Qaeda Central, but who nevertheless carried out attacks supporting Al-Qaeda's global ideology.[28] Individuals praised by al-Suri included El Sayyid Nusayr, an Egyptian- American who shot and killed the American-Israeli politician Meir Kahane in New York in 1990, and Ramzi Yusef, who carried out the first bombing of the World Trade Center in 1993."[29]

Generally speaking, lone wolf-terrorism is not merely a jihadi phenomenon and it can be found with respect to other terrorist groups too. White supremacists

---

25 One of the view media articles mentioning the telegram level of communication (although only using English-language sources) is Mary Ann Russon/Jason Murdock, "Welcome to the bizarre and frightening world of Islamic State channels on Telegram", in *IB Time UK*, posted June 2, 2016 (https://www.ibtimes.co.uk/welcome-bizarre-frightening-world-islamic-state-channels-telegram-1561186) (accessed March 18, 2018).
26 Conclusions are to be modified for the present situation, esp., since it is no more "due to the pressure" but to a continuing process of innovation and adaptation that online activities are promoted by jihadis.
27 Anne Stenersen, "'Bomb-Making for Beginners': Inside al Al-Qaeda E-Learning Course", in *Perspectives on Terrorism* VIIi (February 2013), pp. 25–37, p. 35.
28 We would use the term theology instead of ideology in this context (see theology matters).
29 Ibid., p. 26.

like Tom Metzger and Alex Curtis in the US have actually coined this term in the 1990s. Recent right-wing lone wolves are to be understood as based on certain independence with regards to their planning and operational processes. However, they are nevertheless part of a swarm connected through the mutual acceptance of a certain ideology or varieties of an ideology, facilitated via the media – especially the Internet –[30] and face-to-face connections.[31] The structure of a swarm is to be detected among jihadi lone wolves whose 'loneliness' is a tactical means.

What apparently *is* new in the present situation, is the fact that lone wolf-resources are put online without attempting to organize online courses for tasked like bomb-making, as discussed by Stenersen. Courses are put online to allow for the acquisition of practical knowledge by letting the user study on their own and then joining the swarm and its operations. This is due to the fact that the relatively controlled environment of jihadi fora has changed to a more open environment on platforms like *telegram*.[32]

Former attempts of disseminating knowledge on terrorist operations – as they are well known from the online magazine *Inspire* (and others) – have been restricted in their scope. The special issue on the package bomb, which brought down a UPS cargo plane in 2010, included a detailed technical description of the bombs used (*Inspire* No. 3 – Special Issue)[33], handling of pistols, remote control explosion, legitimizing of jihadi based on "Targeting the populations of countries that are at war with the Muslims" (all *Inspire* No.8), the praise of the "knights of lone jihad", torching parked vehicles, causing road accidents, creating lethal poison as a means of "open source jihad" (all *Inspire* No.10), or the praise of the Boston bombings (*Inspire* No.11) (see below), all indicate an awareness of the strategic importance of individual jihadist operations for the jihadi subcultures (see below).[34]

But there are also weapons that are as dangerous as the individual jihad, i.e. chemical and biological weapons. Here we must take the emergence of a new

---

30 Anders Breivik is the prime example of a right-wing milieu although the striking difference is the media framing trying to deny the influence of the right-wing extremist online milieu on his attacks (see the very instructive contributions in Rainer Just/Gabriel Ramin Schor (Hg.), Vorboten der Barbarei: Zum Massaker von Utoya, Hamburg: Laika-Verlag 2011).
31 Cf. Armin Pfahl-Traughber, "Das 'Lone-Wolf'"-Phänomen im Rechtsterrorismus in Skandinavien: Eine vergleichende Betrachtung von Fallbeispielen aus Norwegen und Schweden, in *Interventionen* 8 (December 2016), pp. 4–17: 16.
32 We are aware that invite links may be regarded as a restriction of access. But empirical evidence from our onging research shows that this actually no fundamental problem to get these files.
33 All Jihadi material quoted is archived at the Oriental Institute, University of Vienna, Austria.
34 This holds true for other contexts see Warren Hinckle, Guerilla-Krieg in USA, Stuttgart: Deutsche Verlagsanstalt 1971 for the readings of US-underground fighters.

group of blue-collar jihadi technicians (see below) into account we mentioned before. The overall assessment of the possible use of chemical and biological weapons by jihadists made in 2007 by Stenersen still holds true to some extent:

> "Online CBW manuals and discussions indicate that jihadists display a particular interest in easily obtainable chemical agents, such as cyanide, rather than sophisticated agents that require considerable skill and resources to produce and deploy. Participants in online discussions also tend to draw ideas and inspiration from past CBW plots. While this is not surprising, it is notable that on jihadist websites, news articles of plots to use crude chemical agents are posted along with simple, do-it-yourself recipes of the same agents. The online manuals and discussion forums raise the possibility that the most imminent chemical-biological threat now comes from Al-Qaeda-inspired enthusiasts, especially those with relevant academic or professional backgrounds, rather than professional jihadist planners. That the online manuals seem too vague to result in a successful attack does not preclude the possibility that more sophisticated weapons are being developed offline."[35]

Looking at the technical capabilities of jihadi engineers, which has emerged in the last years in other fields (see below) "the possibility that more sophisticated weapons are being developed offline" is to be taken for granted.

A historical remark has to be made in order to stress the present state of play in jihadism research. The strategy of isolated fighters using sabotage in guerrilla warfare has already been mentioned by Alberto Bayo Garoud (d. 1967), the teacher of Fidel Castro and Ernesto Che Guevara[36], in Question no. 120 of his *One Hundred Fifty Questions to a Guerrilla*.[37] Thus, stressing the novelty of "lone wolves" can only be considered the result of a lack of historical knowledge and falling into the trap of trying to reconstruct jihadi activities without understanding basic sabotage and Guerrilla techniques. Bringing together the lone wolves acting in swarm-like collective organization, the technical capabilities of jihadi engineers, and the tradition of terrorist operations, we will have to turn to other technical innovations of jihadis. A good example of this approach to jihadism research is the case of drones.[38]

---

35 Stenersen, Anne (2007), Chem-bio Cyber-class: Assessing Jihadist Chemical and Biological Manuals, in *Jane's Intelligence Review* September 2007, pp. 8–13: 13.
36 Himself learning from the North African guerrillas of Abd-el-Krim (see Er, Mevliyar, "Abd-el-Krim al-Khattabi: The Unknown Mentor of Che Guevara", in *Terrorism and Political Violence* 27 (2015), pp. 1–23), reminding us of the network of influences in modern terrorism.
37 http://www.latinamericanstudies.org/bayo.htm (accessed September 25, 2016).
38 We should bear in mind, however, alternative methods of using drones, e.g., Radjawali, Irendra/Pye, Oliver, "Drones for Justice. Inclusive Technology and river-related action research along the Kapuas", in *Geographica Helvetica* 72 (2017), pp. 17–27, Radjawali, Irendra/ Pye, Oliver/ and Flitner, Michael, "Recognition through Reconnaissance? Using Drones for Counter-mapping in Indonesia", in *Journal of Peasant Studies* 44 (2017), pp. 817–83.

Drone Wars Jihadi-Style

The issue of using drones for warfare is relevant to the discussion due to the large number of publications related to the use of drones as a weapon by IS especially. Those who have not read or seen any of the related material apart of the group's official videos may only know that IS has utilised drones as a tool for producing impressive video footage. Yet, they were also used for reconnaissance and intelligence gathering purposes and the step of using them as weapons was to be expected. As predicted, the weaponisation of drones occurred and spread throughout the year 2016. After two Kurdish soldiers were killed in the same year, this development could no longer be ignored and the Combating Terrorism Center (CTC) published the first overview on the issue in January 2017.[39] However, despite previous experiences the CTC report attempted to downplay the role of consumer drones whilst Jake Godin has pursued a more realistic approach, calling drones "the industrial revolution of terrorism".[40]

A very apt commentary reads: "Some here also say they don't possess enough of a skill level to do it, or that toy/hobby grade aircraft/drones will never be used by terrorist."[41] This very commentary could truly be the motto of most terrorism research trying to catch up with terrorists until it is too late. We can furthermore interpret the case of utilizing drones for Jihadi purposes as yet another example for terrorism research trying to catch up with jihadi innovations and not following the insights gained from other fields of consumerization of warfare.[42]

IS has used jihadi-attack-drones, whilst other jihadi forces have also used them for an attack on a Russian airbase near Latakia in early 2018.[43] The number of drones[44] used for the attack was reported to be 13 – a small swarm. Out the

---

39 https://fortunascorner.com/2017/01/31/the-islamic-states-drone-documents-management-acquisitions-diy-tradecraft/ (accessed August 07, 2017).
40 https://www.newsy.com/stories/isis-drones-and-the-industrial-revolution-of-terrorism/ (accessed August 07, 2017). For an overview of the products of this 'industrial revolution' see Nick Waters, "Types of Islamic State's Bombs and Where to find them" (https://www.bellingcat.com/news/mena/2017/05/24/types-islamic-state-drone-bombs-find/?utm_content =buffer4d8e0&utm_medium=social&utm_source=twitter.com&utm_campaign=buffer) (accessed August 07, 2017).
41 https://www.rcgroups.com/forums/showthread.php?2833203-Some-Here-Say-This-Kind-of-Thing-is-Untrue-and-Not-Really-Happening (accessed August 07, 2017).
42 For a recent example of Jihadis dropping bombs from drones see the most recent files since it is an ongoing practice.
43 https://www.almasdarnews.com/article/jihadist-drone-attacks-russian-airbase-southwest-latakia/ (accessed February 8, 2018). This source uses the word "rebels" to cover the adherence of forces participating to other jihadi forces than ISIS.
44 https://www.almasdarnews.com/article/russian-military-shoots-13-jihadist-drones-hmaymim-airport/ (accessed February 8, 2018).

borders of the Syrian/Iraqi area of operation, more drone attacks are to be expected. An article from September 2017 reads:

> "The terror group's technicians claim to have perfected modifications which would allow a drone to carry a devastating payload of up to 20 kg – some 20 times the current maximum. The jihadists' online material now regularly exhorts sympathizers to use the devices to launch attacks and experts have told that a successful atrocity using a drone against countries including the UK is one of the terror group's highest priorities."[45]

Also on a *telegram* channel entitled "Islamic State" (*al-dawla al-islāmiyya*) we could watch a series of tutorials on drones as early as in March 2016.[46] However, the use of drones by IS goes back to even 2014 and we may argue that this knowledge on the possible utilisation of drones was out there in the jihadi swarm already at very early stages – yet often ignored.[47] This spreading of information on drone-warfare within jihadi circles can be interpreted as an example of virtual leadership.

Drones are discussed in jihadi magazines (see below). In *al-Īhāʿāt al-jihādiyya*, a magazine published by the Centre for Jihadi Preachers (*markaz duʿāt al-jihād min ard al-Shām al-mubāraka*) close to the jihadi preacher al-Muhaysinī, a leading figure in the al-Qaʿida related organizations in Syria, published some comprehensive articles on drones.[48] The first article describes the ways in which drones might be operated whereas the following article attempts to convince jihadis of its feasibility. Another interesting article in this part of the magazine discusses operational art in times of drone surveillance. By analyzing the way in which they reflect on new developments of warfare, we could easily understand how jihadist operate. In fact, this is the only way of achieving such an understanding.

Moreover, an essential aspect of this approach is to holistically consider that jihadis produce a coherent theology as discussed in the issue of *al-Īhāʿāt al-jihādiyya*. Consequentially, the following article in this magazine covers the role of women in the jihadi subculture, whilst another two-pager displays Arab calligraphy and demonstrates the importance of the Arabic language for the jihadi *imaginaire*. Jihadi magazines are still an important part of jihadi communication even at operational level. This apect of jihadi communication will be discussed later in this chapter.

This communication ultimately contributes to the overall coherence of jihadi

---

45 https://inews.co.uk/news/uk/drone-terror-attack-jihadists-britain-matter-time-security-sources-warn/ (accessed February 8, 2018).
46 See *telegram.me*, channel *al-dawla al-islāmiyya*, March 24, 2016.
47 For a first report on the ISIS drone program see http://www.icsve.org/research-reports/isis-drones-evolution-leadership-bases-operations-and-logistics/#_ftn55 (accessed February 8, 2018).
48 *al-Īhāʿāt al-jihādiyya* No.3 (Dhu l-hijja 1437h), pp. 61–67.

virtual guidance and is another example of the need of a historical understanding of terrorist operations. A lack of historical knowledge means being surprised again and again by jihadi operations in reality.

Virtual Guidance

A "community" or a "network" has been identified as the source of most terrorist attacks. The attempt to identify a "community of criminals" as the force behind the anarchist attacks in France can be seen as an example for a learning network – some kind of an emergent swarm – promoting 'illegal' actions in the 1890s. This "community of criminals" allows us to understanding how a diffuse network of individuals, journals and small groups of activists have been (mis-) understood as an organization with permanent internal structures. This situation in France at the end of the 19th century and at the beginning of 20th century may serve as an example for a learning network – again, a kind of emergent swarm – promoting 'illegal' actions without a permanent internal structure.[49] A situation we may find to be rather similar to the present circumstances.[50]

Although some of the material analysed in this chapter has been disseminated for predominantly organizational purposes, we cannot deny the importance as much as quantity of religious-theological resources online and on conservative Islamic online platforms. Although the material presented here is operational in nature, technical, and military in general, the overall framework of virtual leadership is still based on a theology of violence. This theology of violence produces the coherent way of thinking that is needed for terrorist attacks and the framework within which operatives guide the attackers who in turn carry out these ideas.[51] This coherent theological framework is also distributed across several virtual platforms – first and foremost *telegram* – and create the cohesion needed for Jihadi operations. The virtual guidance aspect of jihadi communication is not to be ignored unless research will not fall into the trap of beginning again after any new jihadi operation occurs. One of these new modes operations has been called virtually planning or remote control terrorism.

---

49 For a detailed account of the development of the illegalist anarchist networks in France at that time in a leftist perspective see Richard Parry, *Die Bonnot-Bande*, Vienna: bahoe books 2017².
50 For an account by a revolutionary socialist see Holitscher, Arthur, *Ravachol und die Pariser Anarchisten*, Frankfurt a. M.: Verlag Freie Gesellschaft s. d. (Reprint of the first edition Berlin 1925), pp. 78–83.
51 Lohlker 2016a, 2016b, 2016c, and 2017 for the larger religious milieu.

Virtually Planning or Remote Control Terrorism

This is another Internet-based mode of operation, which can often perceived as a lone wolves attack at first glance.[52] Later on, one can uncover direct communication lines between the attacker and jihadist organizations. For such operations the terms "remote control", "virtual plot" or "virtual planning"[53] are commonly used. In the Hyderabad plot of 2016, for instance, the structures associated with the virtual planning of operations became visible.[54] In said plot, a promising young jihadi recruit, willing to carry out attacks, had been identified. Virtual planners guided him through every step of the plan, which was thought to be the Islamic State's first attack in India. The planners also helped recruiting other attackers, organized the delivery of weapons and chemicals from Syria to India in order to make explosives. Lastly, they also arranged for the logistics behind the attack and for the delivery and pick up of weapons and explosives. In order to achieve this, they had to remain in constant connection with the attackers until shortly before they got arrested.

> "In the most basic enabled attacks, Islamic State handlers acted as confidants and coaches, coaxing recruits to embrace violence. In the Hyderabad plot, among the most involved found so far, the terrorist group reached deep into a country with strict gun laws to arrange for pistols and ammunition to be left in a bag swinging from the branches of a tree. For the most part, the operatives who are conceiving and guiding such attacks are doing so from behind a wall of anonymity. When the Hyderabad plotters were arrested last summer, they could not so much as confirm the nationalities of their interlocutors in the Islamic State, let alone describe what they looked like. Because the recruits are instructed to use encrypted messaging applications, the guiding role played by the terrorist group often remains obscured."[55]

But the recruitment process may also work in another way:

> "In early August, Kassim posted an audio recording on Telegram in which he instructed future attackers to send him a video message prior to their operation. According to Belgian journalist Guy Van Vlierden, who first reported on the recording, Kassim specified that the video 'must contain an oath of allegiance and a message of dawa' that encourages others to carry out attacks. Kassim promised that once he received the video

---

52 We may add the cases of persons with psychological problems following some elements of online and media discourses driving them to violent action.
53 Bridget Moreng, "ISIS' Virtual Puppeteers: How they Recruit and Train 'Lone Wolves'", in *Foreign Affairs* (https://www.foreignaffairs.com/articles/2016-09-21/isis-virtual-puppeteers) (accessed June 9, 2017) (posted September 21, 2016).
54 I am following the report by Rukmini Callimachi, "Not 'Lone Wolves' After All: How ISIS Guides World's Terror Plots from Afar", in *The New York Times* (https://www.nytimes.com/2017/02/04/world/asia/isis-messaging-app-terror-plot.html?_r=0) (accessed June 9, 2017) (posted February 4, 2017).
55 See Callimachi, "Not 'Lone wolves'."

he would have it translated and broadcast. 'I am involved in this area, which means that in two seconds they will be translated Arabic-French,' he explained in his Telegram message. 'They will be transmitted to the entire world.'"[56]

The report on the Indian case demonstrates that there is a wide range of activities beyond the European (and the US) assessment on the deliberate planning of jihadis – despite some organizational restructuring:

> "As has become clearer over time, ISIS' strategy for external operations in Europe is not haphazard – its methods are deliberate and carefully organized under the direction of one of its wings, the Amn al-Kharji."[57]

This holds true for the organized networks and for groups guided by a central body of IS. However, there are additional activities connected to IS, AQ, and others. There

> "are fundamental differences between centrally planned operations (such as the Istanbul airport attack) and attacks coordinated by virtual planners, with the latter generally being less sophisticated and less lethal. But it is remarkable, and worrisome, how many of the Ramadan attacks [2016] are clearly linked to the Amn al-Kharji. And the group's ability to use encrypted online communications to interact with operatives abroad leaves open the possibility of links that have not yet been discovered."[58]

Taking into account the elements of virtual planning and guidance, there are still other terrorist attackers who operate individually and whom the coherent theologies of violence[59] – IS or al-Qa'ida style – may have inspired.[60] These individual attackers are in need of knowledge and technical resources to carry out their operation. Although there are many non-jihadi resources available online, jihadis put other Arabic-language resources online.

Technical Resources

Some of the resources published online date back to the beginning of Jihadi transnational operations in Afghanistan. We can find five volumes[61] of the

---

56 See Moreng, "ISIS' Virtual Puppeteers."
57 See Moreng, "ISIS' Virtual Puppeteers."
58 Daveed Gartenstein-Ross/Nathaniel Barr, "Bloody Ramadan: How the Islamic State Coordinated Global Terrorist Campaign", in *War on the Rocks* (https://warontherocks.com/2016/07/bloody-ramadan-how-the-islamic-state-coordinated-a-global-terrorist-campaign/) (accessed June 9, 2017) (posted July 20, 2016).
59 For this concept see Rüdiger Lohlker, *Theologie der Gewalt. Das Beispiel IS*, Vienna: facultas 2016.
60 This word is intentionally used to remind the reader of the semantics of the magazine of al-Qa'ida titled *Inspire*.
61 The volumes were published electronically in 1424 hijri.

"Encyclopaedia of Large Weapons" (*mausū'at al-asliha al-kubrā*) about the handling of i. e. machine guns, mortars etc. published by the "Bureau of Services" (*maktab al-khadamāt*) and the "Directorate of Training Camps and Frontiers" (*qiyādat al-mu'askarāt wa'l-jabahāt*) in the Taliban-Islamic Emirate of Afghanistan. The "Encyclopaedia of Large Weapons" is dedicated to Usāma bin Lādin, who contextualised it within the creation and stabilization of a jihadi tradition.

One questions comes to our mind. Is the republishing of such material due to a mere historical interest in somewhat out-dated material? We may consider this to be partly true; but on the other hand, when thinking about the highly diverse global weapons market, knowing how to handle a Sten gun may still turn out to be useful…

A *telegram* channel[62] started on the 25th of November 2016, focuses on such operational issues.[63] It starts with a post on ammunition, a description of the Russian sniper rifle *Dragunov*, some guidelines for fighters on trench warfare, mortars, anti-tank weaponry and missiles. Also, we can find the biography of an early Muslim master-spy; yet again another aspect of Jihadi reliance on early Islamic history in order to create an *imaginaire* supporting the theological cohesion.

Furthermore, the publishers provide us with an example of a subterranean tunnel system taken from the Indochina war including plans of the structure of this system. A post referring to this illustration stresses the high number of losses by the US-troops in Vietnam.[64] Lastly, a text of twenty pages demonstrates how to launch anti-tank operations, whilst another post contains a tiny spy drone.

In this channel we can also find the reminder that "it is true that god obliged us to lead jihad, but obliged us to prepare for it…"[65] and the descriptions for practical preparations within theological programs of jihadism.

Several other posts are dealing with Kalashnikov rifles,[66] whereas cross-organizational references are available from Jihadi online sources. For instance, a series of videos by an offshoot of the Free Syrian Army (FSA)[67] offers an online course on urban warfare. Amongst the videos we can find the content on: secure handling of guns (video No. 02), asymmetrical sniping (video No. 034), physical fitness (video No. 059) using and cleaning of handguns (video No. 066), a sub-

---

62 At the time of writing having 484 members.
63 *Taktīkāt 'askariyya: ma'lūmāt yahtajuhā al-mujāhidīn*.
64 A more regional approach exploring the experience from the tunnels in and out of Gaza and its application in Syria is to be found in "al-Anfāq bayna al-Shām wa-Ghazza", in *al-Īhā'āt al-jihādiyya* No.3 (Dhu l-hijja 1437h), pp. 56–59.
65 *Taktīkāt 'askariyya: ma'lūmāt yahtajuhā al-mujāhidīn*, telegram.me, December 1, 2016.
66 See for a detailed history C. J. Chivers, *The Gun: The Story of the AK-47*, London et al.: Penguin 2011.
67 We will not discuss here the present status of the FSA, its affiliations, etc., a discussion that is futile in our context.

Spy Drone

terranean (video No. 072), self defense (video No. 076; several additional videos), handling and constructing a flamethrower operating with napalm (video No. 077).

Without assessing the practicability of the information provided in these videos we could consider them a resource for, a) fighters on the ground in Syria, and b for) fighters worldwide who are seeking information and training in urban warfare. Also, referencing non-Jihadi resources has happened in earlier periods of Jihadi online training.

The aforementioned videos were produced at the beginning of the Syrian uprising. Based on the general title the videos are indented for "the protection of the peaceful Syrian revolution" – this part of the title was, however, dropped in later videos. Having said this we may turn to guides to produce explosives; the importance of IEDs we mentioned before.

Explosives

Since the Afghanistan period of violent jihad we are aware of the (offline) courses on explosives, which have been transferred to other media outlets like jihadi magazines in the real world or in cyberspace. At first we will have to take a look into jihadi magazines as an important hub of jihadi communication and part of the collective organizational process of the jihadi swarm.

Magazines

We have introduced the idea of collective organizers with a quotation on the role of a newspaper in the beginning of this chapter. Hence, it may be appropriate to turn out attention to jihadi magazines in order to understand the operational aspects of jihadism, which are not limited to propaganda but can also include action.

Jihadi magazines have a long tradition, which dates back to the early 2000s. The most prominent publications of this time period ones are the Saudi "Voice of Jihad" (*sawt al-jihād*)[68], a religio-theological magazine, and "al-Battar[69] Training Camp" (*muʿaskar al-battār*) (see below), which was once called "a representative example of the way insurgents are using the internet to spread their ideas."[70] This description clearly demonstrates the close relation of religious and military-operational ideas at the very beginnings of modern jihadism. By looking into some of these journals we shall attempt to analyse this dimension of jihadi knowledge.[71]

The Journal *al-Waʿd al-ākhir*[72], one of the lesser known jihadi magazines as it is published in Arabic published a series of articles on the "engineering art of explosives" (*handasat al-mutafağğirāt*) in their general section on "military culture" (*al-ṯaqāfa al-ʿaskariyya*). The first article provides us with a short introduction on the various categories of explosive "for a general study of [explosives] in respect of their use and application".[73] The second article deals with hollow charge ammunition used in RPG-7, RPG-29, or in the 9M133 Cornet anti-tank guided missile and with some remarks on their effective use.[74] The third and fourth article describes cluster bombs used against light to medium armed transporters, arriving at the conclusion that they are not useful against civilians

---

68 The first – and up to now only – comprehensive study of this magazine is Nico Prucha, *Die Stimme des Dschihad*, Hamburg: Dr. Kovać 2010 with an introduction by the author of this chapter.
69 The name is referring to a sword of the prophet Muhammad, another reference to the religio-theological aspect of jihadi thought.
70 http://misc.survivalism.narkive.com/EnEmtHRr/mu-askar-al-battar-al-queda-training-manual (accessed February 6, 2018).
71 A recent attempt of analysis focussing only at magazines in English (and one in English and Somali, I. e., the English language part of it) ignoring the much more important Arabic language magazines is Maura Conway/Jodie Parker/ Sean Looney, Online Jihadi Instructional Content: The Role of Magazines, in Conway, Maura et al. (eds.,) *Terrorists' Use of the Internet: Assessment and Response*, IOS Press, Amsterdam 2017, pp. 182–193. The focus on bomb-making is erroneous. The conclusions are insufficient as it is demonstrated below.
72 Another religious reference in the title. The magazine is covering the Palestinian jihadi movement. The Internet site has the transliteration wrong.
73 *al-Waʿd al-ākhir* No. 1 (Jumāda al-āḫira 1436), p. 13.
74 *al-Waʿd al-ākhir* No. 2 (Rağab 1436), p. 17.

and only to be used against armoured vehicles. Lastly, also the range and possible targets of the explosives and the best way in which to penetrate armoured protection are mentioned.[75]

Another article from this series describes remote ignition explosives and their utilisation against individual humans,[76] whilst next issue's article deals with hand grenades.[77] The following issue contains an article on rockets and on how to inspect the functionality of the related electronics.[78] The eighth instalment of this series deals with the basic components of explosives[79] and further discusses other aspects of military operative art. One series of articles – possibly hinting at the Palestinian context – has been entitled "Know your enemy!" and describes units of the Israeli army, to whom the journal refers to as the elite of the enemy. "Information about guerilla warfare" is provided by another series, which describes basic tactics, elements of guerrilla warfare and the its stages of this kind of warfare etc.

In summary, we could say that *al-Waʿd al-ākhir* is offering some basic knowledge on guerrilla warfare with respect to tactics and operations and that adds some useful intelligence on the most dominant enemy – the Israeli Defence Forces.[80] Aspects on operational security, mobile phone security amongst other practical information are further intended to prepare the mind-set of the future fighters. This may also be considered a kind of true virtual guidance that has reached completion by theological, historical, and political articles.

In this regard, *Fustāt al-muslimīn* is another interesting magazine. In its first issue[81], we can find an Arabic summary of one chapter of *The Revolution in Warfare* by Liddell Hart[82] on the "strategy of indirect approach". This is an example of the jihadi study of military knowledge (see below), whilst a second article on the ideas of the Syrian army succeeds the presentation of Liddell Hart's work.

The second issue of *Fustāt al-muslimīn*[83] provides the reader with a description of minesweeping technology used in the Russian armed forces, including one article on an armoured bridge layer. Yet another example of how hard one tries to "know your enemy". Consequently, another part of the analysis

---

75 *al-Waʿd al-ākhir* No. 3 (Ramadan 1436), p. 20 und *al-Waʿd al-ākhir* No. 4 (Shawwāl 1436), p. 21.
76 *al-Waʿd al-ākhir* No. 5 (Ḏu l-Qaʿda 1436), p. 24.
77 *al-Waʿd al-ākhir* No. 6 (Ḏu l-ḥijja 1436), p. 21.
78 *al-Waʿd al-ākhir* No. 7 (Ṣafar 1437), p. 24.
79 *al-Waʿd al-ākhir* No. 8 (Rabīʿ al-awwal 1437), p. 25.
80 The counter intelligence of jihadis is still a field of research that may be called an *assemblage* (Latour) of *lacunae*.
81 *Fustāt al-muslimīn* No. 1 (Dhu l-qaʿida 1438h.).
82 Basil Henry Liddell Hart, *The Revolution in Warfare*, London: Faber and Faber 1946.
83 *Fustāt al-muslimīn* No. 2 (Dhu l-qaʿida 1438h.).

of Liddell Hart's *The Revolution in Warfare* has been included. Issue no. 3[84] and the fourth instalment of this series continue to take the same line and thus another article in the "military studies" section of the same magazine includes a detailed description of the Steyr-Mannlicher HS-50 .50 BMG single-shot anti-materiel sniper rifle and its effectiveness against US forces in Iraq.[85] Furthermore, one info-graphic on the SA-21 Growler anti-aircraft system has been made available, whilst the succeeding 5th issue of the magazine contains a description of the Russian T-60 tank and the shoulder-launched anti-tank weapon, commonly known as a rocket-propelled grenade (RPG). Lastly, an info-graphic on the GBU 43/B Massive Ordnance Air Blast – the acronym "MOAB" has commonly also been referred to as "Mother of all Bombs" – a large-yield bomb only once used by the US up to now.[86] Indeed, particularly the last example shows how *Fustāt al-muslimīn* offers information on the weaponry of the most important enemies like the US or Russia. A series of articles on strategic approaches also include approaches towards understanding their movements on the ground, whilst this information may also be aimed at the individual fighters or the command level on the ground in order to increase the operative abilities of jihadi units.

Newer magazines less frequently offer militarily relevant info-graphics. The new *al-Anfāl* ISIS-related magazine publishes one-page articles and just a few examples should be sufficient at this point. No. 3[87] describes the production and mixture of acetone peroxide, a primary high explosive including the necessary security precautions. No. 4[88] provides a guideline on how to produce an acetone peroxide device, which is introduced with some instructions of which appropriate religious formula is to be recited at the beginning of this process. No. 5 contains another one-page article on the preparation of an explosive device using acetone peroxide, which receives further attention in follow-up articles in the next issues.[89] How to build a do-it-yourself-pepper is thoroughly explained in the issue no. 8, which also includes some necessary security remarks and the mentioning of the proper religious formula, which is to be quoted before starting the mixing process.[90] With respect to the assessment of the Site Institute, which

---

84 *Fustāt al-muslimīn* No. 3 (Muharram 1439h.).
85 *Fustāt al-muslimīn* No. 4 (Safar 1439h.).
86 *Fustāt al-muslimīn* No. 5 (Rabīʿ al-awwal 1439h.).
87 *Al-Anfāl* No. 3 (22. Rabīʿ al-awwal 1439h.), p. 2.
88 *Al-Anfāl* No. 4 (2. Rabīʿ al-ākhir 1439h.), p. 15.
89 *Al-Anfāl* No. 5 (13. Rabīʿ al-ākhir 1439h.), p. 16.
90 *Al-Anfāl* No. 8 (14. Jumādā al-ūlā 1439h), p. 16.

concluded that *al-Anfāl* provides "weapons manuals", one might be tempted to consider it slightly overstated.[91]

The Somali magazine *Gaidi Mtaani* (also partially available in English and thus accessible to 'experts') and its symbols refer to ISIS and only offer a small number of articles. Issue no. 9, however, contains a piece on martial arts combat training and physical fitness,[92] whilst no. 3 reflects on mysteriously disappearing drones and helicopters, which is explained as a supernatural intervention. A short guide on how to build Molotov cocktails and one on mobile phone security are to be found under the telling headline 'Irhab wa Ghetto'[93] and one can find ads for a guide on how to use AK-47 rifles. In sum, *Gaidi Mtaani* can be considered as a propaganda magazine, which only minimally contributes to operational aspects.

The Arab magazines are one of the resources English language jihadi magazines are based on. We may have a short look at *Inspire*, *Dabiq* and *Rumiyah* since they are the most prominent magazines of the jihadi subcultures, and better known to most experts.

Considering *Rumiyah* as the first English-speaking example and leaving aside its distribution in other languages aside, we can find a one-pager on the military use of white phosphorus including appropriate safety measures in issue No. 12.[94] In No. 9[95] We are provided with an article on "Just Terror Tactics", which advices the reader on how to operate in the US or Europe. The article covers the topics of hostage-taking, the acquisition of firearms, possible targets, executions, conducting operations without firearms, deception and luring targets into traps. This article is followed by a separate entry on truck attacks but instructions are not provided in such great detail as we could find it in in *Inspire* (see below). For now, lets move on to some other publications.

Due to the lack of a sizeable amount of operational material in *Dabiq* we may characterize this magazine as primarily theological and in line with the tradition dating back to *Sawt al-jihād* (see above). Also the IS-news magazine *al-Nabā'*, still one of the most important IS magazines is not covering operational issues explicitly, whilst in South Asia, the structures of the Taliban-related magazines are quite different.

Booklets are collected in order to give practical advice to fighters or would-be-fighters. The guide to the *Hijrah to the Islamic State*, now only of historical interest, may be a good example as it provides detailed information on the travel

---

91 https://news.siteintelgroup.com/Jihadist-News/pro-is-magazine-anfal-borrows-naba-news-format-features-threats-and-weapons-manuals.html (accessed March 1, 2018).
92 *Gaidi mtaani* No. 9 (Dhul hijja 1438h), p. 41.
93 *Gaidi mtaani* No. 3 (Rabiʿ al-Thani 1434h).
94 *Rumiyah* No. 12 (Dhul-Qaʿdah 1438h), p. 39.
95 *Rumiyah* No. 9 (Shaʿban 1438h).

routes to Syria so that those interested can find their way to the Islamic State (in 2015). The traveling routes, suggestions for packing including the advice of using an informal piece of language, experiences gathered on passing the border controls in Turkey, and reports of successful travellers can be found.[96]

Even more famous yet, the *Lone Mujahid Pocketbook*, published in 2013 as a collection of articles taken from *Inspire* No. 1 to No. 10 has become part of the series on the *open source jihad*. The angle and approach taken by the publishers is clear: "Well, there is no need to travel abroad, coz the frontline has come to you." Some of the possible operations discussed concern torching parked vehicles using petrol and matchsticks, causing traffic accidents by spilling oil on the road or by at busting tyres with thick nails. Another suggestion is starting forest fires including precise information on how to specifically start the most devastating fire. Furthermore, a special feature describes pickup trucks as the "ultimate mowing machine", whereas the next article mentions the destruction of buildings through chemical explosions. How to make the actual bombs is discussed in the following article entitled "kitchen fun" and "make a bomb in the kitchen of your mom". A very detailed description, including a guide on how to make acetone peroxide or on how to construct a remote control detonator can also be found.[97] We can further find instructions on the handling of handguns and Kalashnikovs and some general advice on how to operate in the US, followed by a Q&A section. The last section concerns secure communication on the Internet using an encryption program called Asrar al-Mujahideen.[98]

Inspire No. 11 (see above) is mainly praising the Boston Marathon bombings without giving any further information on technical details or the modus operandi.[99]

Inspire No. 12 sets out to establish a new concept entitled the "city wolves". The articles on the "Open Source Jihad" deal with car bombs in the US – but also in the UK and France – and they further identify several targets, followed by the detailed yet infamous illustrative guides.[100]

Inspire No. 13 contains programmatic articles on economic targets in the US. These parts on economic warfare are followed by another detailed and illustrated guide on how to build a DIY-hidden bomb. The guide shows the reader how to assemble all parts of the bomb including the main charge and its components, the explosion starter, a quick burning fuse or the detonator. Lastly, some experiments are conducted with bomb, using security scanners at airports, a thorough analysis on which airlines best to attack and the steps needed in order

---

96 *Hijrah to the Islamic State*, s.l.: 2015.
97 As mentioned in Arabic-language magazines (see above).
98 *Lone Mujahid Pocketbook* Spring 1434 (2013), s.l.: al-Malahem Media 2013.
99 *Inspire* No. 11, Spring 1434 (2013).
100 *Inpire* No. 12, Spring 1435 (2014).

to succeed in this endeavour. The article ends with an identification of potential targets for an attack on important economic figures in the US.[101]

Inspire No. 14 begins with an introduction to the "Open Source Jihad" (OSJ) and with a hint that a water bottle might be more likely to be confiscated by a security officer than a bomb. The OSJ section furthermore covers a guide to assassination operations in the already established usual detailed manner. A guide on how to build a homemade hand grenade with a timer follows, whilst this issue concludes with a more detailed identification of high profile economic targets previously discussed in issue no. 13.[102]

The cover of Inspire No. 15[103] features a threatening illustration of a man with a hoodie, looming in the dark and watching a family home with all its windows illuminated. The issue has been titled "professional assassinations" with the subtitle "home assassinations." The first article related to the context of our research is a call for a "knife revolution" in the US referring to the knife attacks of Palestinians in Israel. In the following article on the "lone jihad" and the proposed strategy and tactics we can find this definition:

> "It is a term made up of two parts: The first is Jihād: It is to make every effort to strive, and to endure in fighting the enemy. The second is fardy (individually): and what is intended by Lone Jihād is that the brother should implement jihād, as we have defined, but individually and independently in the land of the kuffar without having to report to the Mujahideen leadership. And this individualism and independence is the main reason for it (Lone Jihād) to be termed as a Lone Wolf attack."[104]

The reference to the "mujahideen leadership" indicates that the concept means to not engage in centralized operations, which, however, does not mean *non-organized* operations. This is a good example of the collective organization of *lone* wolf attacks. *Inspire* No. 15 consequently continues with a guide to professional assassinations, with the techniques associated with home assassinations and with illustrated guides on how to build parcel bombs, magnetic car bombs or door-trap bombs.

Inspire No. 16[105] introduces the *Inspire Guides* series featuring attacks in New Jersey, Minnesota, and in the Chelsea neighbourhood of New York by stabbings and pressure cooker bombs. The next article contains an illustrated overview of the use of pressure cooker bombs, whereas later in this issue, the rulings for this kind of operations, embedding them explicitly in the coherent jihadi theology of violence, become a central theme.

---

101 *Inspire* No. 13, Winter 1436 (2014).
102 *Inspire* No. 14, Summer 1436 (2015).
103 *Inspire* No. 15, Spring 1437 (2016).
104 *Inspire* No. 15, Spring 1437 (2016), p. 43.
105 *Inspire* No. 16, Autumn 1438 (2016).

Inspire No. 17[106] deals with "train derail operations" and US railways are consequently identified as a crucial part of the country's infrastructure. Indeed, transportation is described as a primary target for economic warfare[107] and a tabular presentation offers an overview over four lone wolf operations. The attached interview with the leader of the al-Qaeda of the Islamic Maghrib (AQIM), Abu Musab Abdel Wadud, states the following:

> "For example, America, France and other countries which have faced this form of Jihadi operations have not been able to devise fool-proof methods of countering this phenomenon. Intelligence is often useless with regards to an individual Mujahid, since he doesn't need mobile communication or social media networks. Investigation is also ineffective because in most situations he doesn't need weapons, storage dumps or explosives. So before the execution phase, it is very difficult for even the most professional of intelligence agencies to detect the likelihood of such an operation."[108]

This passage may indicate the confidence Abdel Wadud may have in the operations and showcase the insecurity he aims to likes to instil within the European and North American societies. In the next part of the journal, which features a timeline of train accidents in the US since 1904, further encouragement can be distilled from the writings. The following article deals with the "security for the lone mujahid" and especially with "psychological security", linking it to jihadi theology. Derailing operations and their preparation is central to the next section, especially since the focus has ben put on building a homemade derail tool and on the fact that is approach does not involve suicide and can thus be repeated. The section concludes with an overview of the US railway network.

To the complex of publications related to *Inspire* we may add the – now offline – *telegram* channel *Inspire Muslims* and the related *Inspire Guides:*
- No. 1 "Orlando Operation" includes a) a description of the attack on the nightclub in Florida, b) analysing the "advantages", c) stressing characteristics, and d) a guideline for future attacks[109].
- No. 2[110] "Nice Operation, France" contains a) a description of the attack, b) stressing characteristics, c) the message of the attack and d) reference to *Inspire* No. 2 (see above) for additional ideas for attackers.
  No. 3[111] "Commenting on the arrests od Muslim sisters in France" is basically a short commentary on the arrests in France.

---

106 *Inspire* No. 17, Summer 1438 (2017).
107 Economic warfare is understood as a vital aspect in other – Arabic language (!) – communication of AQAP. See Rüdiger Lohlker, *Roadmap to Terror in Saudi-Arabia* (https://islamicstudiespapers.files.wordpress.com/2016/02/astop-8.pdf) (accessed March 17, 2018).
108 *Inspire* No. 17, Summer 1438 (2017), p. 51.
109 *Inspire Guide No. 1: Orlando Operation*, June 17, 2016.
110 *Inspire Guide No. 2: Nice Operation, France*, July 17, 2016.
111 *Inspire Guide No. 3: Comment on arresting Muslim Sisters in France*, September 10, 2016.

- No. 4 is to be found in *Inspire* No. 16 (see above).
- No. 5[112] "The British Parliament Operation in London" features a) a general analysis of the attack, b) its message, and c) comments and advice.

Some of the guides and articles from the *Inspire* magazines[113] are translated into Arabic, which closes the cycle reaching the military practice of al-Qaeda in the Arab Peninsula (AQAP) in Yemen in the Arabic language using original sources in English. We shall not discuss the cross-organizational reference to AQAP materials by IS-related online communication at this point.

In sum, looking at the aforementioned summaries of jihadi magazines we might say that the impact of Arabic language communication, contrary to evidence-based research, is still widely ignored. Indeed, only considering English-language as a valid expression of the overall strategy of i.e. IS propaganda magazines appears to be a rather limited and narrow approach.[114] Burying ones head in the sand is – and has never been – a valid strategy for understanding jihadism. The "implications" of such a strategy may in fact be negligent since magazines are just a small part of the military information that circulates within jihadi circles. Of far greater importance is the Arabic-language material disseminated via *telegram* and on other platforms in cyberspace. The impact of that ignorance may be demonstrated by the 'news' of jihadi weapons markets.

How to buy Weapons via telegram-channels

In November 2017 the – not so new – news of a market for weapons and other military ordnance at *telegram* were published by *Foreign Policy*.[115] Leaving aside the fact that not 5000 users are buying and selling in the group "Market of Mujahideen – Weapons- Souq Sham" any more, we have to state only 189 members are still active. Quite a loss of customers. Still available are firearms, mobile phones, ammunition, sandals, running shoes, a German passport and some sheep (may an error?). There are other similar groups available on *tele-*

---

112 *Inspire Guide No.5: The British Parliament Operation in London*, March 23, 2017.
113 E. g., *Harrid* No. 8 (2011/1432h).
114 Haroro J. Ingram, *Islamic State's English-language magazines, 2014-2017: Trends & implications for CT-CVE strategic communications*, March 2018 (ICCT Research Paper) (https://icct.nl/wp-content/uploads/2018/03/ICCT-Ingram-Islamic-State-English-Language-Magazines-March2018-1.pdf) (accessed March 17, 2018).
115 Adam Rawnsley et al., The Messaging App Fueling Syria's Insurgency, in *Foreign Policy* (http://foreignpolicy.com/2017/11/06/the-messaging-app-fueling-syrias-insurgency-telegram-arms-weapons/) (accessed May 10, 2018).

gram established in May 2018, none of them active. These black markets evidently do not work. Arms trafficking in Syria is done by using other channels.[116]

Comparing these 'shocking' newsbit with the reality of arms trafficking in the Arab world, the importance evidently is in decline. On *Facebook* you easily find news about arms being sold, e. g., in Cairo[117] or in Libya, calling itsellf "Facebook the principal market for weapons in Libya". Arab Facebook groups on weapons have 115,846 likes (*sūq al-silāh al-'arabiyy li-muhibbi l-asliha al-nariyya*) or – run by a gun store in New York, NY (!) (*al-silāhlīk*), having 49,157 likes.[118] Grabbing the headlines may be a way to promote *telegram* as the ultimate evil – leaving aside the ominous dark web – online without understanding the Arab contexts of a peripheral region of the world system breaking apart – when *Facebook* is available. Let us return to serious research about jihadi military knowledge disseminated online!

Military Knowledge

Talking about *lone wolves* etc. should not lead us to the idea that virtual warfare does not include an attempt to understand the military apparatus and concepts of jihadis. Indeed, jihadi *telegram*-channels provide a basic reminder in this regard since they also explain how to take care of weapons.[119] Some basic rules are:

1) clean the weapon regularly and without being negligent
2) check and test the weapon before and after it is used
3) clean the weapon with oil
4) avoid the weapon being exposed to high humidity
5) wrap the weapon in a piece of cloth soaked with a little bit oil when not using it.

This example for a virtualized training camp (see above) provides information to the mujahids, which can be applied in combat situations. We will discuss some examples and additional material in future research.

Of immediate concern for the mujahidin on the battlefield is a precise iden-

---

116 E. g., Small Arms Survey, *Fire and Forget: The Proliferation of Man-portable Air Defence Systems in Syria* (The Proliferation of Man-portable Air Defence Systems in Syria) (accessed May 05, 2018).
117 http://aswatmisriya.com/new/details/55676 (posted March 13, 2013) (accessed June 02, 2018).
118 Via https://www.middleeast-online.com/ (posted April 09, 2016) (accessed June 02, 2018).
119 *Taktīkāt 'askariyya: ma'lūmāt yahtajuhu l-mujāhidīn*, telegram.me, September 23, 2017.

tification of the weaponry used by the enemy.[120] This is can be achieved through technical briefs and illustrations of i. e. F-18 Hornet fighters, unmanned Boeing X-45, B2 and B 52 bomber together, F-22 Raptor fighter, A-10 Thunderbolt II, MIG-29, Sukhoi T-50 amongst other aircrafts mentioned. Cluster bombs are of concern too, which is demonstrated in a video and in great detail featuring iron arrows. We can compare this to the magazines mentioned above. Magazines and online information of this kind can be regarded as reinforcing each other through feedback loops.

Often discussed (see below) are training instructions for snipers and the principles of sharpshooting.[121] The same channel debates long distance guns like the Steyr-Mannlicher HS-50.[122] Yet another channel contains detailed descriptions of a twin-barrelled anti-aircraft ZU 23-23-2 autocannon which is used by the Iranian armed forces. This may be another example of knowing the enemy and his weapons in case of their acquisition by jihadis. An illustrated guide on how to construct a handle for a gun is also mentioned[123] aside of a series of posts that deal with a detailed explanation of other weapons and further means of warfare. In this regard, a very detailed 86 pages booklet on "military chemistry" – a necessary prerequisite for bomb-making – has been made widely available on several *telegram* channels.[124] In the following parts of this series of articles we can continue tracing the readily available military guides and their different character. For now, we will turn our attention to two comprehensive packages of files that represent jihadi military knowledge.

The second package of files has been titled "lone wolves" (see above) but we shall turn to another one first. Carrying the title "making small and high explosive IEDs" the package contains an illustrated guide in twelve pictures. We can assume that this knowledge has already been available before the actual magazines mentioned above were published. This part of the audio-visual-scriptural complex of jihadi knowledge,[125] a complex discernible in the material analysed below, will be looked at in connection with an impressive repository of jihadi

---

120 The following data are to be found in the *telegram* channel *Taktīkāt 'askariyya: ma'lūmāt yahtajuhā al-mujāhidīn*, telegram.me.
121 E. g, *Al-qunnāsa 'al-rimāya'*, telegram.me, interestingly the same channel offers a guideline for the use of radar by the Yemeni army (*Taktīkāt 'askariyya: ma'lūmāt yahtajuhā al-mujāhidīn*, posted January 10, 2018) another case of knowing if you are able to acquire his weaponry and technical means.
122 *Taktīkāt 'askariyya: ma'lūmāt yahtajuhā al-mujāhidīn*, posted January 1, 2018.
123 *Abū Khattāb al-'Irāqī li'l-akhbār al-'āmm*a, posted March 5, 2018. This channel is now offline.
124 *Mukhtasar Kitāb Dalīl al-Kīmiyā' al-'askariyya* via *Taktīkāt 'askariyya: ma'lūmāt yahtajuhā al-mujāhidīn*, posted March 5, 2018.
125 *'ubuwwāt nāsifa saghīra shadīdat al-infijār* via different channels on telegram.me (accessed March 6, 2018).

Lone Wolves

military knowledge. Lets continue in the correct order now and focus on the first package entitled "lone wolves".

The Knowledge of Lone Wolves

The collection of the numerous files titled "Lone Wolves" (*al-dhi'āb l-munfarida*) starts with an animated cover stating: "It is not allowed to use the content against Muslims" – Thinking of the many feuds among jihadi groups, this advice appears to not be followed strictly.

In a separate section, we can find videos on jihadi training camps, i.e. of the *Tehreek-e Taliban Pakistan* including a mixed soundtrack of mostly Arabic religious hymns and depicting physical training, combat training, and even medical check-ups of the fighters. These kinds of videos demonstrate the readiness of the fighters and try to increase the appeal of the group and its "Mujahideen Special Group" (MSG) for young men who are seeking an opportunity and context in which to act as true men.[126] Furthermore, the video can also be understood as a counter-propaganda attempt and showing the skilful prowess of the MSG in comparison its enemies.

In the text section of the "Lone wolves" collection, we can find a booklet on security and intelligence within an Islamic context[127], followed by a second and third issue.[128] The next booklet discusses general principles of security, like

---

126 Research into jihadi masculinities is still to be done.
127 Markaz al-fajr li'l-i'lām, *Barnāmaj sinā'at al-irhāb*, Vol.1: July 24, 2010 (Sha'bān 13, 1431h).
128 Same dates.

mindfulness and prevention of faulty operations.[129] Two other booklet deal with the same issues.[130]

The first English-language videos feature instructions on how to build simple detonators, fuses, etc. and further present several examples of various bombs, which is intended to demonstrate the wide range and different kinds of explosions. Most of these explosions are shown in the open countryside, a few detonations happen underwater, others destroy buildings or detonate somewhere in the woods, but most of them are merely collected from the Internet and put into a new jihadi context.

Another video from the old *Shumūkh al-islām* und *al-Fallūja* jihadi forum shows the mixing of some basic material needed for explosives. A course for building these explosives is called "Explosives made easy" (*al-mutafajjirāt al-sahla*),[131] which provides detailed introduction, rich illustrations and very precise descriptions. A list of the material used concludes the course, whereas some other issues that are discussed include IEDs (see above), suicide bomber vests, hand grenades etc. Another, similar course is called "Explosives popular" (*al-mutafajjirāt al-shaʿbiyya*).[132] Here, a video demonstrates how to build a detonator by using a remote centerlock device. In the background we can hear music – a jihadi *nashīd*. An Arabic version on "How to make a bomb in your mother's kitchen" (see above) has been provided too – An English/Arabic blend of jihadi military information (see above).[133]

Turning to texts again we can encounter a short written piece on IEDs – especially cluster bombs – and on how to be apply them.[134] A one-pager lists the prerequisites for building a smoke bomb.[135] Another text contains a detailed description of cylindric IEDs, focussing on bullets and shrapnel,[136] whilst a text on the different kinds of hollow charges is also available.[137] Remote-controlled mines, like Claymore mines are described in another text[138], some thoughts on how to build a directed charge are available too[139] and a variety of explosives are described as IEDs that can be used against armoured vehicles.[140] Truly, we have a comprehensive encyclopaedia of explosives at our disposal.

---

129 *Mabādiʿ al-ʿāmma li'l-amn*, Vol.2; October 2010 (Shawwāl 1431h).
130 Same dates.
131 ʿAbdallāh b. ʿAbdallāh, *al-Mutafajjirāt al-sahla*, s.l. Rabīʿ al-awwal 1430h.
132 Tāriq Ismāʿīl Kākhiyā, *al-Mutafajjirāt al-shaʿbiyya*.
133 *Isnaʿ qunbula fī matbakh wālidatika*.
134 *al-ʿUbuwwa ʿadsiyya*.
135 *ʿUbuwwa dukhkhāniyya al-sāmma*.
136 *al-ʿUbuwwa al-ustuwāniyya*.
137 *al-ʿUbuwwa al-jawfāʿ*.
138 *al-ʿUbuwwa al-talfīziyūniyya*.
139 *Tasnīʿ al-ʿubuwwāt al-muwajjaha*.
140 *al-ʿUbuwwa al-sihniyya*.

Another group of texts discusses cluster bombs (*'unqūdiyya*)[141], some basic knowledge on rockets[142], toxicology[143], and – yet again – an introduction to explosives.[144] Other texts provide us with short introductions to explosives[145], which gives the aspiring jihadi a more general idea where more detailed guides might be found. We could continue to explore this large number of files on explosives but for now we must close this section with the "Special course on Explosives for the beginning jihadi" by Dhu l-bijadayn, a well-known jihadi writer on this very issue.[146]

This special course available as several Arabic-language videos introduces the use of binoculars (even offering a Q&A session), night-vision goggles and some multi-purpose tools – as usual, embedded in a religious context. Another Arabic-language and web-harvested video includes tutorials on kick-boxing, which in turn has been supplemented by a video on self-defence. A special text covers the military use of knives.[147]

A chapter of the older and slightly out-dated jihadi magazine *Muʿaskar al-battār* (see above) encompasses a good introduction to the handling of an RPG – the most-frequently used anti-tank weapon system[148] – and an analysis of Russian tanks hints towards selecting these tanks for the next attack.[149] The analytical part, however, does not stop there and also includes Russian rocket launchers,[150] which once more illustrate the jihadi attempt to know the enemy.

A five-part series also offers a course in sniping, which has been published by the Palestinian ʿIzz al-dīn al-Qassām brigades.[151] The very detailed course covers basic principles of camouflage (part 1), training in precision shooting (part 2), precision shooting of rifles and their handling (part 3), sniper rifle stand, mechanics and the riflescope (part 4) and lastly the influence of wind and movements (part 5).[152] Slightly out of focus, yet also available in this

---

141 *al-Unqūdiyya*.
142 *ʿIlm al-sawārīkh*.
143 *ʿIlm al-sumūm*.
144 Abū Hafs al-Lubnānī, *ʿIlm al-mutafajjirāt* with several pages introduction on jihadi theological contexts.
145 *al-Hashwa al-mutafajjira maʿa al-suwar*, *al-Mutafajjirāt*, *al-Mutafajjirāt al-qāsima*, *al-Mutafajjirāt al-sahla* (mentioned above), and *Sawāʿiq al-mutafajjirāt*.
146 Rüdiger Lohlker, "Al-Qaeda Airlines: Jihadi Self-Assessment and the Ideology of Engineers", in Rüdiger Lohlker/Tamara Abu-Hamdeh (eds.), *Jihadi Thought and Ideology*, Berlin: Logos 2013, pp. 5–15.
147 Abū al-Hasan al-Hanafī, *al-Sikkīn al-ʿaskarī: silāh al-muqātil al-salafī*, s. l.: s. d.
148 Al-Barrāʿ al-Qahtānī, *Mudāddāt al-durūʿ*; older versions of RPGs are described.
149 *al-Dabābāt*; interesting the use of some German language illustration.
150 *Rāgimat al-sawārīkh al-mutaʿaddida al-mahāmm*.
151 The military wing of the Palestinian HAMAS.
152 *Silsilat "wa-ʿiddū"* 2, part 1–5. The title of the publication is referring to the Quran.

package, is a video about/against Copts in Egypt making sense if we contextualize in jihadi theology.

A jihadi theological collection of texts gives answers to questions on the legitimacy of the military jihad.[153] The text has been written by the most prominent – at least for some time – author of IS named Bin'alī.[154] Again, we can notice the fusion of theological and military aspects, whilst a wide range of other theological texts is also readily available. For example, one of these other texts (evidently referring to Saudi Arabia) links the military forces, police units, national guard to pure unbelief as they are considered to be a force against true Islam (=jihadism).[155]

Mobile phones and Internet security is also frequently discussed in many texts – most prominently, in this very collection, we can find a twelve-part course on mobile phone security.[156] Other texts deal with "Electronic Warfare and the Negligence of Supporters of the Islamic State"[157], security on Twitter[158], or with a ten-pages text on mobile phone protection.[159] The platform *telegram* is also discussed and the writer engages in a monologue on its usefulness and problems. Of utmost importance are the documents on chemical and biological warfare, which we will assess in the following part of this series. For the moment, we shall restrict ourselves to only mentioning an article on anthrax, which in turn contains an analysis on the Aum Shinrikyo attack in Japan[160], one document on nerve gas[161], one on nicotine[162] and a fundamentals document on concentrating liquids.[163]

---

153 Turkī bin Mubārak al-Bin'alī, *al-Qindīl fī radd al-abāṭīl*, s. l.: al-Wafā' 2014–15.
154 For him and his theological positions see Lohlker, *Theologie* and more recent postings on jihadica.com.
155 *al-Āyāt wa'l-aḥādīth al-dālla 'alā kufr*.
156 *Dawrat amn al-hawātif al-dhakiyya*. Compare the contribution of Clemens Holzgruber in this volume.
157 *Al-Ḥarb al-iliktrūniyya wa-ghaflat ansār al-dawla al-islāmiyya*.
158 *Kayfa tugharrid fī Twitter bi-amān (bi'dhn allāh)*.
159 *Dalīl al-himāya al-iliktrūniyya li'l-hawātif al-dhakiyya*.
160 *al-Jamra al-khabītha*. For the case of Aum Shinrikyo see Ian Reader, *Religious violence in contemporary Japan: the case of Aum Shinrikyo*, Richmond: Curzon 2000; for their biological and chemical weapons program see Richard Danzig et al., *Aum Shinrikyo: Insights into how Terrorists develop biological and chemical Weapons*, Washington, DC: CNAS 2012².
161 'Abdallāh Dhu l-Bijadayn, *Hal kammiyya 27 cm³ min ayy mādda sāmma aw mushsha'a kāfiyya*, Shabakat al-Fallūja 1431 h.
162 *Samm al-nīkūtīn*.
163 *Tarkīz*.

Collective Organizers: Lone Wolves, Remote Control, and Virtual Guidance

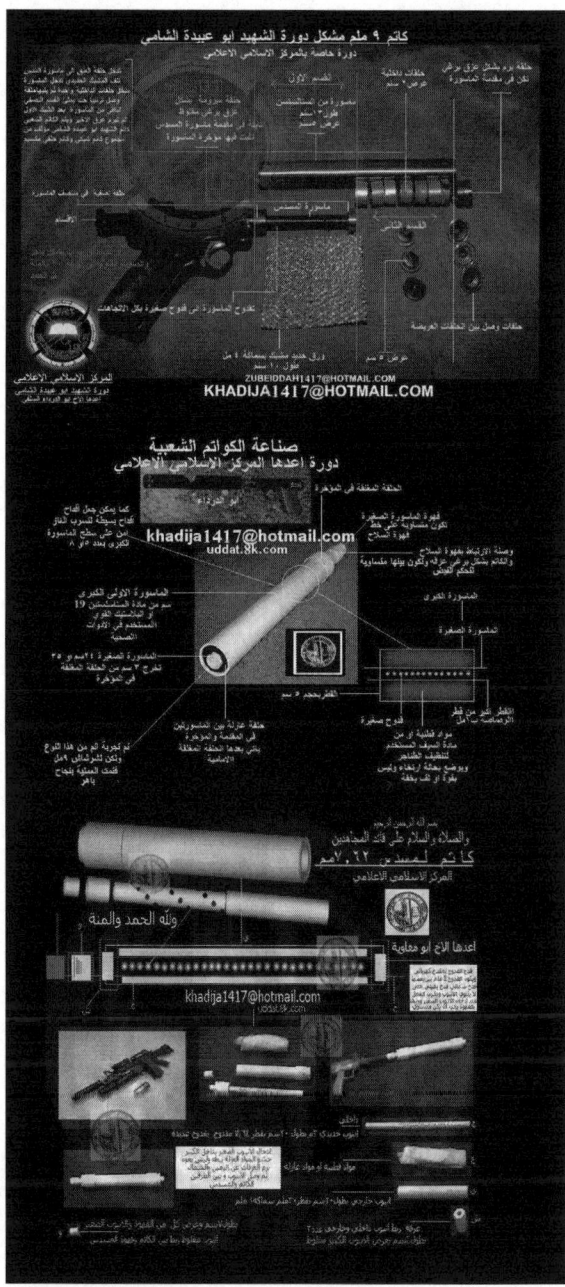

Silencer

Jihadism and Arabo-Islamic Mainstream

As seen in many other fields and activities, jihadis pick up materials that may appear like mainstream Arabic-language texts on the first glance. After a careful re-contextualization jihadi channels use these works, distribute them as jihadi ideas and embed their thought in Islamic thought and history.[164] One important aspect of jihadi thought in this regard is the appropriation of Arab heroes of the early Arabo-Islamic conquest as a point of reference. The prominent military commander Khālid b. al-Walīd, for example, has often been referred to by jihadi groups, linking the jihadi framework to Arabo-Islamic tradition.[165]

As mentioned above some comprehensive general courses on jihadi warfare, strategies, operational art, tactics are commonly available. A series of audio files (39 MP3 files) provides us with insights ranging from principles of security to a detailed description of guerrilla warfare – partly based on the history of different theatres of war. The title of the series is quite programmatic "The Art of terrorism" (*sinā'at al-irhāb*) and very prominent among jihadi media products.

In this context, we can consider such publications an important aspect is jihadi tradition building. One important element essential to this process is the republication of older jihadi magazine like *Mu'askar al-battār* (see above). We can find several articles referring to the Palestinian-Israeli conflict (another cross-conflict movement), an article on different varieties of Uzi submachine guns, texts on physical training, advices on identifying urban targets, techniques of camouflage and general security and counterintelligence matters in issue No. 7 of this very publication. Also Arabo-Islamic poetry and traditions are interspersed in the *Mu'askar al-battār*[166] and we can immediately identify the unique jihadi blend of political analysis, operational art, weapons, counterintelligence and the theological input, which in sum produces a coherent worldview.

Other issues of the magazine that have been republished are No. 1 up until No. 6. Some of the issues cover specific problems like rural or mountain warfare (No. 5), the M-16 gun (No. 4), or moving secretly in urban areas and cities (No. 6). Many other issues of the 'classical' jihadi magazine *Mu'askar al-battār* are available and now link the newer 'lone wolves' to the jihadi tradition of urban warfare. A recent series of posts thus include audio files by the 'historical' leader of al-Qaeda in the Arabian Peninsula (AQAP), Yūsuf al-'Ayerī (d. 2003) and on his

---

164 To give one example: Bassām al-'Asalī, *Fann al-harb al-islāmī*, Vol.1–4, Beirut: Dār al-fikr 1988. The publishing house is a large Arabic publisher. Interestingly the fourth volume reaches until the crusades being a link to contemporary jihadi ideas – at least for jihadis.
165 See Ahmad Bek al-Lahhām, *'Abqariyya Khālid b. al-Walīd al-'askariyya*, Jeddah: Dār al-manāra 1986.
166 *Mu'askar al-battār* No 7 (Safar 1325h).

views on guerrilla warfare in general and urban warfare in specific.[167] Hence we can recognise the multidimensional republishing of sources from the jihadi tradition, which has been tailored towards the operational needs of present day jihadis.

The lone wolves repository – we have only selected a few resources to give us an idea of what is readily available – demonstrates the ability of jihadis to construct and use a wide range of weapons, military materials and devices to attack their enemies. With regards to the utilization of drones, the ability to produce ammunition and possibly engage in gunsmithing in the future on a large scale, we can conclude that all the information that has been put on the Web and what has been practiced and thought by well trained and experienced technicians, capable to disseminate their knowledge, may paint a more comprehensive picture of what jihadism means online – and in Arabic – today.

A last remark: Regarding the most recent attacks using cars (not car bombs![168]) another perspective may be useful in order to understand the relationship between jihadi operations and the broader specter of societal violence. Since even *Wikipedia* provides entries on "vehicular homicide," "rampage killing," and "road rage" it is clearly case of misattribution if one attempts contextualize these attacks as mere varieties of jihadi operations. Some recent cases committed by a driver in Germany, killing civilians and ultimately ending in the suicide of the driver (Münster, Cottbus 2018) gave birth to the discussion if this suicide method by car and committed by drivers with psychical problems could perhaps be caused by the "echo chamber" of jihadi car attacks. However, this simply ignores decades and numerous cases of attacks in which cars have been used as weapons.[169] Indeed, another example that illustrates the common refusal to understand that jihadis are adopting societal possibilities in their pursuit of attacking societies.[170]

The material we presented is collected through careful research of many different jihadi online resources and tries to give an idea of the ongoing highly interconnected Arabic-language discussion of Jihadis online. Without knowing this discussion a thorough understanding of what is meant by jihadism and the operational capabilities of jihadis globally is impossible.

---

167 Published on *telegram* channel *dawla al-khilāfa* (posted April 14, 2018).
168 Although car bombs are part of the *imaginaire* of cars as weapons (see Mike Davis, Buda's Wagon: A Brief History of the Car Bomb, London/Brooklyn, NY: Verso 2017 who gives some other links to the history of jihadism) attacks by cars driving into groups oh humans are often separated from it.
169 E. g., Josef Augstein, "Auto-Attacke in Münster: Islamistische Hintergründe", in *Der Spiegel* April 9, 2018 (http://www.spiegel.de/politik/deutschland/muenster-islamistische-hinter gruende-kolumne-von-jakob-augstein-a-1201922.html) (accessed April 10, 2018).
170 We may remember that *Inspire* was created by an US citizen being well aware of the role of cars in US society.

Ali Fisher

Interrogating the electronic ribat: Data Science in the study of the Jihadist movement

> *The internet has become a great medium for spreading the call of Jihad and following the news of the mujahideen.*
> Anwar al-Awlaki[1]

In the 1980s scholars had to find ways to physically gather print material, audio tapes, VHS and later DVD. However, the growing use of the internet by the Jihadist movement since the 1990s created the opportunity for sympathisers and scholars around the world to accesses, read, watch, listen and engage with that content digitally. What began as electronic scans of print material and video content transfered from VHS and DVD, is now a digital publishing system delivering content simultaneously in physical and digital form.

The rationale for this was set out in a statement issued by *al-Fajr* on May 6th 2011;

> Internet is a battlefield for jihad, a place for missionary work, a field of confronting the enemies of God. It is upon any individual to consider himself as a media-mujahid, dedicating himself, his wealth and his time for God.[2]

Anwar al-Awlaki in his *44 Ways to Support Jihad* suggested a range of ways in which the brothers and sisters could be "internet mujahideen" by contributing in one or more of the following ways:
- Establishing discussion forums that offer a free, uncensored medium for posting information relating to Jihad.
- Establishing email lists to share information with interested brothers and sisters.
  Posting or emailing Jihad literature and news.
- Setting up websites to cover specific areas of Jihad, such as: mujahideen news, Muslim POWs, and Jihad literature.[3]

---

1 Anwar al-Awlaki, 44 Ways to Support Jihad, Victorious Media.
2 Quoted in; Nico Prucha, "Online Territories of Terror – Utilizing the Internet for Jihadist Endeavors", *ORIENT IV* (2011), p. 46.
3 Anwar al-Awlaki, 44 Ways to Support Jihad, Victorious Media.

As the available technology has changed, the Media Mujahidin have continued to evolve, reconfigure, and explore the opportunities as part of the Swarmcast.[4] They have purpose-built programs such as the 2007 release of *Asrar al-Mujahidin* intended to facilitate secure communication with Islamic State Iraq amongst other jihadist groups, the *Dawn of Glad Tidings* Twitter app, Telegram bots, and browser plugins for Chrome and Firefox. Equally, the volume of content and range of platforms used to disseminate content has expanded rapidly including beacons such as Twitter and Telegram, and content stores such as YouTube and Vimeo, Archive.org, Amazon Cloud and OneDrive.

This has created the potential for researchers to access and study the content which circulates within the Jihadist information ecosystem, and indeed to take a macroscopic view of the information ecosystem itself. Unfortunately, while the opportunity to gather data on the authoritative elements of the jihadist movement exists, few studies which claim to conduct data analysis have genuinely embraced the opportunity of Data Science based approaches.

Instead of genuine data science, there has been an explosion in 'tweet-ready' punditry which fails to grapple adequately with the challenge of integrating genuine subject matter expertise with the methodological rigor required for Data Science. Dogged by poor data acquisition, substandard analysis and misleading graphs, many studies have become entangled in the challenges identified in the articles which created the foundations for 'Critical Terrorism Studies'. As a result, Just as John Vasquez noted in *The War Puzzle*, "much has been written about the causes of war; little has been learned about the subject" similar could be said for the volume of content and commentary produced about the use of the internet by the jihadist movement.[5]

This chapter examines current uses of data in the study of the Jihadist movement and highlights some significant limitations in studies which are emblematic of wider problems in the field. It then provides an outline of what data science is, and how the study of the jihadist movement must be built on data science which provides an authentic representation of the movement. It concludes with a framework for how data science could be employed to produce an authentic representation of the movement to avoid the many methodological shortcomings exhibited by current analysis which has pushed claims of decline and 'total collapse'.

---

4 Ali Fisher, "How jihadist networks maintain a persistent online presence." *Perspectives on Terrorism*, 9.3 (2015).
5 John Vasquez, The War Puzzle (Cambridge: Cambridge University Press, 1993) p. 3.

The online Jihadist movement

Reviewing the massive increase in articles since 9/11, Richard Jackson observed "the vast majority of this literature can be criticised for its orientalist outlook, its political biases and its descriptive over-generalisations, misconceptions and lack of empirically grounded knowledge".[6]

Over generalisation and lack of empirical grounding in the extensive archive of Jihadist documents in Arabic has lead the attempt to understand the jihadist movement in terms of street criminals, gangsters, individuals obsessed with computer games (particularly first-person shooters), and a desire to go from zero-to-hero.[7] As highlighted by Nico Prucha:

> these interpretations often lack any attempt to address the theological aspects of the movement ... and prominence of scholars within the Jihadist movement's overall interpretation of theological concepts, including an Islamic State model of governance.[8]

---

6 Jackson, Richard. "The Study of Terrorism 10 Years after 9/11: Successes, Issues, Challenges." *Uluslararası İlişkiler* 8.32 (2012): 1–16. Jackson, R. 'Constructing Enemies: "Islamic Terrorism" in Political and Academic Discourse', Government and Opposition, 42, 394–426 (2007).
7 https://onlinejihad.net/2017/08/28/part-4-understanding-the-resilience-and-appeal-of-islamic-state-electronic-propaganda-and-beyond/.
8 https://onlinejihad.net/2017/08/28/part-4-understanding-the-resilience-and-appeal-of-islamic-state-electronic-propaganda-and-beyond/.

Interpreting the work of the media mujahidin as marketing or in terms of their 'brand', fails to comprehend the role of their work within the movement.⁹ Similarly, focusing social media, images, infographics and videos as ways of branding the jihadist movement, confuses the purpose of Jihad and da'wa;¹⁰ As Abdullah Azzam highlighted in one of the modern foundational documents of the Jihadist movement,

> Jihad is Da'wah with a force, and is obligatory to perform with all available capabilities, until there remains only Muslims or people who submit to Islam.¹¹

Da'wa is not focused on marketing or nor branding jihad – it is the purpose toward which Jihad is conducted. The confusion stems from, as Richard Jackson wrote about the study of terrorism more generally, "large numbers of new scholars lacking adequate grounding in the existing literature; and a persistent tendency to treat the current terrorist threat as unprecedented and exceptional".¹²

Instead of building the understanding of the foundational documents of the Jihadist da'wa, research falls back onto familiar western frames of reference such as Hollywood, rather than deep-rooted research on Islamic theology.¹³

These interpretations originate from the attempt to view the subject matter – Jihadist media – through a Western and predominantly English language lens. In this lens, not even Latinized Arabic key words from the rich blend of Arabic dominated theological motifs are reflected upon sufficiently. This traps the interpretation within specific perceptive dispositions that Pierre Bourdieu calls

---

9 van Lieshout, Jan, and Robert Beeres. "Strategic Counter-Marketing to Fight ISIL." *Netherlands Annual Review of Military Studies 2017*. TMC Asser Press, The Hague, 2017. 181–194.Gates, Scott, and Sukanya Podder. "Social media, recruitment, allegiance and the Islamic State." *Perspectives on Terrorism* 9.4 (2015). Ingram, Haroro J. "Three traits of the Islamic State's information warfare." *The RUSI Journal* 159.6 (2014): 4–11. Liang, Christina Schori. "Cyber Jihad: understanding and countering Islamic State propaganda." *GSCP Policy Paper* 2 (2015): 4. Saltman, Erin Marie, and Charlie Winter. "Islamic state: The changing face of modern jihadism." *London: Quilliam Foundation* (2014): 1–71. Charlie Winter (2018) Apocalypse, later: a longitudinal study of the Islamic State brand, Critical Studies in Media Communication, 35:1, 103–121, Winter, Charlie. "The virtual 'caliphate': Understanding Islamic State's propaganda strategy." (2015). Atwan, Abdel Bari. *Islamic state: The digital caliphate*. Univ of California Press, 2015. Speckhard, Anne, and Ahmet S. Yayla. "Eyewitness accounts from recent defectors from Islamic State: Why they joined, what they saw, why they quit." *Perspectives on Terrorism* 9.6 (2015).
10 https://twitter.com/ICSR_Centre/status/866222658169524224; https://twitter.com/ICSR_Centre/status/911201218101481472.
11 Hashiyat ash-Shouruni and Ibn al-Qasim in Tahfa al-Mahtaj 'ala al-Minhaj 9/213Quoted by Abdullah Azzam, *Defence of the Muslim Lands*, (English translation work done jihadist media).
12 Richard Jackson, The Study of Terrorism after 11 September 2001: Problems, Challenges and Future Developments, *Political Studies Review*, 7, 2, (171–184), (2009).
13 Marshall, Alex. "How Isis got its anthem." *The Guardian* 2015 (2014).

habitus.[14] These interpretations frequently lack any attempt to address the theological aspects of the movement, even the simple references in the titles of media products go unnoticed.

This, as a consequence, leaves the analysis dislocated from the repeated referencing of the concepts, which link together to construct chains that anchor contemporary media to the foundations created by scholars stretching back through the history of Jihadist writing, (and furthermore, the selective, yet coherent use of historical writings used by jihadists to enhance and enrich their posture).

For example, most discussion and interpretation of the series *Salil al-Sawarim (SAS)*, located in a Western habitus, focused on the Hollywood style or slick production values – just as understanding of the movement often revolves around ideas of 'brand' and 'marketing'. However, *Salil al-Sawarim*:

> is particularly illustrative of this emphasis on theology. Readers sufficiently initiated into the mainly Arabic language corpus of Sunni extremist theology will understand the title's particular reference right away; it refers to the book *al-Sarim al-maslul 'ala shatim al-rasul*, "the Sharp Sword on whoever Insults the Prophet." Its author is 13th century Islamic scholar Ibn Taymiyya (1263–1328 AD).[15]

Equally consider the sound effect used to underscore references to Ibn Taymiyya's writings in numerous AQ and IS videos. It is no coincidence that it is a high pitched metallic sound effect which recreates a sword being drawn from its scabbard. Without an attempt to address the theological aspects of the movement, nor encoded cultural understandings, and the meaning evident to those from (or sufficiently initiated into) an alternative habitus.

As William Rowlandson argues, definitions are "really a debate about who owns the words".[16] Framing the interpretation of Jihadist media within a Western habitus focuses interpretation firmly within the comfort zone of English speaking commentators who often have little familiarity with the theological and historical reference points used by the movement, nor a nuanced understanding of the concepts expressed by Jihadists in over 300,000 pages of Arabic. To maintain their ownership over such interpretations, it has become increasingly important for some commentators to downplay the role of theology, talk up the importance of pictures, and research the use of western languages.[17]

This matters to data science as the use of western constructs and languages

---

14 http://www.tandfonline.com/doi/full/10.1080/17539153.2017.1337326.
15 https://onlinejihad.net/2017/11/16/notes-on-the-salil-al-sawarim-series-the-theological-framework-from-amsterdam-to-the-islamic-state/.
16 Rowlandson, W. 2015. Imaginal Landscapes: Reflections on the Mystical Visions of Jorge Luis Borges and Emanuel Swedenborg. London: Swedenborg Society.
17 https://www.nzz.ch/international/bei-islamistischer-radikalisierung-schauen-zu-viele-weg-ld.1328748.

– along with content easily found by western researchers – attempts to wrest the analytical locus of the jihadist movement away from the complex, and unfamiliar Arabic core – instead locating understanding within a Western habitus. This approach fences off alternative world views and further seeks to extend Western hegemonic ownership over meaning – developed since 9/11 became a moment of universal temporal rupture.[18]

The impact of an approach dominated by a western habitus, further exacerbates the frequently observed imbalance between the level of subject matter and data analysis expertise and often leads to western assumptions about the movement impacting study design, data acquisition and limiting the utility of any research. For example, the data analysis of ISIS networks on VK, deployed a robust data analysis approach for the online phase of the research, but from the outset the research struggled with the subject matter. The authors appeared surprised to find women prominent in the digital outreach efforts. However, as Saudi former Usama bin Laden bodyguard and first-generation leader of AQAP Yusuf al-'Uyayri wrote in 'The Role of the Women in Fighting the Enemies':

> the woman is an important element in the struggle today, and she must participate in it with all of her capacity and with all of her passion. And her participation does not mean the conclusion of the struggle – no. Rather, her participation is counted as a pillar from amongst the pillars that cause victory and the continuation of the path.[19]

The document highlights women as fighters and participants in battle (mujahidah being the female form of mujahid):

> [T]o show the importance of your role in this clash today between the religions of Kufr and the Religion of Islam, and especially in the new crusade that the world is waging against Islam and the Muslims under the leadership of America, then we must remind you of an aspect of your role, reflected in the image of the Mujahidah of the Islamic Golden Age.[20]

While acknowledging limitations on the involvement in battle – outside of specific circumstances – the document states

> … we want you to follow the women of the Salaf (female companions of the prophet) in their incitement (inspire) to fight and their preparation for it and their patience on this

---

18 Toros, Harmonie. ""9/11 is alive and well" or how critical terrorism studies has sustained the 9/11 narrative." *Critical Studies on Terrorism* 10.2 (2017): 203–219. http://www.tandfonline.com/doi/full/10.1080/17539153.2017.1337326.
19 Yusuf Bin Salih Al-'Uyayri, The Role Of The Women In Fighting The Enemies, (Translated version) At-Tibyan Publications http://advances.sciencemag.org/content/2/6/e1501742.full.
20 Yusuf Bin Salih Al-'Uyayri, The Role Of The Women In Fighting The Enemies, (Translated version) At-Tibyan Publications http://advances.sciencemag.org/content/2/6/e1501742.full.

path and their longing to participate in it with everything in return for the victory of Islam.[21]

Far from being unlikely to be involved in online activities, this emphasis on incitement, preparation, and participation should highlight the expected role women may play within the online struggle – including on VK. Familiarity with these texts is not just a niche historical interest. It is essential if research is to continue without exhibiting *content blindness*.

AQAP theologians such as Yusuf al-'Uyairi and their many writings have long mattered to ISI(S) (not just in the time since they caught the attention of commentators as they swept into Syria). Many of the Arabic language productions by ISIS have strong lingual and theological ties to content produced by the original incarnation of AQAP, yet ISIS was the first group to have the room, territory and thus resource to apply the otherwise theoretical theology that was brought into organized existence by key leaders and theologians such as al-'Uyairi. His study circles, strategic writings, and sober analysis of U.S. intervention into Iraq are reflected in the structure and output of contemporary ISIS media releases and notions. Furthermore, a eulogy of al-'Uyairi (died 2003) by his brother in arms al-'Awshan (who was also killed shortly after) was downloaded nearly 3,000 times in just one core IS-Telegram channel.

Increasingly problematic for the production of authentic data science research, are what Caron E. Gentry and Katherine E. Brown have shown to be the dominance of particular approaches, including cultural essentialism and neo-Orientalism, which can cause a 'subordinating silence' which veils particular groups or perspectives from view.[22] These, like many of insights derived from the work on subordinating gendered narratives about terrorists who are perceived to be biologically female, provide valuable perspectives and parallels closely the issue of which parts of Jihadist ideational content matter to, or get attention from, Western researchers and policymakers.

In the research on the electronic ribat, there is an ongoing disconnect between Arabic sources and European language research, which is reflected in the obsession with English language magazines such as Dabiq,[23] Rumiyah[24] or com-

---

21 Yusuf Bin Salih Al-'Uyayri, The Role Of The Women In Fighting The Enemies, (Translated version) At-Tibyan Publications http://advances.sciencemag.org/content/2/6/e1501742.full.
22 Brown, Katherine E. 2011. "Blinded by the Explosion? Security and Resistance in Muslim Women's Suicide Terrorism," in Laura Sjoberg and Caron E. Gentry, eds. *Women, Gender, and Terrorism*. Athens: University of Georgia Press, 194–226.
23 Krishna-Hensel, Sai Felicia. "Legitimizing the Caliphate and its politics: Moral disengagement rhetoric in Dabiq." *Authoritarian and Populist Influences in the New Media*. Routledge, 2017. 148–174. Nadia Al-Dayel & Aaron Anfinson (2017) "In the Words of the Enemy": the Islamic State's reflexive projection of statehood, Critical Studies on Terrorism, 11:1, 45–64. Droogan, Julian, and Shane Peattie. "Mapping the thematic landscape of Dabiq magazine."

paring AQ and ISIS through their magazines such as Inspire and Dabiq.²⁵ Despite the hundreds of thousands of pages of content produced in Arabic, researchers such as Haroro J. Ingram focus their analysis on English magazines, to "explore the strategic logic of Islamic State (IS)" and specifically how "IS uses Dabiq to 'sell' [their] vision to English-speaking audiences, especially in the West".²⁶ This echoes what Caron E. Gentry has shown from analysing which female participants in martyrdom operations, gain media attention. The women who gain attention are those "that present threats to the Western 'us' and not the Middle Eastern 'other'." By contrast, for 'women who did not (yet) pose a threat to Western interests…, virtually no image exists in the public eye. They almost do not exist'.²⁷ One finds similar emphasis in the comparison of European language content and 'Foreign Fighters' compared to Arabic documents and Arab fighters. However, as the late Reuvan Paz noted in 2007, the movement is "almost entirely directed in Arabic and its content is intimately tied to the socio-political context of the Arab world".²⁸ Yet the vast majority of research focuses on European language or secondary sources (or English Language social media accounts), with significantly fewer studies of the Arabic sources and online presence – despite Arabic being the primary and vastly more heavily used language of the Jihadist movement.²⁹

Australian Journal of International Affairs 71.6 (2017): 591–620. Gambhir, Harleen K. "Dabiq: The strategic messaging of the Islamic State." *Institute for the Study of War* 15 (2014). Ingram, Haroro J. "An analysis of Islamic State's Dabiq magazine." *Australian Journal of Political Science* 51.3 (2016): 458–477. AZMAN, NUR AZIEMAH. "ISLAMIC STATE'(IS) PROPAGANDA: DABIQ AND FUTURE DIRECTIONS OF 'ISLAMIC STATE." *Counter Terrorist Trends and Analyses* 8.10 (2016): 3–8. Musial, Julia. ""My Muslim sister, indeed you are a mujahidah"-Narratives in the propaganda of the Islamic State to address and radicalize Western Women. An Exemplary analysis of the online magazine Dabiq." *Journal for Deradicalization* 9 (2016): 39–100.

24 Wignell, Peter, et al. "A mixed methods empirical examination of changes in emphasis and style in the extremist magazines Dabiq and Rumiyah." *Perspectives on Terrorism* 11.2 (2017): 2–20. Mahzam, Remy. "Rumiyah–Jihadist Propaganda & Information Warfare in Cyberspace." *Counter Terrorist Trends and Analyses* 9.3 (2017): 8–14.

25 Haroro J. Ingram (2016) An Analysis of *Inspire* and *Dabiq*: Lessons from AQAP and Islamic State's Propaganda War, Studies in Conflict & Terrorism, 40:5, 357–375, Vallee, Charles. "Digital Jihad: Al-Qaeda and the Islamic State Dabiq vs. Inspire." *International Institute for Counter-Terrorism* (2015). Reed, A. G., and Haroro J. Ingram. *Exploring the Role of Instructional Material in AQAP's Inspire and ISIS'Rumiyah*. Europol, 2017.

26 Ingram, Haroro J. "An analysis of Islamic State's Dabiq magazine." *Australian Journal of Political Science* 51.3 (2016): 458–477.

27 Gentry, Caron E. 2011. "The Neo-Orientalist Narratives of Women's Involvement in al-Qaeda." In Laura Sjoberg and Caron Gentry, eds. *Women, Gender, and Terrorism*. Athens: University of Georgia Press, 176–193.

28 Paz, Reuven. "Reading Their Lips: The Credibility of Jihadi Web Sites as 'Soft Power' in the War of the Minds." (2007).

29 Emblematic of this phenomenon see: Berger, J. M., and Heather Perez. *The Islamic State's*

Perhaps this is the content Western researchers are able to find, or because so few researchers are able to listen to and understand the nuances of spoken Arabic nor read Arabic quickly enough to digest the volume of content which circulates in Arabic each week. It is hard to tell definitively which of these two interrelated problems cause the phenomena, but the result is a vast overexposure of sources in English compared to those texts meaningful to the core of the movement – written in Arabic. This veil of silence significantly skews some computer science based work towards English language sources, rather than the full breadth of the movement.

For the understanding of the electronic ribat (and the movement more broadly) the focus of analysis must first be core Arabic content. Any subsequent transition to translations or content shared in other languages based on the analysis of the core. Credible data science cannot focus on proxy metrics derived from the periphery of the movement as a substitute for the much deeper and more complex understanding required to penetrate the core.

Here the study of rhetoric in gender subordination provides a valuable explanation of how such a process can cause a 'veil of silence' to descend over an entire area of study perpetuating content blindness around Arabic Jihadist archive.

As Caron E. Gentry wrote:

> Across time and place in global politics, rhetoric has often been used to perpetuate certain social 'truths' and norms. A speaker or author uses language to direct an audience toward a manufactured truth, one in which some information is emphasized while other information is concealed. In this way, the speaker designates certain ideas, norms, and events superior to others and ignores actions or events that might challenge them.[30]

With a particular focus on neo-Orientalist Narratives, Gentry highlights:

> The othering so intrinsic to neo-Orientalism is deeply troubling because it blinds scholars, researchers, and law enforcers to any deeper realities or nuances in people's lives.[31]

Diminishing Returns on Twitter: How Suspensions are Limiting the Social Networks of English-speaking ISIS Supporters. George Washington University, 2016. Gambhir, Harleen K. "Dabiq: The Strategic Messaging of the Islamic State." *BACKGROUNDER* (2014). Wignell, Peter, et al. "A mixed methods empirical examination of changes in emphasis and style in the extremist magazines Dabiq and Rumiyah." *Perspectives on Terrorism* 11.2 (2017): 2–20.

30 Gentry, Caron E. 2011. "The Neo-Orientalist Narratives of Women's Involvement in al-Qaeda." In Laura Sjoberg and Caron Gentry, eds. *Women, Gender, and Terrorism.* Athens: University of Georgia Press, 176–193.

31 Gentry, Caron E. 2011. "The Neo-Orientalist Narratives of Women's Involvement in al-Qaeda." In Laura Sjoberg and Caron Gentry, eds. *Women, Gender, and Terrorism.* Athens: University of Georgia Press, 176–193.

No matter the particular cause, a persistent blindness amongst researchers to the nuances and complexities of the jihadist movement contained in the Arabic texts, undermines attempts to analyse the movement.

Solving the problems of the State

In addition to the veil cast over Arabic content, the research specific to the jihadist movement and the electronic ribat (if ribat is understood at all) is dominated by what Cox called a 'problem-solving' approach.[32] Specifically relevant to the electronic ribat, "much of the research inquiry is largely restricted to the assembling of information and data that would solve or eradicate the 'problem' as the state defines it".[33]

As the earlier discussion of female bombers highlighted, threats to Western interests can dominate research questions, rather than a genuine attempt to understand a Jihadist group as the research subject. As Richard Jackson noted,

---

32 Robert Cox, 1981. "Social Forces, States and World Orders: Beyond International Relations Theory", Millennium: Journal of International Studies, vol.10, no.2, pp. 128-9. Gunning, Jeroen. "A case for critical terrorism studies?" *Government and Opposition* 42.3 (2007): 363-393. Richard Jackson, The Study of Terrorism after 11 September 2001: Problems, Challenges and Future Developments, *Political Studies Review*, 7, 2, (171-184), (2009). Richard Jackson, Harmonie Toros, Lee Jarvis & Charlotte Heath-Kelly (2017) Introduction: 10 years of *Critical Studies on Terrorism*, Critical Studies on Terrorism, 10:2, 197-202.
33 Richard Jackson, Jeroen Gunning, Marie Breen Smyth 'The Case for a Critical Terrorism Studies', Paper prepared for delivery at the 2007 Annual Meeting of the American Political Science Association, August 30 Gunning, Jeroen. "A case for critical terrorism studies?" *Government and Opposition* 42.3 (2007): 363-393.

"It is fair to say that the vast majority of terrorism research attempts to provide policy-makers with useful advice for controlling and eradicating terrorism as a threat to Western interests". This problem-solving approach can "be a real problem when it distorts research priorities, co-opts the field and turns scholars into 'an uncritical mouthpiece of state interests'".[34]

Gender studies approaches have also highlighted the problem of adopting a Western habitus. For example, as Katherine E. Brown showed the Western State security frame in the discussion of istishhadiyyat (female martyrdom operatives):

> in this mainstream view in which the principal frame of reference is the state, and in particular Western states, female suicide terrorism simply becomes a variant of an already known threat to the state. This security approach consequently leads to homogenization based on method of attack and its security impact rather than a recognition of the politics of those involved.... Research that adopts the security approach is thus blinded by the glare of the explosion: the corporality and immediacy of the violence and state responses are overexposed at the expense of other features of the phenomenon.[35]

In the current study of the movement on the electronic ribat, for example, the security frame takes the form of scouring ISIS English language magazines for European locations, which repeats the overexposure of threats to Western States and prioritises a Western security frame of reference.[36] This is a problem that is further exacerbated by the focus on (returning) Western Foreign Fighters where the research priorities become distorted away from the core of the movement and focus instead on the priorities of the Western state.[37] As with the linguistic

---

34 Jackson, Richard, "The Study of Terrorism 10 Years After 9/11: Successes, Issues, Challenges", Uluslararası İlişkiler, Volume 8, No 32 (Winter 2012), p. 1–16 quoting, Ranstorp, "Mapping Terrorism Studies after 9/11", p. 25.
35 Brown, Katherine E. 2011. "Blinded by the Explosion? Security and Resistance in Muslim Women's Suicide Terrorism," in Laura Sjoberg and Caron E. Gentry, eds. *Women, Gender, and Terrorism*. Athens: University of Georgia Press, 194–226.
36 http://www.voxpol.eu/online-jihadi-instructional-content-iss-rumiyah-2017/.
37 Klausen, Jytte. "Tweeting the Jihad: Social media networks of Western foreign fighters in Syria and Iraq." *Studies in Conflict & Terrorism* 38.1 (2015): 1–22. Benmelech, Efraim, and Esteban F. Klor. *What Explains the Flow of Foreign Fighters to ISIS?*. No. w22190. National Bureau of Economic Research, 2016. Byman, Daniel, and Jeremy Shapiro. *Be afraid. Be a little afraid: the threat of terrorism from Western foreign fighters in Syria and Iraq*. Brookings, 2014. Briggs, Rachel, and Tanya Silverman. *Western foreign fighters: innovations in responding to the threat*. Institute for Strategic Dialogue, 2014. Rich, Ben, and Dara Conduit. "The impact of jihadist foreign fighters on indigenous secular-nationalist causes: Contrasting chechnya and syria." *Studies in Conflict & Terrorism* 38.2 (2015): 113–131. Weggemans, Daan, Edwin Bakker, and Peter Grol. "Who are they and why do they go? The Radicalization and Preparatory Processes of Dutch Jihadist Foreign Fighters." *Perspectives on Terrorism* 8.4 (2014). Hegghammer, Thomas. "Should I stay or should I go? Explaining variation in Western jihadists' choice between domestic and foreign fighting." *American*

bias toward European languages, this method of understanding the jihadist movement through the emphasis on Western fighters and threats to Western interests, only touches on the periphery of the movement, which cannot be used as a proxy for the Arabic core.

For the data analysis of the electronic ribat, one of the issues which has dominated articles in recent years has been providing advice for controlling and eradicating terrorist content online, to paraphrase Richard Jackson. This effort has focused on ways to measure or show decline and is often predicated on framing devices of the state, such as the emphasis on 'official propaganda'. This, as shown below, has resulted in a series of studies using proxy metrics to produce a two dimensional 'measurement' of content – the purpose of which is defined through western concepts such as 'Utopia'. These two-dimensional approaches have over the years taken the form of measuring the average number of followers on Twitter or counting the number of pictures published. This produces a proxy metric rather than an authentic view of the aims of the movement. An authentic view needs to be based on assessing the success of ISIS or Jihadist strategy, based on the discussion of Jihadist strategy in Arabic documents, audio and video all of which is currently almost entirely missing from the research design, data acquisition and data analysis.

Versions of these measures have been used, co-opted or adopted by Western policymakers, such as the White House promotion of the RAND study.[38] This study, the findings from which were promoted by the White House, "claimed to detect 'a clear decline in the number of Islamic State supporters tweeting on a daily basis' starting in April 2015".[39] The problem solving approach to the study of the jihadist movement had problems with both data acquisition and data analysis.

From a data acquisition perspective,

Political Science Review 107.1 (2013): 1–15. Bakker, Edwin, and Roel De Bont. "Belgian and Dutch jihadist foreign fighters (2012–2015): Characteristics, motivations, and roles in the War in Syria and Iraq." *Small Wars & Insurgencies* 27.5 (2016): 837–857. Bakker, Edwin, et al. *Dealing with European Foreign Fighters in Syria: Governance Challenges & Legal Implications*. The Hague: International Centre for Counter-Terrorism, 2013. Bakker, Edwin, and van Zuijdewijn J. de Roy. "Jihadist Foreign Fighter Phenomenon in Western Europe: A Low-Probability, High-Impact Threat." *ICCT-Research papers* 2015 (2015): 22. Basra, Rajan, and Peter R. Neumann. "Criminal Pasts, Terrorist Futures." *Perspectives on Terrorism* 10.6 (2016): 25–40.

38 Bodine-Baron, Elizabeth, et al. *Examining ISIS Support and Opposition Networks on Twitter.* RAND Corporation Santa Monica United States, 2016. Islamic State's Twitter traffic drops amid US efforts, AP, 09 July 2016. https://apnews.com/21c9eb68e6294bdfa0a099a0632b8056/ap-exclusive-islamic-states-twitter-traffic-plunges.

39 Frampton, Martyn, Ali Fisher, and Dr Nico Prucha. "The New Netwar: Countering Extremism Online" (London: Policy Exchange, 2017) pp. 59–60.

the RAND study focuses on a variety of terms for ISIS. However, during the time period of the study, ISIS supporters increasingly used tags relating to a specific province, which are not included in the list of search terms used in the study .... An apparent lack of access to the nuances of jihadist strategy, meant that, however good the lexical analysis, data collection was not looking in the right place.[40]

From the data analysis perspective,

> the report's authors suggested two potential causes [for the drop in pro-ISIS Twitter content]; 'first, the reduction may be a result of the Twitter suspension campaign', and second, 'the trend may partly be an indication of reduced global support for Islamic State'.[41]

Both suggestions assume the Western backed response to ISIS are the cause of the results. No suggestion is made that ISIS and the Media Mujahidin could have changed tactics or that changes in content were the result of strategy. In fact, not only had the way ISIS tagged content changed, but they had moved away from core communication via Twitter to engaging with their vanguard via Telegram.[42]

Looking beyond the US government, a UK Government backed report produced by VOX-Pol, sought to assess whether is it worthwhile for pro-IS users to return to Twitter in 2017.

As a result of disruption,

> one of the stated aims of the Global Coalition against Daesh is to undermine ISIS by making them appear unsuccessful. This creates the potential for research to become co-opted and could turn scholars into 'an uncritical mouthpiece of state interests' were the research focus and Coalition goals to become closely aligned. In the extreme, the potential distortion of research priorities and co-opting of the field would be particularly problematic if any individual or institution were posing as academic researcher(s) or independent journalists but had an undeclared conflict of interest, as has occurred in previous conflicts.[43]

Were that to happen, for example with researchers commenting on the success of operations conducted by the Global Coalition against Daesh and its members or making claims about the decline of ISIS, while they were also collaborating with

---

40 Frampton, Martyn, Ali Fisher, and Dr Nico Prucha. "The New Netwar: Countering Extremism Online" (London: Policy Exchange, 2017).
41 Frampton, Martyn, Ali Fisher, and Dr Nico Prucha. "The New Netwar: Countering Extremism Online" (London: Policy Exchange, 2017).
42 Prucha, Nico. "IS and the Jihadist Information Highway–Projecting Influence and Religious Identity via Telegram." *Perspectives on Terrorism* 10.6 (2016).
43 Previous examples of undisclosed conflicts of interest are documented in: Saunders, Frances Stonor. *Who paid the piper?: the CIA and the cultural Cold War*. Granta Books, 2000. Lucas, Scott. *Freedom's war: The US crusade against the Soviet Union, 1945–56*. Manchester University Press, 1999. The CIA's Cultural War: how the CIA secretly funded the magazine Encounter, BBC World Service, 19 Nov 2015, https://www.bbc.co.uk/programmes/p037t501.

or working for the Coalition – without disclosing the conflict of interests to the readers – there is a risk this would cease to be distortion or co-option of the field, and become covert collusion.[44] Such covert collusion could influence the available information about the fortunes of groups such as ISIS, in a similar way to the UK government information operation to pay for content in "the Arabic broadcast media and posted online with no indication of British government involvement" as reported by the *Guardian*.[45]

The focus on European languages, along with the potential distortion of research priorities by the 'problem solving' approach, creates significant inhibitions to an authentic understanding and interpretation of the movement, but these are only half the challenge with Data science. Appropriate data collection and analysis methods are also a vital component in robust data science.

Data quality

Rather than detailed data science, much of the work over recent years has taken the form of 'tweet-ready' punditry, providing ad hoc responses based on what an individual personally saw on Twitter, (or Nashir channels on Telegram) rather than explanations based on research that carries predictive value. Finding problem-solving proxy metrics that could show ISIS digital presence in decline began with the specific claims of disruption in September 2014 in which J.M.Berger claimed "It's very clear now that Twitter suspensions have seriously degraded IS ability to game hashtags and distribute content".[46] Six months later, Berger and Morgan still doubted the "purported resilience of the ISIS social network".[47] As 2016 began, almost eighteen months after those first claims of serious degradation and disruption, there was optimistic talk of cyberbombs and wiping ISIS off the internet.[48] 2016 also witnessed a CTC study produce a massive

---

44 Conflicts of interest in this sense should be read as those defined here: https://authorservices.taylorandfrancis.com/what-is-a-conflict-of-interest/.
45 https://www.theguardian.com/world/2016/may/03/how-britain-funds-the-propaganda-war-against-isis-in-syria.
46 https://twitter.com/intelwire/status/513303666368196608.
47 Berger, Jonathon M., and Jonathon Morgan. "The ISIS Twitter Census: Defining and describing the population of ISIS supporters on Twitter." *The Brookings Project on US Relations with the Islamic World* 3.20 (2015): 4–1. https://www.brookings.edu/wp-content/uploads/2016/06/isis_twitter_census_berger_morgan.pdf.
48 Richard Forno and Anupam Joshi, 'How U.S. "Cyber Bombs" against Terrorists Really Work', The Conversation, Scientific American, 13 May 2016, https://www.scientificamerican.com/articl e/how-u-s-cyber-bombs-against-terroristsreally-work/.

underestimate of the content being produced, likely due to the failure to examine content from Telegram, despite ISIS using it consistently for almost a year.[49]

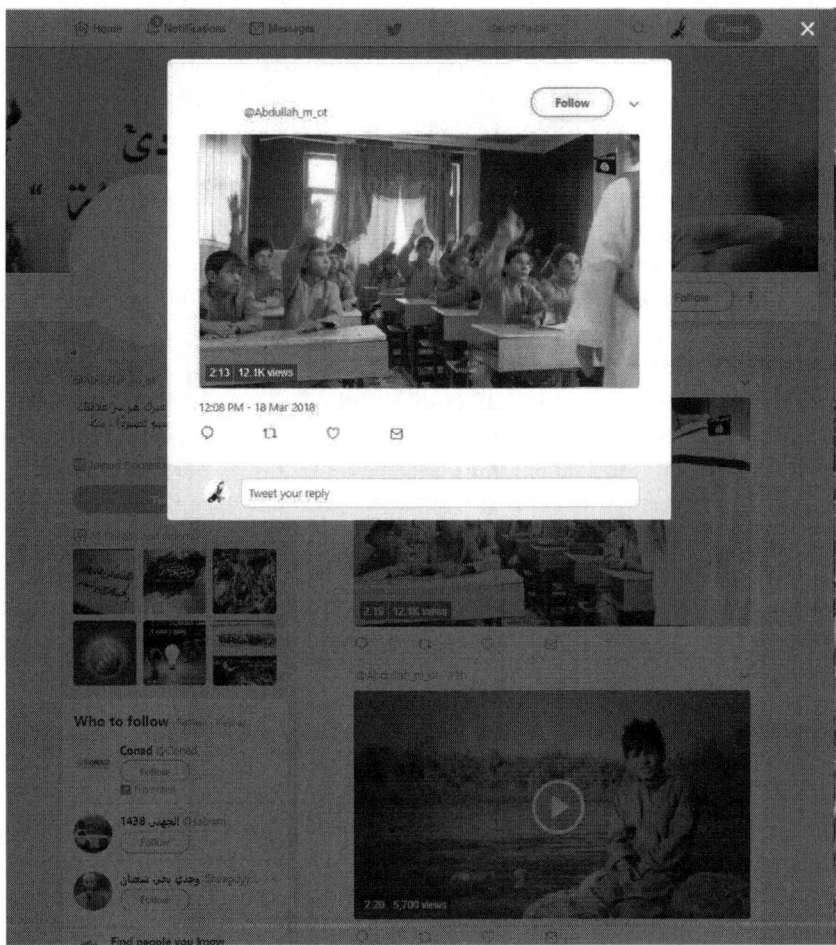

18th March 2018–12,100 views

In 2017 a VOX-Pol study "pro-IS accounts are being significantly disrupted and this has effectively eliminated IS's once vibrant Twitter community". Furthermore, "IS's ability to facilitate and maintain strong and influential com-

---

[49] Milton, Daniel. *Communication Breakdown: Unraveling the Islamic States Media Efforts*. US Military Academy-Combating Terrorism Center West Point United States, 2016. For comparison see: Frampton, Martyn, Ali Fisher, and Dr Nico Prucha. "The New Netwar: Countering Extremism Online" (London: Policy Exchange, 2017 p. 38.

munities on Twitter was found to be significantly diminished".[50] However, during the same period of the VOX-Pol study, Twitter represented 40 % of known referrals to ISIS content.[51] As predicted, in 2014 the Swarmcast reconfigured. The failure to find the accounts and recognise the methods through which ISIS was driving traffic to content meant the report's "up-to-date account of the effects of Twitter's disruption strategy on IS supporter accounts" reflects western assumptions on what ISIS are doing – rather than an authentic representation of what ISIS is doing.[52]

In January 2018 Jade Parker and Charlie Winter announced "a full-fledged collapse" in ISIS media.[53] January 2018 also witnessed a 48 % increase in ISIS content production and in March 2018 ISIS videos are getting over 12,000 views on Twitter.[54] Ironically, in May the same researchers were producing updates on what ISIS were producing – four months after the purported 'total collapse'.

It is hard to square the large-scale viewing of ISIS videos via Twitter and recent month-on-month increase in ISIS branded productions, with the pronouncements of degradation, decline and collapse made over the last three and a half years. Instead of degradation and collapse, the nature of the ISIS Swarmcast means it can appear to be degraded, but it has really only reconfigured, as it has repeatedly since the phenomena was first identified in 2014.[55]

Unfortunately, while there has been no let-up in the quantity of analysis being published about ISIS media activities, there have been limitations in the quality of that analysis. Particular in the way such research contributes to an authentic representation of the Jihadist movement.

These studies often rely poor statistical work and linear approaches. The lack of appropriate and genuine data science has led to persistent content blindness amongst computer science-based analysis, while subject matter specific research has suffered from the *Falling Follower Fallacy*, and the *6th Grader Problem*.

A few recent examples of problems of data collection are emblematic of a

---

50 Conway, Maura, et al. "Disrupting Daesh: measuring takedown of online terrorist material and it's impacts." (2017): 1–45. http://doras.dcu.ie/21961/1/Disrupting_DAESH_FINAL_WEB_VERSION.pdf.
51 Frampton, Martyn, Ali Fisher, and Dr Nico Prucha. "The New Netwar: Countering Extremism Online" (London: Policy Exchange, 2017).
52 Fisher, Ali, and Nico Prucha. "ISIS is winning the online jihad against the West." *The Daily Beast* 10 (2014). https://www.thedailybeast.com/isis-is-winning-the-online-jihad-against-the-west.
53 https://www.lawfareblog.com/virtual-caliphate-rebooted-islamic-states-evolving-online-strategy.
54 Analysis: IS media show signs of recovery after sharp decline, BBC Monitoring, (23rd February 2018) https://monitoring.bbc.co.uk/product/c1dov471#top.
55 Fisher, Ali, and Nico Prucha. "ISIS is winning the online jihad against the West." *The Daily Beast* 10 (2014). https://www.thedailybeast.com/isis-is-winning-the-online-jihad-against-the-west.

wider problem. First, the difference between what is 'found' and what is 'produced'. In October 2017 graphics were published which purported to show that "#IS's media machine is contracting. A large proportion of the propaganda apparatus is now almost totally dormant".[56] 'Almost totally dormant' in this context actually meant any foundation or Wilayah from which the researcher had found 4 or fewer pieces of content. The methodological problems behind this claim, include accuracy of data acquisition, counting all content as having the same value and a profound misunderstanding of timeseries research. In the case of data acquisition, based on what the researcher found, al-Furat, Somalia, Khurasan, Bayda', Anbar, & West Africa were all claimed to be 'almost totally dormant'. However, all these actually produced more than the four pieces of content in September required for them to be considered active. It was not that the entities were dormant, but that the researcher had not been able to find the content. Hence what this research was measuring was the researcher's ability rather than ISIS production. This echoes, previously published findings which showed ISIS *weekly* content production actually exceeded the CTC estimate of *monthly* production. This was because CTC, just like these more recent claims of decline, were based on tracking the declining ability of the researchers to find content, not the ability of ISIS to produce it.[57]

In addition, basing the claim on four pieces a month highlights a clear misunderstanding of timeseries data. This is because any magazine which is published weekly (for example *The Economist*) would be dormant for 8 months of 2018.[58] In the case of the Economist, founded in 1843 and publishing 51 issues a year (there is a Christmas double issue), there are only 4 months in which there are sufficient Fridays for it to be published more than four times.[59] Yet in the terms of the research, the economist would be considered 'almost totally dormant' – an obvious nonsense. Furthermore, it is problematic to count different types of content as the same. For example, the organisation that published the 46 minute speech by Abu Bakr al-Baghdadi, at the end of September 2017 is recorded as dormant because it *only* produced the first recording of Abu Bakr al-Baghdadi to be released in the last 10 months. Claiming it was dormant does not

---

56 https://twitter.com/charliewinter/status/920651518172332032.
57 Milton, Daniel. *Communication Breakdown: Unraveling the Islamic States Media Efforts*. US Military Academy-Combating Terrorism Center West Point United States, 2016. For comparison see: Frampton, Martyn, Ali Fisher, and Dr Nico Prucha. "The New Netwar: Countering Extremism Online" (London: Policy Exchange, 2017 p. 38.
58 The exact number of publications on the day of publication of this book cannot be given due to the ongoing process of publication.
59 *The Economist* is published weekly, 51 times a year, with the Christmas double issue remaining on sale for two weeks. The issue is dated Saturday and goes on sale each Friday.

provide an authentic view of content production, nor the authority and relative value of the particular types of content.

Equally, because the content is undifferentiated, photos represent around to 80 % of the content. As such, any change in photo production will massively impact the overall impression regardless of proportionally larger fluctuations in other media types. For example, the emphasis on decline between 2015 and February 2017 is based on the number of photos, as video production increased. By adding all media types together, a decrease in easily produced photographs hides an increase in the higher resource requirement and greater impact of video production.

The impact of the methodological limitations, in design, data acquisition and analysis are subtle, but they make all the difference in producing an authentic understanding of the jihadist movement through credible data science.

Counting Content

A further aspect of the problem-solving approach has been the attempt to make links between changes in ISIS activity and the activity of the Global Coalition, just as previous connections were made between content found on Twitter and ISIS global support. For example, it has been claimed "the destabilization of the Islamic State's territorial strongholds is correlated to a decrease in the volume of media production".[60]

For a data scientist interested in the electronic ribat there are a number of problems with this type of research. Beyond the issues of data acquisition and analysis;
- There is no calculation of correlation in the published research, so it is an assumed pseudo-correlation which is not based on any demonstrable relationship in the data.
- The apparent relationship between territory and production can only be maintained by cherry picking certain points in time.

To show how the pseudo-correlation is produced we need to understand how the timeline is constructed, and then how it is compared to territory.

The use of cherry picking particular timepoints is particularly illustrative of the impact of the distortion caused by the 'problem solving' approach. The familiar narrative of anti-ISIS forces and problem solving research is that ISIS reached a highpoint in 2015, and has been in decline ever since.

---

60 Mehdi Semati & Piotr M. Szpunar, ISIS beyond the spectacle: communication media, networked publics, terrorism, Critical Studies in Media Communication Vol. 35, Iss. 1,2018.

This narrative is built on a range of cherry picked points which highlight the problems of contemporary applications of data science. As Richard Jackson noted there is "persistent tendency to treat the current terrorist threat as unprecedented and exceptional" and ISIS activity in the electronic ribat is a particularly good example.[61] Specifically the 'highpoint' argument gives little attention to the period before August 2015. However, the Jihadist movement online has been learning and refining its operations for two decades.

Beyond the unreliability of counting content as a measure of success, the attempt to present ISIS as new belies the need to consider a wider history of jihadist media and analyse whether 2015 was a two dimensional 'highpoint' or an outliner in a much more complex and three-dimensional information ecosystem.

From a historical perspective, for example, this video of 'oh allah bestow on us paradise' (يا الله الجنة) published in 2013 features a now familiar nashid, with familiar themes that appear in contemporary ISIS collections and videos. This despite most commentary beginning with ISIS in 2014 or in some cases 2015 and presenting it as something unprecedented.

Previous research has already shown why the summer of 2015 is cherry picked

---

61 Richard Jackson, The Study of Terrorism after 11 September 2001: Problems, Challenges and Future Developments, *Political Studies Review*, 7, 2, (171-184), (2009).

as a start point if your goal is to contribute to claims of decline.[62] As discussed in depth elsewhere, Summer 2015 was Ramadan, 1 year of the Caliphate, and witnessed a major push to launch wilayat media production. When this is considered the two dimensional 'highpoint' becomes an obvious outlier based on a confluence of factors within the ongoing fluctuation of content production.

In addition to using an outliner rather than an authentic representative of the content production, the claims of decline, including those by the Global Coali-

---

62 Frampton, Martyn, Ali Fisher, and Dr Nico Prucha. "The New Netwar: Countering Extremism Online" (London: Policy Exchange, 2017).

tion, then head straight to 2017. This allows them to present "huge and steady decrease" by drawing a metaphoric straight line between 2015 and 2017.[63]

This presents a range of problems. First, journalists writing about the 2015 'highpoint' have claimed ISIS "was producing more than 200 videos, radio programmes, magazines and photo reports each week" resulting in "just under a thousand [892] unique data points, ranging from radio bulletins and electronic magazines to videos and photographic essays".[64] However, in September 2017 Charlie Winter, who claims 2015 as the 'highpoint' told a Wired security event about the 'Virtual Caliphate' that there are "hundreds and hundreds of unique media products, videos, magazines, radio bulletins, in lots of different languages coming out every single day".[65]

It does not take a data scientist to calculate 'hundreds a day', will be higher than the 200 a week highpoint, but it is the second problem, that is particularly troubling: The way problem-solving researchers have presented 2015 and 2017 data. This is particularly illustrative of the challenge posed by claims of 'decline'. To produce the effect, problem-solving researchers have had to become creative with their display longitudinal data, which fall well outside the accepted standards of academic research.[66]

Contrary to the ideas about displaying time series data, the bars in the graph are spaced evenly. The effect is the impression of a steep, linear decline, even though the chronological space between data points varies significantly.[67] In fact, while two of the time points are only a single month apart, the other gaps were 6 and 17 months respectively.

When the image is redrawn, so all months are represented equally – both months with and without data – the problems become evident. First, the impression of sharp decline is reduced. Second, what happened to 2016? It is now easy for the viewer to realise 2016 is completely missing.

Using data previously presented elsewhere, weekly data from February 2016

---

63 Lakomy, Miron. "Cracks in the Online "Caliphate": How the Islamic State is Losing Ground in the Battle for Cyberspace." *Perspectives on Terrorism* 11.3 (2017).
64 Winter, Charlie. "Apocalypse, later: a longitudinal study of the Islamic State brand." *Critical Studies in Media Communication* 35.1 (2018): 103–121. Actual number (892) added for clarity.
65 https://onlinejihad.net/2017/11/23/how-decliners-get-data-so-wrong/#_edn7.
66 Edward Tufte, has "set out a detailed analysis of how to display data for precise, effective, quick analysis" in his *Visual Display of Quantitative Information*. This includes demonstrating that inappropriate use of data can lead to an apparent, but entirely spurious, connection between the fortunes of the New York Stock Exchange and the level of Solar Radiation.
67 http://www.wired.co.uk/article/isis-islamic-state-propaganda-content-strategy. The same trick was also used to the same effect at other occasions suggesting it was not a just a miscommunication between author and designer: https://twitter.com/charliewinter/status/920651729393389568.

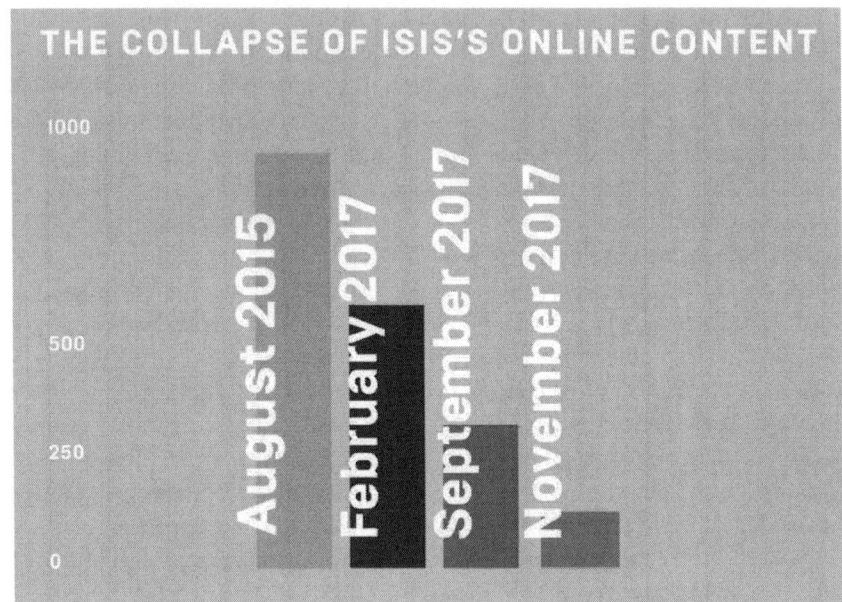

Original graph featured in Wired

to March 2017 shows production fluctuated, despite claims of a "huge and steady decrease" or 30 % to 40 % reduction.[68]

Equally the issue of outliers and a problem with an interpretation which claims a single direction of 'decline' becomes more pronounced. Genuinely longitudinal data, rather than cherry-picked, seemingly random, points show

---

68 Lakomy, Miron. "Cracks in the Online "Caliphate": How the Islamic State is Losing Ground in the Battle for Cyberspace." *Perspectives on Terrorism* 11.3 (2017)Charlie Winter, ICSR Insight: The ISIS Propaganda Decline, 23rd March 2017. http://icsr.info/2017/03/icsr-insight-isis-propaganda-decline/.

there is much more to the story than drawing an imaginary line across a 17-month gap and claiming correlation.[69]

Content fluctuated on a daily, weekly, and monthly basis. This means you can cherry pick points to claim large-scale decline or increase. Taking a longer-term view, there were times in 2016 where the rolling mean of weekly content production was rising, at others falling. Fluctuation, often during periods of reconfiguration, is entirely consistent with content production by the Jihadist movement during the last two decades. The persistent tendency to treat ISIS as 'unprecedented and exceptional' means this history and nuance are entirely missing from the linear, decline centric, data analysis whether from Coalition Information Operations or recent journalism.

Using rolling mean to examine how production changed over 2016 uncovers some important results. Most important, there was an increase of 132 % in the rolling mean of content production between the low points of September / October 2016 and the cherry-picked month of February 2017.[70] This means, as previous research has shown, February 2017 occurred during a period of rising content average production.[71] An authentic representation of ISIS production during 2016 directly contradicts the claims of a single downward direction, as the Global Coalition imply and some punditry explicitly claims.[72] While the individual fluctuations are interesting, the more important conclusion is that fluctuations in content production by jihadist groups are normal, they do not necessarily represent the impact of western activity, and cannot be used to draw conclusions about the movement. It may be possible to pick two points and accurately calculate the difference in the total numbers but this does not provide an authentic representation of the movement, nor meaningful understanding of the content.

The other part of the problem with a claimed correlation between media and territory, is that it implies (rather than calculates) a relationship between the two.

The problem-solving logic of correlation requires there to be a single downward direction and that these would occur in a way that indicates a relationship between them, distinct from confounding by other factors.[73]

However, a different picture has long been evident to anyone embedded in an

---

69 Mehdi Semati & Piotr M. Szpunar, ISIS beyond the spectacle: communication media, networked publics, terrorism, Critical Studies in Media Communication Vol. 35, Iss. 1,2018.
70 Frampton, Martyn, Ali Fisher, and Dr Nico Prucha. "The New Netwar: Countering Extremism Online" (London: Policy Exchange, 2017).
71 Frampton, Martyn, Ali Fisher, and Dr Nico Prucha. "The New Netwar: Countering Extremism Online" (London: Policy Exchange, 2017).
72 https://twitter.com/charliewinter/status/935082777040642050.
73 Without an actual calculation, claims of correlation have no weight. The following is therefore emblematic of the problem. We also won't spend any time on whether they were claiming a correlation based on the Spearman or Pearson method.

Arabic context and "crystal clear to virtually anyone who has the linguistic capacity to grasp and the opportunity to witness what jihadists are actually saying, writing and doing, both online and offline".[74]

The Global Coalition has reported on the reduction in ISIS territory as a percentage area held at the territorial highpoint of August 2014.[75] Yet, decliners claim summer 2015 as the media highpoint, which occurs while ISIS was losing ground, including parts of Sinjar and Kobane (14 % in total during 2015).[76] Put simply, the count of content was increasing toward the claimed 'highpoint' while territory was decreasing, which casts doubt on the pseudo-correlation.

Furthermore, as content production has fluctuated, for there to be even a pseudo-correlation, logic dictates that territory would have to fluctuate too. This is problematic as claims of a relationship between territory and media production after the 2015 media 'highpoint' rely on a 'decline' narrative. Yet, content production went up 132 % between October 2016 and February 2017, while territory held by ISIS went down. The Coalition territorial estimate for October 2016 shows that the territory ISIS had lost was 56 % Iraq 27 % Syria, by February 2017 this had become 63 % and 35 % respectively.[77]

As a result, not only do the claimed 'highpoints' occur a year apart, but the claimed pseudo-correlation between the two evaporates when the change in production and territory are compared with genuinely longitudinal data rather than cherry-picking. Indeed, the study of the jihadist movement requires data science capable of producing an authentic representation of the phenomena rather than tweet-ready problem-solving which presents ISIS as unprecedented, thus removing the need for detailed analysis of what came before. The importance of focusing on an authentic representation was highlighted only days after Jade Parker and Charlie Winter announced "a full-fledged collapse" in ISIS media.[78] During the month they pronounced the full-fledged collapse ISIS content production showed a month-on-month increase of 48 %.[79]

---

74 Rüdiger Lohlker, "Why Theology Matters – The Case of ISIS," Strategic Review, July –September 2016; http://sr-indonesia.com/in-the-journal/view/europe-s-misunderstanding-of-islam-and-isis.
75 https://www.defense.gov/Portals/1/features/2014/0814_iraq/docs/20160512_ISIL%20Areas%20of%20Influence_Aug%202014%20through%20Apr%202016%20Map.pdf.
76 http://www.businessinsider.com/how-much-territory-has-isis-lost-2016-10?IR=T.
77 October 2016: http://theglobalcoalition.org/en/maps_and_stats/daesh-areas-of-influence-october-2016-update/; February 2017: http://theglobalcoalition.org/en/maps_and_stats/daesh-areas-of-influence-february-2017-update/.
78 https://www.lawfareblog.com/virtual-caliphate-rebooted-islamic-states-evolving-online-strategy.
79 Analysis: IS media show signs of recovery after sharp decline, BBC Monitoring, (23rd February 2018) https://monitoring.bbc.co.uk/product/c1dov471#top.

Summary

The Jihadist movement distributes their strategy in their own words, these words should not be obscured by disciplinary siloes, a failure to collaborate, nor an attempt to force the understanding of the movement into a Western, predominantly English language, habitus.

Lacking a nuanced understanding of the movement, both "counter-narratives" and takedowns have become trapped in a tactical paradigm, while research has struggled to grasp the strategy of the movement. However, while once derided as a 'straw man argument', the need to understand how ISIS networks of influence operate at a strategic level is now evident to almost all.[80]

It requires data science based on the collaboration between data analysts and subject matter experts to achieve it. Understanding the information ecosystem is about more than peering down soda straws at handpicked examples; it is about the way different parts of the ecosystem co-exist and intersect; it is about the way the humans behind the screens interact and fundamentally about the content they share. This includes the documents which outline the strategy and tactics which the Jihadist movement currently intends to use. It is not about providing the latest proxy metric to government but developing an authentic understanding of the movement on the (electronic) ribat.

What is Data Science

Many contemporary perspectives on data science highlight the importance of computer data, programming languages, maths and statistics. For example, Mike Loukides argues "data science requires skills ranging from traditional computer science to mathematics to art".[81] This vision is shared by Jeff Hammerbacher who described the reason for adopting the 'data science' label at Facebook:

> … on any given day, a team member could author a multistage processing pipeline in Python, design a hypothesis test, perform a regression analysis over data samples with R, design and implement an algorithm for some data-intensive product or service in Hadoop, or communicate the results of our analyses to other members of the organization.[82]

---

80 https://www.brookings.edu/wp-content/uploads/2016/06/isis_twitter_census_berger_morgan.pdf.
81 Mike Loukides, What is data science? The future belongs to the companies and people that turn data into products. June 2, 2010 http://radar.oreilly.com/2010/06/what-is-data-science.html.
82 Jeff Hammerbacher, 'Information Platforms and the Rise of the Data Scientist', in Toby Segaran, Jeff Hammerbacher, *Beautiful Data* (O'Reilly Media, Inc. *July 2009*) p. 84.

These perspectives on Data Science place heavy emphasis on Computer Science. In the study of the Media Mujahidin, this type of approach has lead to endless presentations by computer scientists focusing on what is purported to be 'core content' of the jihadist movement – magazines such as Dabiq, Inspire, or Rumiyah, or Twitter accounts with pictures of Lions and detection of tweets using terms such as 'Islamic State'. Such computer science driven big data approaches, often focus on challenges characterised by three Vs: volume, velocity, and variety – with the veracity of data being a common fourth 'V'.[83]

However, the use of data science must maintain a focus on delivering meaningful and authentic representations of the phenomena being studied, whether or not these insights are immediately considered relevant by policy makers. The focus must be on the challenges posed by the Jihadist movement, rather than the data collection challenges. To this end, the use of data science will require teamwork between computer or data specialists and subject matter experts.

Fortunately, this is not the only approach to Data Science. In his valuable *An Introduction to Data Science*, Jeffrey Stanton writes:

> Data Science refers to an emerging area of work concerned with the collection, preparation, analysis, visualization, management, and preservation of large collections of information. Although the name Data Science seems to connect most strongly with areas such as databases and computer science, many different kinds of skills – including non-mathematical skills – are needed.[84]

To ensure the data science returns an authentic representation of the phenomena being studied, Jeffrey Stanton outlined the four A's of data as useful categories through which team members can identify the roles and responsibilities at each stage of a research project:
- *Architecture* refers to the form and format of the data and the design of the research.
- *Acquisition* includes the identification, collection, and storage of data, including how that data will be presented for analysis. This consideration is particularly important when the subject area specialist is not also technically capable of accessing the data from the format in which it is being stored.
- *Analysis* combines data science elements such as the summarizing the data, using samples to make inferences about the larger context, and data visualization. It also includes the process through which data will be made available

---

83 3 Vs https://hbr.org/2012/10/big-data-the-management-revolution/ar; for Veracity: http://www.ibmbigdatahub.com/sites/default/files/styles/xlarge-scaled/public/infographic_image/4-Vs-of-big-data.jpg?itok=4syrvSLX.
84 Stanton, Jeffrey M. "Introduction to data science." (2013). https://ischool.syr.edu/media/documents/2012/3/DataScienceBook1_1.pdf.

to the subject matter expert, in this case diplomacy, to be analyzed within the context of that field.
- *Archiving* refers to preservation, long-term storage and, where appropriate, making the data reusable.

As team members are often significantly more familiar with one part of the project than the other, defining clear roles can help ensure that important aspects of research do not fall down the cracks between computer or data specialists and subject matter experts. In addition, laying out the responsibility at each stage of the project can help ensure that a data science approach can best contribute to greater understanding of the activity of the Media Mujahidin. The table below is intended to be illustrative rather than exhaustive. Understanding the role of the 'other' specialisms in the collaboration are fundamental to effective data science. This is not only to ensure they receive what they require to do their part of the project, it is to ensure the project is a genuine collaboration rather than a list of individuals working in parallel with little understanding of the other elements of the project.

As this chapter has shown, the problems in the current study of the electronic ribat are seriously impacting the understanding of the Jihadist movement. As the 'internet has become a great medium for spreading the call of Jihad and following the news of the mujahideen' so the methods used to study the phenomena must follow suit to produce an authentic representation of the movement.

To study the electronic ribat, data science must be a genuine collaboration made up of teams with a range of skills; genuine Arabic language abilities (not faux Arabic), in depth knowledge of the hundreds of thousands of pages of Arabic documents, and the back catalogue of video, audio and nashid. Statistical specialists capable of ensuring that data is appropriate, that graphical representations are authentic representations of the data and that statistical techniques such as time series and correlation are executed accurately and adequately understood by subject matter specialists.

The time for fumbling in the dark, proxy metrics and poor data work is over – dawn is coming.

Ali Fisher / Nico Prucha

A Milestone for "Islamic State" Propaganda: "The Clanging of the Swords, part 4"

Introducing the theological framework of "Clanging of the Swords" – from Amsterdam to the "Islamic State"

This chapter is an in-depth analysis of a four-part video series named *Salil al-sawarim*, or the "clanging of the swords". This series is worthy of such detailed attention as it provides an excellent example of a certain form of ISIS (=IS) propaganda. More specifically, it is a key example of how IS uses theology to justify the actions of its fighters and legitimise its occupation of territory in Syria and Iraq.

Sunni extremists, referred to as jihadists or Salafi-jihadists, have a long and rich tradition of written theological explanations of what it means to be a "true" or "proper" Sunni Muslim. However, IS uses theology to justify its day-to-day operations to a greater degree than other Sunni extremist groups, including Al Qaeda (AQ).

The series *Salil al-Sawarim* is particularly illustrative of this emphasis on theology. Readers sufficiently initiated into the mainly Arabic language corpus of Sunni extremist theology will understand the title's particular reference right away;[1] it refers to the book *al-Sarim al-maslul 'ala shatim al-rasul*, "the Sharp Sword on whoever Insults the Prophet." Its author is 13th century Islamic scholar Ibn Taymiyya (1263–1328 AD), who is often referred to as *shaykh al-Islam* ("the scholar of Islam") in the conservative Arabic-Islamic framework.

---

1 Rüdiger Lohlker, Why Theology Matters – the Case of Jihadi Islam, in: *Strategic Review* (July-September 2016) (http://sr-indonesia.com/in-the-journal/view/europe-s-misunderstanding-of-islam-and-isis) (accessed May 05, 2018).

Ibn Taymiyya is renowned for his "characteristically juridical thinking"[2] and viewed as a highly competent legal scholar. His writings are based – at least in part – on Islamic jurisprudence (*fiqh*).

Ibn Taymiyya has featured prominently in Sunni extremist thought since the 1980s, when AQ established this theology. The "Islamic State" has based all of its audio-visual output on the theology penned by AQ. The crucial difference is that IS has (had) the territory to implement and enforce this corpus of theology on the population of the self-designated "caliphate".

Ibn Taymiyya provides a legal framework based on jurisprudential findings for killing "an insulter of the prophet, regardless whether he is a Muslim or a disbeliever".[3] Whoever insults the Prophet, according to Ibn Taymiyya, "must be killed, no matter if he is a Muslim or disbeliever, and has no right to repent."

Within the Sunni extremist mind-set, the sword must be drawn upon anyone who opposes their worldview and specific interpretation of Qur'anic sources or the hadith (sayings and deeds of Prophet Muhammad). In various AQ and IS videos, a specific sound effect subtly underscores references to Ibn Taymiyya's writings. This sound effect, popular within jihadist online subculture, is that of a sword drawn from its shaft, clanging in the process.

Jihadists have also used the writings of Ibn Taymiyya to justify specific attacks. For example, Muhammed Bouyeri cited Ibn Taymiyya's book before killing Dutch filmmaker and Islam critic Theo van Gogh in November 2004 in Amsterdam:

> "Shortly before he [Bouyeri] killed van Gogh, he circulated the theological tractate on the "heroic deed" of Ibn Maslama[4] per e-mail to his friends. It is one of the 56 texts Bouyeri wrote or distributed. The fatwa of Ibn Taymiyya was among them also in a short leaflet-form downloadable from tawhed.ws titled "The drawn sword against the insulter of the Prophet" (al-sarim al-maslul didda shatim al-rasul). It is likely that the text not only influenced Bouyeri's decision to assassinate van Gogh, but also his method.
> The text details how and why to kill targets, first of all because of insult (shatm, sabb, adhan) of Islam. Bouyeri tried to sever van Gogh's head with a big knife after he had

---

2 Wael b. Hallaq, *Ibn Taymiyya against the Greek Logicians*. Translated with an introduction by Wael Hallaq, New York: Oxford University Press, 1993, p. xxxiii.
3 The book is available online on various websites and outlets, for example *Durar al-Sunniyya*, www.dorar.net. A print version is available in most religious book shops in Arab countries. The image is a book cover illustration of a commented version published as: Ibn Taymiyya, *al-Sarim al-maslul 'ala shatim al-rasul li-shaykh al-Islam Taqiyy al-Din Ahmad bin 'Abd al-Halim Ibn Taymiyya al-Harrani*, Shubra al-Khayma: Alexandria/Medina, 2008.
4 As the author of the citation Philipp Holtmann explains, "terrorists are called upon to identify with the Muslim Ibn Maslama who volunteered to kill Muhammad's critic Ka'b bin al-Ashraf." Philipp Holtmann, *Virtual Leadership in Radical Islamist Movements: Mechanisms, Justifications and Discussion*. Working Paper, The Institute for Policy and Strategy, Herzliya Conference February 6–9, 2011 (http://www.herzliyaconference.org/eng/_Uploads/dbsAttachedFiles/PhilippHoltmann.pdf) (accessed May 05, 2018).

shot him several times. In the text, we find the passage: "the cutting of the head without mercy is legal if the Prophet does not disapprove it." Moreover, the text advises multiple times to use assassination as an act of deterrence. The slaughter of van Gogh in open daylight seems like a one-to-one translation into reality of the directives we find in the text."[5]

User-created content on Twitter praising the killing of Theo van Gogh, outlining the theological obligation to hunt anyone who insults Prophet Muhammad or God.[6]

---

5 Ibid.
6 The text praises Muhammad Bouyeri as a jihadist role model. Not only has he acted to avenge

In addition, AQ alluded to the writings of Ibn Taymiyya in a video claiming responsibility for a suicide bombing targeting the Embassy of Denmark in Pakistan in 2008[7] after a Danish newspaper published cartoon depictions of Muhammad.

Ibn Taymiyya is among several traditionalists and historical scholars who have explored the subject of avenging the Prophet Muhammad. The work by Jordanian-Palestinian jihadist scholar Abu Muhammad al-Maqdisi stands out in its attempt to clearly outline who can be killed legitimately for insulting Prophet Muhammad. Al-Maqdisi extends this beyond individuals, and says any government deemed to have insulted either the Prophet, God or religion in general is a legitimate target for reprisal.[8]

In January 2015 two brothers, apparently trained in Yemen by Al Qaeda in the Arabian Peninsula, opened fire in the offices of the French satirical magazine Charlie Hebdo. After the attack, a bystander filmed the Kouachi brothers shouting, "We have avenged the Prophet" (*li-intiqamna al-rasul*), before fatally shooting wounded French police officer Ahmad Merabet.[9] A video published on January 11, 2015 by the IS-affiliated media outlet, *Asawirtimedia*, praised the attacks. The video is entitled "The French have insulted the Prophet of God – thus a merciless reaction."

There is a coherent message across jihadist writings, videos, and theological decrees that say vengeance restores the dignity of Prophet Muhammad. They command individuals worldwide to demonstrate their faith by responding violently to those who insult the Prophet.

This report focuses on IS' fourth *Salil al-Sawarim* movie, in which retribution for insulting Prophet Muhammad is the underlying principle of a brutal and rapidly emerging sectarian war (*harb ta'ifi*). The film shows IS fighters seeking to exterminate the Shiites, portrayed as a group that has insulted the prophet, his companions, God, and in sum, Islam, since the early days of the religion.

---

the violation of van Gogh against religion in general, but rather he, according to the text, denounced the worldly law in the Dutch court, claiming to only acknowledge *shari'a law*.

7 A video entitled *al-qawla qawla ul-sawarim*, "the words [are now about action and hence] words of the sword", shows the testimony of the suicide operative identified as a Saudi by the nom de guerre Abu Gharib al-Makki [the Meccan]. The one-hour video justifies the attack; "the time to talk is over, the time for actions (i.e the swords must be drawn) has come to avenge the insults of Prophet Muhammad".

8 Abu Muhammad al-Maqdisi, *al-Sarim al-maslul 'ala sabb al-rabb aw al-din aw a-rasul sala l-llahu 'alayhi wa-salam*, via Minbar al-Tawhid wa-l Jihad.

9 A detailed overview is provided by the BBC, also outlining in depth the attack by IS member Amedy Coulibaly who executed several hostages in a Jewish supermarket in Paris: http://www.bbc.com/news/world-europe-30708237 (accessed May 05, 2018). Amedy Coulibaly uploaded a video where he pledges allegiance to al-Baghdadi. Part of his video is used in one of the 'official' IS videos to applaud the January 2015 Paris attack, Risala ila Fransa, Wilayat Salah al-Din, February 14, 2015.

"The French have insulted the Prophet of God"

For example, SAS4 shows several sequences in which murdered Iraqi soldiers are described as Shiites, or rejectionists (*rafida*), a degrading term in Sunni extremist literature. The film brands Shiites as inferior humans who constitute the "interior enemy" because they are Arabs. It follows that they are Islam's most important foe and must be fought first and foremost.

IS cites historical scholars such as Imam al-Sam'ani or Ibn Hazm to justify the execution of Iraqi soldiers

Text and videos are not the only means of spreading the theoretical principle of avenging the Prophet; two of the most popular jihadist songs, or *nashid*, on YouTube reference Ibn Taymiyya and the notion of killing all those who insult Islam. A *nashid* by Abu Yaseer has over 1.5 million views and can easily be retrieved online by searching for "Salil al-Sawarim".[10] A related *nashid* with the title "the words [are now about action and hence] words of the sword" by Abu

---

10 Hosted by the YouTube Channel "The Great Breakfast War", https://www.youtube.com/watch?v=ZQoJvI8XUa0 (accessed May 05, 2018).

'Ali has over 3.5 million views.[11] The reference of the "sword" is part of both *nashid*.

Popular jihadist songs on YouTube. 1.5 million views (left), 3.5 million views (right)

The four-part *Salil al-sawarim* series conveys two main themes:
1. Punishment: It is legitimate to kill anyone considered a non-Sunni Muslim, in particular the Shiites of Iraq.
2. Shiism by Sunni extremist standards is portrayed as a sect that has deviated from Islam and seeks to destroy Sunni Islam from within.
3. Inclusion and representation: IS is shown operating carefully within Sunni territories in Iraq and Syria, assassinating key government figures and offering the Sunni majority a chance to reintegrate into the true Sunni community – represented solely by the "Islamic State" – by repenting (*tawba*) their sin of having worked for non-Sunni Muslims.

The chance to repent has become an integral part of IS strategy to consolidate newly-conquered territory. Key IS ideologues such as Abu Muhammad al-'Adnani have supported this strategy; it consists of annihilating key figures of the Iraqi government; punishing Sunnis who collaborated with the Americans or Shiites; and offering Sunni police and soldiers a chance to be cleansed of their sins and restored as true members of the Sunni community by renouncing their past actions and swearing allegiance to al-Baghdadi.

Salil al-sawarim has turned into a popular and active meme online. It fosters IS identity and creates role models in a fandom-styled environment where users can create and upload their own images to praise videos like SAS and the worldview they depict.

IS has become more than an idea or a physical movement. It has managed to spread its "values" and theological reference points across a wide range of online platforms in a number of languages, primarily Arabic.

---

11 This singer was featured in Al Qaeda in the Arabian Peninsula videos as far back as 2003/4.

For example, the two screen-grabs below highlight how IS establishes role models and turns its audio-visual propaganda into memes that are readable and comprehensible to a wide group of consumers – ranging from hard-core sympathizers to lesser initiated followers and even those who simply seek to make fun of IS. The screen-grabs feature the same sequence of SAS4, where a young foreign fighter from Bahrain (Salman Turki) addresses the audience in Arabic.

The first image is a cat meme showing several IS sympathizers watching SAS4 on a smart phone. The second image identifies a role model; it praises the Saudi man standing next to the young Bahraini for making the ultimate sacrifice by committing a suicide bombing to help IS gain control of an area in Raqqa.

Cat memes and role models – IS projects influence online and has a fandom base

Salil al-Sawarim, part 1

The first part of *Salil al-sawarim* (SAS1) was released by "Islamic State in Iraq" (ISI) in 2012. After Al Qaeda in Iraq consolidated control over the Sunni province of Anbar, it declared the establishment of ISI, *al-dawlat al-Iraq al-Islamiyya*. Anbar province has an extensive border with Syria that includes the Syrian town of Minbaj, which became one of the main hubs for cross-border activity.

SAS1 features a rich blend of narratives that have formed an integral part of Sunni extremist identity since the U.S. occupation of Iraq in 2003/4. SAS1 features several prominent jihadist figures, including IS godfather Abu Mus'ab al-Zarqawi and IS spokesman Abu Muhammad al-'Adnani. The video portrays the

Shiites as mere agents and henchmen of the Americans and shows a number of attacks on police posts and individuals accused of apostasy and collaboration.

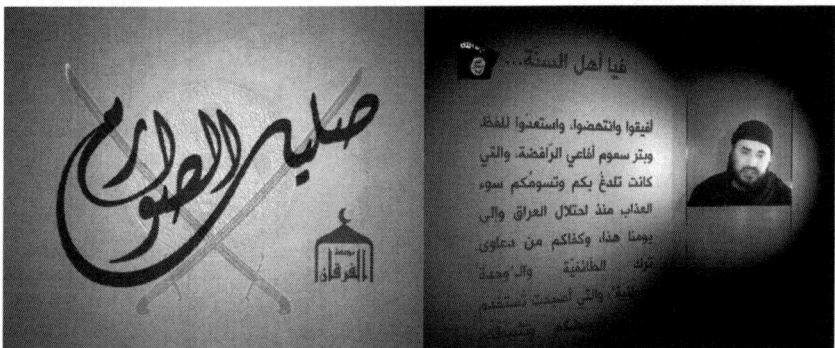

Salil al-Sawarim 1 fostering sectarian tensions and praising the "Islamic State" Godfather Abu Mus'ab al-Zarqawi

The first movie features two sequences that would later become "Islamic State" *modus operandi*, and appear prominently in SAS4. The first type of sequence depicts well-planned, well-organized and well-executed rapid attacks on police and army checkpoints in urban and remote areas of the country. For example, the film shows fighters killing uniformed officers in Baghdad in hit-and-run and execution-style shootings. The film uses audio recordings of Abu Muhammad al-'Adnani or Abu Mus'ab al-Zarqawi to justify these killings. The second type of sequence shows fighters raiding army outposts in remote areas. The aftermath of these attacks is also shown, including close-ups of dead Iraqi soldiers as proof of the success of the Sunni extremists.

In other parts of SAS1, suicide bombers give their testimony (*wasiyya*) while crude bombs and handgun silencers are proudly shown as "industrial produce of the State for the oppressed," whom IS claims to be fighting for. Sniper scenes are an integral part of the first SAS movie, as in SAS4.

SAS1 features a coherent blend of elements of Iraqi-based Sunni extremist theology, notably the offer to fellow Sunni Muslims, including those in the ranks and service of the Iraqi army, police and government, to repent (*tawbu*) and become "true" Muslims again. This form of *repentance* and *inclusion* is important throughout the series, but reaches a climax in the fourth SAS video, which shows the mass repentance of Sunnis in areas that IS conquered in Iraq in early 2014.

This is a form of *applied theology*, an idea that originated with AQ, though it lacked the territory to fulfil its *implementation*. By contrast, SAS1 features former *Sahwa* ("Awakening Council") soldiers repenting and joining IS while its spokesman, Abu Muhammad al-'Adnani, calls on all Sunnis to renounce their loyalty to the then Iraqi Shiite-led government of president al-Maliki.

A targeted assassination in SAS1 set the precursor for what was about to hit Iraq, in particular the region of Anbar and the cities of Fallujah, Ramadi, Mosul and smaller towns such as Hit. The screen-grabs below show Muhammad al-Sab'awwi, allegedly a *Sahwa* leader and head of security for the city of Mosul. He was marked as an enemy in SAS1 and allegedly subsequently killed.

Screengrab of SAS1 showing the Mosul security chief (left) and a popular YouTube video (right, 860,000 views) claiming he was killed after SAS1 was released

SAS1 also features a speech by Abu Muhammad al-'Adnani entitled "we renew our invitation (*da'wa*) to every apostate, traitor and deviant to repent and to return [to the state of being a Sunni Muslim." This offer is especially directed at "policemen and Sahwa members" and ceases to be valid when IS overpowers or captures them. According to jihadist reasoning, repentance can only be considered sincere and potentially accepted if the individual does so without coercion – so as not to violate the jihadist interpretation of Qur'an, verse 5:34:

> "unless they repent before you overpower them – in that case bear in mind that God is forgiving and merciful."[12]

The first *Salil al-sawarim* video ends with a slogan that has since become commonplace in IS propaganda: "the Islamic State will remain" (*baqiyya*). The conclusion of SAS1 also makes clear the ambition of the "Islamic State in Iraq" to expand into *Sham* (Syria) and liberate Sunni Muslims from the regime of al-Assad.

---

12 For a detailed discussion of this principle in jihadist videos: Nico Prucha. *Online Territories of Terror – How Jihadi Movements Project Strategic Influence on the Internet and the Battlefield and Why it Matters*, Dissertation, University of Vienna, June 2014.

A Milestone for "Islamic State" Propaganda: "The Clanging of the Swords, part 4"   81

A speech by IS spokesman Abu Muhammad al-'Adnani and the direct application in the video.

Salil al-Sawarim, parts 2 and 3 – making a state

SAS2 shows fighters conducting hit-and-run missions, infiltrating Iraqi cities, such as Hit, Ramadi, or Haditha to capture and execute Iraqi counter-terrorist or government officials, and then withdrawing to the remote desert.

The second video also introduces footage that would become a common theme in "Islamic State" propaganda: a professionally-laid out shooting range where many masked men are training. The weapons shown include the classic Kalashnikov assault rifle, as well as the much glorified – and often seen in jihadist videos – Pulemyot Kalashnikova (P.K.) heavy machine gun. SAS2 is more sophisticated than its prequel; the attacks by the *Mujahidin* appear more precise, professional and deadly.

SAS2 emphasizes the importance of media work, featuring an IS media operative preparing crates of DVDs to give out to Sunnis in the towns and cities that will be attacked but not immediately occupied. A *Mujahid* is interviewed and introduced as a "soldier of the Islamic State". Iraqi cars, gear and elite police SWAT equipment are handed out to the graduates of the training course.

A Mujahid in full SWAT gear gives an interview; apparently looted SWAT boots and uniforms being handed out.

The video also features action footage in various towns and cities at night. Iraqi soldiers and policemen approach IS fighters disguised in special police uniforms to greet them, believing they are comrades, only to be executed.

Those who IS considers high-value targets, predominantly collaborators and *Sahwa* officers, are at the centre of the movie which showcases IS laying the groundwork to eventually take over the territory cleansed of functionaries loyal to the central Iraqi government.

Iraqi SWAT pick-up trucks, uniforms and equipment – in the hand of IS operatives.

A blog named "Islamic News Agency – *da'wa al-haqq*" described the second SAS movie as a documentary in Full HD, with 49 minutes of IS fighters in special counter-terrorism vehicles conducting assaults in various cities and killing dozens of Iraqi soldiers.

The third video of the *Salil al-sawarim* series was released on January 17, 2013. By this time, the "Islamic State" was seeking to consolidate control of territory in Iraq and the purpose of SAS3 was to document its proclaimed campaign *Hadim al-aswar* ("take down the walls!").

The video opens with a band of *Mujahidin* singing and the movie sequence is introduced as:

> "a new phase in the conduct of jihadi operations, starting in the beginning of Ramadan, a.H. 1433. The *Mujahidin* have arisen anew and returned to areas from which they had previously withdrawn. This film is a documentary of some of the military operations in this important and historical phase for jihadist work in Iraq."

The campaign "take down the walls" consisted of systematic attacks on prisons and had two strategic objectives:
1. Exacting revenge for Sunnis, perceived as excluded, marginalized and persecuted by the ruling Shiite majority of Iraq;
2. Replenishing fighter ranks with freed inmates who have little choice but to support and join IS.

SAS3 features freed inmates of the Tasfirat prison in Tikrit who have assumed or resumed leadership roles within IS. These men inform the audience of the

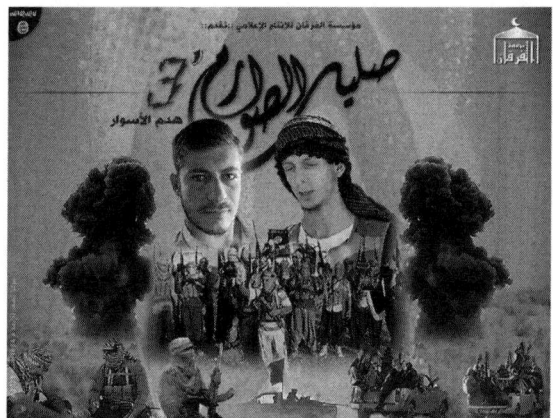

The official banner of the al-Furqan release in the light of the campaign "take down the walls!"

hardship and torture endured in prison while relaying theological interpretations framed in terms of the need to act.

The Sunni community is repeatedly portrayed as driven to extinction by Iranian-backed Shiites and Western enmity. In addition, every IS armed operation is framed as an altruistic act for the Sunnis in Iraq and Syria.

The specific Sunni extremist interpretation of the Qur'an and the *Hadith* are put in practice; for example, a *Mujahid* issues a call to prayer while standing next to slain enemies. Such footage is intended to portray IS as the only Sunni group willing to resist the Shiite takeover of Iraq and Syria.

The 80-minute long SAS3 concludes with a massive suicide bombing attack on an Iraqi army barracks near or in Mosul, undertaken by a Tunisian foreign fighter. He is identified as Abu Ziyyad al-Bahhar "from Tunis, the Muslim city where real men are made." He describes his emigration (*hijra*) into Syria and then Iraq in 2013 and claims he did not face any problems while traveling. Using classical Sunni extremist rhetoric, he urges others to follow his example:

> "This is not the end of the path – no (…) Many of our brothers have spent many years in prison (…). *Hijra, jihad*, hardships and combat; being imprisoned, blood, flesh [and sacrifice], this is the path. This is the path of Muhammad."

The "Islamic State" is the first Islamist movement to make highly professional use of the Internet for "missionary purposes" (*da'wa*) related to territory seized from a sovereign state. The control of strategic towns and even huge cities such as Mosul, parts of Ramadi (2014–2015), Fallujah, and Raqqa, the capital of the "Caliphate", allows IS media workers to continuously produce new video propaganda from both the 'hinterland' as well as from the frontlines.

This enables jihadist media strategists to convey several messages; firstly, they showcase IS members building and maintaining critical infrastructure for civilians, while fighting, bleeding and dying for this pseudo-altruistic project on the frontlines. They also show IS fighting a rich blend of enemies, including air force raids by the "crusader alliance" and various Shiite, Kurdish and Christian militias on the ground. These sequences are intended to convey a sizeable Islamic state populated by people who have adopted a real Muslim identity.

Salil al-Sawarim, part 4

Individuals who gained fame with the release of SAS4, such as Salman Turki or Lavdrim Muhaxheri, rose within IS ranks and quickly became the 'real face' of IS – offering the group's theology in their own words. As a result, IS media has a wider appeal than that of predecessor groups, like AQ or the first generation of "Islamic State in Iraq".

The release of the video *Salil al-Sawarim, part 4* by ISIS's media department *al-Furqan* demonstrated sophisticated use of social media to disseminate video content. *Al-Furqan*'s sister department, *al-I'tasimu* announced the release of the fourth instalment of the film on *Twitter* on Saturday, 17 March 2014. A few hours later, it was published via *al-I'tasimu*'s high-profile *Twitter* account and the tier-one jihadist forums.

In the first twenty-four hours after the fourth instalment was posted on YouTube, it was viewed 56,998 times with an average user watching a little over 17 minutes of the hour-long film. This means that collectively *YouTube* users spent the equivalent of 686 days watching this one video. It has subsequently been reposted a number of times on *YouTube*, and was published on other file sharing sites such as *archive.org* and links for download were broadcast via *justpaste.it*. It was published in different sizes and formats. A high-definition format, about one gigabyte in size, carries death and mayhem to homes and portable devices worldwide.

Approximately one month later, this major video production was available for download and on YouTube with English, Dutch, German, French, Russian and Bahasa Indonesia subtitles.

Ensuring a high number of views on the first day after publication takes coordination across a range of social media channels. Analysis of the dissemination of SAS4 allows us to determine:
- The volume of tweets related to the video release.
- An estimate of the size of the network-of-interest surrounding the video release.
- The prominent languages used to spread word of the video release.

- The frequently shared URLs that led to content access across a range of platforms.
- The users most frequently mentioned in connection to the video.
- The key actors in the *Twitter* network-of-interest that spread word of the video release.
- The platforms that users utilised to tweet.
- The likely location (proximity) of *Twitter* users sharing the video.

The Framework and Context of Sunni Extremist Media

Sunni extremist groups such as AQ and the "Islamic State" use the Internet as a communication hub to broadcast their messages. Online jihad is a phenomenon that has spread on a massive scale and pace in the past fifteen years. "Islamic State", in particular, invests a great deal of effort in its online operations including maintaining/re-establishing accounts and networks on *Twitter*, *Facebook*, *YouTube*, *telegram* and elsewhere. Large amounts of jihadist audio, video and written content can be found on these networks, mostly in Arabic.

For most of the past 15 years, jihadist material was concentrated within classical websites, blogs, and online forums. It has recently expanded to the full range of social media. This content conveys a coherent jihadist worldview, based on theological texts penned by AQ ideologues as far back as the 1980s.

Following the terrorist attack on September 1, 2001, the Internet became the general platform for AQ to spread its Sunni extremist theology. This theology, established by AQ in the 1980s, entered a new evolutionary phase in mid-2014 when ISIS declared a "Caliphate".[13] This AQ offshoot then became its primary

---

13 Statement regarding the Relationship of the Qa'idat al-Jihad group to ISIS (in Arabic) Markaz al-Fajr li-l I'lam, https://alfidaa.info/vb/showthread.php?t=92927 (accessed February 02, 2014). Al-Qaeda Central issued this statement distancing themselves from *the Islamic State of Iraq and al-Sham* with the refusal of ISIS' leader Abu Bakr al-Baghdadi to pledge allegiance (*hay'a*) to AQ-*amir* Ayman al-Zawahiri. As a consequence, the Syrian revolution against al-Assad was further divided with various 'rebel' factions turning on each other – including *Jabhat al-Nusra*, the official branch of AQ turning on ISIS and vice versa. The clash – or *fitna* (tribulation) – between ISIS and JN as well as other factions is the manifestation of two torrents: the claim of seniority posed by AQ and its Syrian franchise *Jabhat al-Nusra* versus the practicality of the "Islamic State" which advanced what AQ pledged to fight for: the establishment of a Caliphate. Joas Wagemakers refers to ISIS as the *Zarqawiyyun*, practical military orientated individuals who seek to implement their principles of faith by brute force versus the *Maqdisiyyun*, adherents of Abu Muhammad al-Maqdisi who criticized the "Islamic State" for its apparent rapid move in declaring a Caliphate. For further reading: Joas Wagemakers, *A Quietist Jihadi: The Theology and Influence of Abu Muhammad al-Maqdisi*, Cambridge University Press: Cambridge/New York/Melbourne 2012. Cole Bunzel referred to this rift as "two tendencies predominate among jihadis insofar as the Syrian war is con-

rival, developing a massive foothold on social media sites, mainly Twitter[14], while AQ lost significant support online and offline.[15]

Under Abu Bakr al-Baghdadi, IS[16] adopted al-Qaeda's iconography and doctrine without being subject to its formal leadership.[17] The Internet served as a powerful tool that allowed the jihadist network to morph and spread in many directions.

IS' professional and coherent decentralized use of the Internet involves the continuous and tireless deployment of media-workers and media-dedicated brigades embedded with fighting jihadi units in the real-life battlefields. The media departments – or the designated individual *media mujahid* (sg.) – facilitate all means possible to transport, broadcast and thus project *strategic influence* by enabling individuals worldwide to tune into the jihadist *monopoly of truth*. This *monopoly* is a dominant form of projecting only one *truth*, or *haqq*, in jihadist parlance, while remaining that every Muslim outside this tight definition is either treading on the "path of falsehood (*batil*)", is an apostate (*murtadd*), or simply earmarked to be excommunicated (*takfir*) as a disbeliever (*kafir*). The jihadi monopoly of "truth" only allows onea specific interpretation and implementation of the corpus of *Qur'an* and *Sunna*, claiming absolute authority over common Islamic habits and traditions to widen their potential impact.

Symbols, icons, gestures, and key words from religious texts are hijacked and used to legitimise extremist reasoning and acting. The jihadist strives by all means, foremost by violent actions, to implement an orthodox and selective

---

cerned: one favoring the al-Qaeda-affiliated Jabhat al-Nusra (JN) and cooperation with all rebel groups, and another favoring ISIS and its exclusionary political designs as the reborn Islamic state, or proto-caliphate." Cole Bunzel, The Islamic State of Disunity: Jihadism Divided, in: *Jihadica*, (2014) (http://www.jihadica.com/the-islamic-state-of-disunity-jihadism-divided/) (accessed May 05, 2018). See also: Khalil Ezzeldeen/Nico Prucha, Relationship between ISIL and local Syrian rebels break down, in *IHS Jane's Islamic Affairs Analyst*, Islamic World Web Watch, April 2014.

14 Ali Fisher, How Jihadist Networks Maintain a Persistent Presence Online, in *Perspectives on Terrorism* (2015) (http://www.terrorismanalysts.com/pt/index.php/pot/article/view/426) (accesed August 01, 2015).

15 Jabhat al-Nusra (JN), the Syrian AQ affiliate was first to use Twitter on a noticeable scale and facilitated the social media platform to disseminate propaganda videos and writings. The JN-IS divide caused JN to lose members, fighters, and media activists to the "Islamic State". Further reading: Nico Prucha and Ali Fisher, Tweeting for the Caliphate, Twitter as the New Frontier for Jihadist Propaganda, in *CTC Sentinel (Westpoint)*, (2013) (http://www.ctc.usma.edu/posts/tweeting-for-the-caliphate-twitter-as-the-new-frontier-for-jihadist-propaganda) (accessed May 05, 2018).

16 At the time the "Islamic State" referred to itself as dawlat al-Islamiyya fi l-'Iraq wa-l Sham (ISIS), then shortened its name after the declaration of the Caliphate to IS or dawlat al-khilafa.

17 See Cole Bunzel, The Islamic State of Disobedience: al-Baghdadi Triumphant, *Jihadica*, October 5, 2013, http://www.jihadica.com/the-islamic-state-of-disobedience-al-baghdadis-defiance/ (accessed by May 05, 2018).

interpretation of Islamic divine texts. This propaganda is disseminated online on a variety of channels and platforms, in an increasing number of languages with differently calibrated appeals to global and local audiences.[18] The most modern means of communication are deployed coolly and skilfully to propagate an antiquated, ancient-medieval yet coherent worldview. This propaganda is meant to address contemporary geopolitical circumstances, as well as local grievances. Resisting and acting against unfair and inhumane realities, including by the use of force, is declared 'missionary work' (*da'wa*). Conducting *da'wa* online, on all channels and layers of the Internet, has proven effective in several past conflicts and is a key operational concern for militant groups, as well as related non-militant movements, often referred to as Salafist groups in the West.

Given the innovative capacity of online forums, social media and in general 'new media' platforms, the jihadist theology is effectively competing with mainstream worldviews for the 'hearts and minds' of young Muslims.

Fighting for Hegemony: Claiming Sunni-Muslim identity and "Prophetic Methodology"

This is a fight for hegemony and identity: what does it mean to be a Sunni Muslim in times of war and sectarianism? To answer this question, the "Islamic State" has taken the lead in producing mainly Arabic language videos to incite a global Arab audience by popularizing their fighters, ideologues and preachers as ultimate role models, modern-day Islamic warriors, or simply as defenders of Sunni communities in a time of suffering.

"Islamic State" is an Arab movement fighting for independence, yet welcoming non-Arab Muslim foreign fighters into its ranks and using them strategically and on a tactical level in jihadist media, on the battlefield and in the hinterland, where they can support state-building efforts.

Foreign fighters tend to address their target audience in their respective language, and are often featured in videos with Arabic and non-Arabic subtitles. This includes British citizens,[19] Germans, Austrians,[20] French,[21] Russians,[22] al-

---

18 Nico Prucha, *'Online Territories of Terror': How Jihadi Movements Project Strategic Influence on the Internet and the Battlefied and Why it Matters*, Dissertation, University of Vienna, (June 2014).
19 IS' magazine *Dabiq* is published in English to ensure maximum readership worldwide, including through mainstream media outlets. British and American foreign fighters appear from time to time (e.g. a video released by Markaz al-Hayyat li-l i'lam, featuring a British, French and German foreign fighter entitled "Wait. We are also waiting." October 16, 2014).
20 For example, a video uploaded from the IS province Wilayat Hims featuring Austrian-

though the overwhelming majority of IS and AQ videos are in Arabic, featuring native Arabs.

The influx of foreign fighters to IS from Europe and the United States has increased the use of social media by the group, and both Arab and non-Arab foreign fighters post a large amount of content on social media sites in various languages. Foreign fighters have the potential to have particular resonance for Islamic communities in their respective countries of origin, as grievances and the framing of "injustice" can vary depending on the local context, while the theology is tied into the Arabic religious reasoning, as expressed by writings and most importantly, as conveyed by audio-visual means.

The Qur'an – understood as the speech of God (*kalimat allah*) – was revealed in Arabic, and therefore is the most important language for Islam. The *lingua jihadica* is, likewise, Arabic; the overwhelming majority of AQ penned texts from the 1980s and the dominant majority of IS videos are in Arabic. As a result, key words in Arabic have become a mainstream substrate in many non-Arabic languages where Islam has found a home, providing non-Arabic speaking sympathizers of *jihad* terms to identify with and use for their religious rituals and codes of identification. This is important when studying Arabic jihadist materials, especially when it comes to the *social media jihad*.[23]

Sympathizers and media operatives use key words strategically to widen the appeal of jihadist theology, while ascribing extremist definitions to the mainly Qur'anic terminology. Deriving from the original Arabic, the key words are transcribed in Latin letters (for example *allahu akbar*) and are the most integral part of any non-Arabic language production. The use of these key words is significant to understand and assess the impact of the Arabic-dominated theology on non-Arab majority societies, expressed both online and offline. For

---

Egyptian Muhammad Mahmud and a German by the nom de guerre Abu 'Umar al-Almani, "Siyahat al-Umma – Der Tourismus dieser Umma", Wilayat Hims, August 5, 2015.

21 For example, the French language *nashid* "Tend ta main pour l'allégeance", with English subtitles. Markaz al-Hayyat li-l 'ilam. May 24, 2015. French is also an important language for IS, which seeks to reach Francophone Muslims. In a video published on July 24, 2015, a French speaking Mujahid addresses France and threatens future attacks. "Wa ma zalamnahum wa-lakin kanu anfusahum yuzlamun". Wilayat Hama, July 24, 2015.

22 With a large number of foreign fighters coming from the Caucasus region, IS has a dedicated Russian-language media department, "al-Furat", that promotes Russian, mainly Chechen, fighters and ideologues.

23 This is most evident in non-Arabic language *nashid* where Arabic key words are built-in references to complex theological concepts. For more details, see Nico Prucha, Die Vermittlung arabischer Jihadisten-Ideologie: Zur Rolle deutscher Aktivisten, in: Guido Steinberg (Ed.), Jihadismus und Internet: Eine deutsche Perspektive, in: *Stiftung Wissenschaft und Politik*, (October 2012), pp. 45–56 (http://www.swp-berlin.org/de/publikationen/swp-studien-de/swp-studien-detail/article/jihadismus_und_internet.html) (accessed May 05, 2018).

example, non-Arab foreign fighters introduce these key words to their target audiences and employ them to define what it means to be a 'true' Sunni Muslim. Social media platforms encourage sympathizers to engage with such videos and role models, hence popularizing specific key words among non-Arab communities within non-majority Islamic societies, for instance in Europe.

Jihadist media strategies were further developed and improved after the rise of IS in 2013/14 as a major player in the Syrian revolution and its subsequent re-emergence in Iraq. IS successfully competes with its rival AQ for hearts and minds – using the media strategies and theology/theology invented by AQ – to broadcast and project influence on an unprecedented level. The deliberate and proficient use of social media outlets, particularly Twitter and since late 2015, Telegram, has furthermore enabled the flow of images and videos from real-life battlefields, sometimes in almost real-time.

As such, IS has adopted the theology of AQ and outrun its mentor in terms of the scale and pace of uploading content while maintaining a persistent presence in the physical world. This content consists mainly of videos meant to depict the application of its theology in territory in Syria and Iraq (and elsewhere such as Libya) that AQ was never able to conquer. Content is shared through a broad support network of media *Mujahidin* in one of the clearest manifestations of *Netwar* since it was first envisaged.[24]

Context of IS Conquest in Iraq: The 'Arab Spring' as a Renaissance for AQ Affiliates in Perspective

Within the framework of the turmoil in the wake of the 'Arab Spring', and especially with the conflict in Syria growing in intensity and scope, AQ has been able to re-emerge with two linked groups, *Jabhat al-Nusra* (JN) and *The Islamic State of Iraq and al-Sham* (ISIS). While JN has pledged allegiance (*bay'a*) to Ayman al-Zawahiri, ISIS under the rule of Abu Bakr al-Baghdadi has morphed into a major manifestations of al-Qa'ida iconography and doctrine by adhering to the theology without being subjected to AQ's formal leadership.[25] The renaissance of al-Qaeda doctrine is largely based on its most powerful tool that allows

---

24 For details on the concept of Netwar: John Arquilla/David Ronfeldt, "The Advent of Netwar (Revisited)", RAND (http://www.rand.org/content/dam/rand/pubs/monograph_reports/MR1382/MR1382.ch1.pdf) (accessed July 8, 2014). John Arquilla/David Ronfeldt. Networks, Netwars, and the Fight for the Future, in *First Monday*, Volume 6, Number 10, October 1, 2001. http://ojphi.org/ojs/index.php/fm/article/view/889/798 (accessed July 8, 2014).
25 See Cole Bunzel, The Islamic State of Disobedience: al-Baghdadi Triumphant, in *Jihadica*, (2013) (http://www.jihadica.com/the-islamic-state-of-disobedience-al-baghdadis-defiance/) (accessed May 05, 2018).

the network to morph and spread in many directions: the professional and coherent decentralised use of the Internet and the continuous and tireless deployment of media-workers and media-dedicated brigades embedded with fighting jihadi units in the real-life battle arenas.

The Islamic State, referring to itself also as the Islamic Caliphate State, considers itself as an avant-garde, an icon (*ramz*) and in parts in its rhetoric even as *awliya'* (friends/saints)[26] of God who are fighting against injustice, suppression, occupation, imprisonment, or the distortion of "Islam". In the words of Ayman al-Zawahiri, contemporary *Mujahidin* are convicted of their re-enactment of Muslims under the command of Prophet Muhammad. He refers to the early Muslims as "the most noble servants in close proximity to God", a sentiment that furthers the contemporary *Mujahid's* self-understanding and perception as having a likewise relationship to God. This role model is outlined in al-Zawahiri's writing "note on the noblest servants in close proximity to God – campaigns of death and martyrdom", published in a second electronic edition by *as-Sahab* on the *Shumukh al-Islam* forum in mid-March 2014.[27] As based on jihadists in their own words, the sentiment is more than merely being "soldiers of God", but rather consider themselves as the "men of [Prophet] Muhammad", calling out by their filmed testimonials for men to join them in their endeavour. These videos, needless to add, are produced, edited, curated and ultimately disseminated digitally – and handed out via USB drives and DVD's to the local audience within the territory held by the Islamic State.

Anyone is invited to tap into this freely available culture on the Internet and be a part, either as passive or active consumer – by various means within the shared space of the inclusive online territories that nevertheless promise the same paradise for the online activist as for offline members. This has led to the construction of a virtual sense of a real (global) community, where individuals may feel compelled to commit acts of terror by themselves out of a presumed personal responsibility for the "Islamic" collective in the West or by seeking to join the *Mujahidin* within Islamic territories deemed as occupied by Western nations or at war with non-Sunni armies in general, as is the case in Syria as of writing.

On this virtual realm, the principles of the al-Qa'ida dominated theology remain active and resilient whereas in real-life, offline-fighting groups, either with direct or indirect connections to the remnants of the AQ network propagates the implementation of these principles framed as "*shari'a* law" by force.

---

26 The *awliya' allah*, "the friends of God" as stated in Qur'an 10:62 is an expression used by jihadists for describing themselves and elevating their deeds for God by approximating themselves to God as representatives exercising His will in this world.

27 Ayman al-Zawahiri, *Risala 'an ashraf qurubat al-'ubbad hamlat al-mawt wa-l-istishhad*, second edition, Markaz al-fajr li-l i'lam, broadcast by *al-Sahab*, https://shamikh1.info/vb/showthread.php?t=220308 (accessed March 13, 2014).

Groups adhering to the jihadist theology and mind-set in general learned their lessons from past conflicts in Iraq and Algeria where the indiscriminate killing of Muslims contributed to the demise of jihadi outlets and emphasize positive elements in their audio-visual incitement material published frequently online.

Content Analysis of Salil al-Sawarim, part 4

As is typical of jihadist videos, *Salil al-sawarim, part 4* begins with the basmala formula:[28] "in the name of God, the most beneficent, the most merciful." The opening sequences of the film are set within the overarching notion of the 37th sura of the Qur'an (*sura al-saffat*)[29], Verses 172–173:

> "Our word has already been given to Our servants the messengers: it is they who will be helped, and the ones who support (*jund*) Our cause will be the winners."[30]

As M.A.S. Abdel Haleem notes, "in classical Arabic *jund* means 'supporters', not just 'armies'." IS, however, implies the meaning of *jund* is "soldiers", hence defining every true legitimate supporter of the "Islamic State" as a soldier. In this manner, IS redefines Sunni Muslim identity and any physical member of the group is presented as a soldier of God (*jund allah*), or soldier of the caliphate (*jund al-khilafa*) with a reference to the above cited passage of the Qur'an.

The video shows a satellite map of the greater Middle East, the territory IS considers the heartland of Islam and hence the most important countries to "liberate". Clearly visible are the rivers Euphrates and Tigris, which according to jihadist doctrine, are the God-given boundaries of what should be referred to as the "Arab Peninsula."[31] Syria and Iraq are part of the Arab Peninsula in jihadist understanding, and defined as the cradle of Islam, including by Ayman al-Za-

---

28 *Bi-smi l-llahi l-rahmani l-rahim* is a common saying for Muslims worldwide; during prayer; when entering a house, when thanking God for their food, etc. Every Sura of the Qur'an with two exceptions (surat al-anfal, "spoils of war" and surat al-tawba, "repentance"), start with the basmala.
29 "Those who set the ranks". The term *saff* (row) is reference to the rows of believers during prayer and is used in jihadist slang likewise to project unity in their war against non-Muslims worldwide.
30 Unless otherwise noted, the English translation of the verses of the Qur'an throughout this study is that of M.A.S. Abdel Haleem, *The Qur'an*, Oxford: Oxford University Press 2004.
31 In Jihadist definition, the Arab Peninsula (*al-jazirat al-'Arab*) comprises an area that includes Iraq. According to the first generation of Al Qaeda in Saudi Arabia, the Arab Peninsula must be cleansed of all polytheists (*mushrikin*) as detailed in AQAP's electronic magazine "the voice of jihad", Vol. 6 & 7. Discussed in: Nico Prucha, *Die Stimme des Dschihad "Sawt al-gihad", al-Qaedas erstes Online-Magazin*, Hamburg: Verlag Dr.Kovač 2010.

wahiri in a 2012 speech commemorating and acknowledging martyred al-Qaeda ideologues and leaders.[32]

This drive to liberate the Arab Peninsula is focused on Mecca and Medina as much as Jerusalem. The Sunni extremists portray themselves as the only Muslim Arabs – in contrast to all Arab regimes – willing to take Jerusalem back and enforce the "true" Islam in the birthplace of Islam in contemporary Saudi Arabia.

The camera zooms into Iraq and takes the audience into the full HD perspective of a drone, hovering over the Iraqi city of Fallujah, where the most severe attacks against U.S. occupation forces occurred. As a result, Fallujah has been at the centre of jihadist narratives in writing and on video since 2003. The U.S. Army suffered many losses in the Iraqi province of Anbar, and was only able to retake the city of Fallujah after two intensive campaigns consisting of house-to-house fighting.

Drones, operated by handheld tablets such as iPads or Android-powered devices, are in to some extent revolutionizing the landscape of jihadist videos. On December 17, 2015, the IS "province" of Anbar, Iraq, published a video message for the Saudi government titled "expel the polytheists from the Arab Peninsula", a phrase popularized by the first generation of al-Qaeda in the Arabian Peninsula (AQAP). At the end of the video, a suicide bomber's farewell ceremony is documented and his advance towards a remote Iraqi Army outpost is filmed by a drone, showing the long drive through the desert plains and the massive explosion at the Army site.

Death on the ground – filmed from above by an IS operated full HD camera drone

The drone, possibly an iPad-controlled AR Parrot drone, provides an overview of the city of Fallujah, suggesting calmness and peace after the IS takeover in January 2014. The drone perspective projects the "Islamic State" as functioning and operational in Fallujah, presenting itself as the only force able and willing to protect the Sunni population – a strategic message in light of the bloody sectarian war in Iraq and the recent history of grievances due to war and conflict since 2003 related to the city itself.

The images of the drone are termed "*Fallujah bi-'adsa al-furqan*", "by the lens

---

32 Ayman al-Zawahiri, *li-ahlina fi manzal al-wahi wa-mahad al-Islam*, al-Sahab, May 16, 2012.

of al-Furqan [media]", the main official media outlet of IS, founded in the days of al-Zarqawi and now one of the group's main media stations, resembling a Caliphate-wide broadcasting company.

The sequence shifts to convoys of mainly Toyota pick-up trucks with armed fighters and .50 caliber guns from various IS controlled cities. This footage underlines the fight for territory within the Sunni Arab heartlands of Syria and Iraq. When the video was published in May 2014, it was meant to show that the "Islamic State" was indeed in the phase of consolidation. The audience is taken from the city of Fallujah to cities across Syria and Iraq, showing columns of IS-cars and fighters parading in various cities.

The "al-Furqan drone" documenting the IS convoy from above and cameramen on the ground in Fallujah

The cities shown include Homs, Raqqa, and Ramadi, which fell to IS in May 2015 and was liberated by Iraqi forces in February 2016[33]. The sequence ends with footage of Fallujah and the black flag of the Islamic State, while the narrator sets the tone of divine guidance for IS:

> "by the voice of truth (*haqq*) and the conquest of the *millat Ibrahim* prying open the true conflict between the opposing military camps and those who fight for *al-haqq* and [against] falsehood (*al-batil*).[34] For jihad is set to establish the *din* (bond to God, etc), this is a shari'a obligation, a duty that can only be achieved by holding fast (*i'tisam*) on to God and by adhering to the *jama'a*.[35] This endeavor entails sacrifice and humbleness

---

33 Iraq liberates city of Ramadi from Islamic State, in *Chicago Tribune*, February 9, 2016, http://www.chicagotribune.com/news/nationworld/ct-iraq-ramadi-islamic state-20160209-story.html (accessed May 05, 2018).
34 For a description of the terms *haqq / batil*: Nico Prucha, Notes on the Jihadists' Motivation for Suicide-Operations, in *Journal for Intelligence, Propaganda and Security Studies (JIPSS)* 4i (2010), pp. 57–68.
35 A religious reference to the *ahl al-Sunna wa-l jama'a*, meaning the Sunni Muslims who are acting on behalf of the prophetic tradition (Sunna), exemplified by prophet Muhammad and his companions. Sunni extremists claim to be in the closest proximity to God by re-enacting the example and guidance, as set by the Sunna of prophet Muhammad and his companions (*sahaba*). The "Islamic State" has taken this AQ crafted concept to a new level by popularizing their slogan "upon the prophetic methodology" (*'ala minhaj al-nubuwwa*), framing every action, ranging from the destruction of Shiite mosques to the execution of non-Sunni

until the judicial rulings prescribed by *shari'a*[36] are retained and safeguarded, the divine physical punishment (*hadd*) are implemented and carried out without any fear of God.[37]"

The focus of the video is Syria and Iraq, where at the time of the video release, "vast territories" had recently been conquered and absorbed into the "Islamic State". The target audience consists of Arabic native speakers who understand the dynamic in Iraq, where IS was able to establish itself as the main lobby for the marginalized Sunni population, particularly in Anbar.[38] The conquest and subsequent consolidation of territory, as allegedly shown in the video, is framed within the grand dream of liberating Jerusalem, a repetition echoed by jihadist groups since the 1980s,[39] stating that "the Mosque of al-Aqsa is just a stone hurl away" from the newly (re-) established Islamic State that seeks to liberate and integrate all parts of the once blossoming caliphate.

The introduction is concluded by a lengthy talk given by a foreign fighter from Kosovo who is fluent in Arabic and holds his passport into the camera like most of his comrades. The group of men waiving black flags and flashing their weapons and passports are framed as sincere believers who "fulfil their covenant to God"[40] and are presented to the audience as ultimate role models.

Muslims, as the only valid model of pieces of divine scripture as well as the alleged prophetic conduct.

36 In Arabic: *ahkam al-shari'a*. The term *ahkam*, singular: *hukm*, refers to the judicial findings based on the interpretations of religious scripture and is often equated to a specific "ruling" or "jurisprudential decree" issued by a religious authoritative scholar (*shaykh*).

37 A core theme in jihadist literature; in particular, the first generation of Al Qaeda in the Arabian Peninsula (AQAP) published a great deal of writings online referring to the fifth chapter (*al-Ma'ida*) of the Qur'an in defining themselves as the only proper Muslims favored by God. "[God] loves and who love Him, people who are humble towards the believers, hard on the disbelievers, and who strive in God's way without fearing anyone's reproach. Such is God's favour." A true believer adhering to the jihadist corpus of writings and videos only fears God and accepts or gives guidance channeled through the formalization of religion and thus enforced as "shari'a law", *ahkam*, or defined as part of *fiqh* (Islamic jurisprudence).

38 Emma Sky, *The Unravelling. High Hopes and Missed Opportunities in Iraq*, Atlantic Books: London 2015. Also: Patrick Cockburn, *The Rise of the Islamic State: ISIS and the New Sunni Revolution*, Verso: London, New York 2014.

39 The importance of fighting within Arab countries to liberate Jerusalem is discussed in: Nico Prucha, 'Abdallah 'Azzam's Outlook for Jihad in 1988 – "al-Jihad between Kabul and Jerusalem", in *RIEAS*, (December 2010) (http://rieas.gr/images/nicos2.pdf) (accessed May 05, 2018).

40 The contract, or '*ahd*, is a central theme throughout the theology of Sunni extremist groups. In jihadist mindset, the only 'true' Muslim is the one who understands and acts on behalf of the "contract [or: covenant] with God", affirming that God in return will recompense the bloodshed and deeds invested by the believer in the afterlife, as based on the extremist reading of verses such as 3:169 or 8:60, to briefly reference two samples.

From Kosovo to the Caliphate – Lavdrim Muhaxheri a Rising Jihadi Video Star

The man featured giving a lengthy talk to the audience in fluent and elaborate Arabic is a recognizable figure for fans of IS videos. In *Salil al-Sawarim 4*, he is neither identified nor otherwise named by a nom de guerre or *kunya*, which is quite unusual. Only his Kosovar passport in his hand portrays him as a non-Arab who otherwise has a high-ranking dual-position of fighter and preacher or ideologue. In a series entitled "Windows into the Epic Battlefield" comprising 50 videos, released by – at the time – the "Islamic State in Iraq and Syria (or al-Sham)" in 2013–2014, he was featured as Abu 'Abdallah al-Kosovi. He starred in the 15th instalment of this series, published via Twitter on October 12, 2013 and broadcast via jihadist forums as well.

Abu 'Abdallah from Kosovo speaks in Albanian and Arabic subtitles appear. He defines his address to the audience as an advice (*nasiha*), a recurring element in jihadist videos and writings. In addition to senior ideologues and leading figures, 'regular' fighters issue *nasiha* to share their personal experiences with a wider audience. Their goal is to explain what *jihad* is about and encouraging their targeted consumers to join the cause.

In explaining his move to Syria he highlights the motivation to help and support the weak, oppressed Sunnites, using the Arabic word *mustada'ifin* to express his religious motivation. This is a direct reference to "the oppressed" in Qur'an 4:97.[41] He then praises the "assembled lions from all over the world" who have come to aid the *mustada'ifin*.

A screengrab of Kosovar foreign fighter Muhaxeri from SAS4 (left) and of the 50 video series (2013) speaking from an IS checkpoint in 'Azaz, North Syria in Albanian (right).

He portrays himself more as a humanitarian than a fighter – a humanist who has emigrated to help people in need, people that the audience can identify and sympathize with. Furthermore, as most jihadists state, the final motivation is

---

41 Nico Prucha, *Die Stimme des Dschihad "Sawt al-gihad": al-Qaedas erstes Online-Magazin*, Hamburg: Verlag Dr.Kovač 2010, p. 151.

instilled by the notion made popular by Abu Mus'ab al-Zarqawi in Iraq and the first generation of AQ in Saudi Arabia, "to fight for the sake of the word of God, that is the highest and met with disbelief by the imbecile [non-Muslims]."[42] This underlines the idea that the identity of the *Mujahid* is based on loyalty to God, as based on the theological concept of *al-wala' wa-l bara*[43], and he states:

> "my Muslim brothers, this is an advice from Syria (*ard al-Sham*), the land of *jihad* and epic battles (*malahim*), and as you have seen here, God has bestowed upon us victory. No authority or [worldly] rule remains for the apostates and disbelievers, all praise be God's."[44]

For one, he declares the area a safe-zone where the proper conduct of prayer and *shari'a* law is exercised without interference by any apostate or negative influence. This liberated territory under IS control and its interpretation of Islamic Jurisprudence (*fiqh*) is:

> "so we can live in the shades of *shari'a* law and for the sake of it. People here [in North Syria] love the Islamic *shari'a*, coming in flocks to be under the judicial rule of the *shari'a*."[45]

In the six months in between the release of the 15th video of the *Nawafidh 'ala ard al-malahim* series and *Salil al-sawarim*, Abu 'Abdallah al-Kosovi has made a career within the ranks of "the state" (*al-dawla*), as it is often referred to on social media. IS made and released the SaS4 video during a period of accelerated territorial conquest in Syria and Iraq, with the objective of uniting and consolidating territory.

With this mind-set, he gives a furious speech in Arabic to the main Arab target audience, expressing his Muslim identity as an adherent of IS theology in his own words for the viewers. This is a powerful rhetorical tool that is used throughout jihadi videos. A 'common' man or fighter speaking about his personal motivation and in his own words appeals to a far broader audience than elaborate addresses by clerics or renowned preachers.

As in most cases, this speech is interesting because it features an individual explaining in his own words why he joined IS and what he is fighting for. His individual motivation expressed in Arabic is particularly important because he calls on the Arab community – as a non-Arab Muslim – to join the fight. Fighters are portrayed as role models "who fulfil their covenant to God". They are shown holding their passports into the camera[46] renewing their *bay'a* to Abu Bakr al-

---

42 *Nawafidh 'ala ard al-malahem*, 15 (http://justpaste.it/drd5) (accessed December 17, 2014). The *justpaste.it* link is a collection of the first 32 video installments of the series.
43 "Loyalty and dissociation", as discussed in this report later.
44 *Nawafidh 'ala ard al-malahem*, 15 (http://justpaste.it/drd5) (accessed December 17, 2014).
45 Ibid.
46 See for example: *Huwa samakum al-Muslimin*, Mu'assassat al-Furqan, April 14, 2014. The

Baghdadi and pledging their allegiance to death as the ultimate fulfilment of the "covenant to God."[47]

Foreign fighters burning their passports has become a regular theme in IS videos and is one of the most dramatic expressions that loyalty (*wala'*) is only for God, manifest by the *bay'a* to al-Baghdadi, while the destruction of the passports is the ultimate dissociation (*bara'*) to governments that are branded "un-Islamic" for various reasons.

As part of the *millatu Ibrahim*, the "community of [prophet] Abraham,"[48] the speaker sends a clear message to the tyrants (*tawaghit*) and disbelievers (*kuffar*) worldwide, assuming the ultimate representation of the *millatu Ibrahim*:

"we tell you as Ibrahim [Abraham] told his father:
"We disown you[49] and what you worship beside God! We renounce you! Until you believe in God alone, the enmity and hatred that has arisen between us will endure!" [Qur'an 60:4] And we say to you what the prophet – peace and blessings upon him – said: "we have come to you with nothing other than slaughter.[50]""

This is the exact same reference that Bouyari used before murdering Theo van Gogh in the streets of Amsterdam. Ten years after this murder, a physical "Islamic

---

title of the video refers to Qur'an 22:78, translating as "God has called you Muslims." Thus, the bearing of any man-given identity, such as a nationality, is considered invalid and sinful.

47 This is a frequent narrative in IS videos; it strengthens the individual's commitment to the doctrine of *jihad* and invites viewers to participate by pledging allegiance to Abu Bakr al-Baghdadi – an act that does not necessarily need to be made face to face but can also take place on the Internet. As stated above, the pledge of allegiance to al-Baghdadi is a pledge of allegiance to God. In some IS videos the *bay'a* is termed as a "pledge of allegiance to death" (*bay'a 'ala l-mawt*), for example: *bay'a 'ala l-mawt*, wilayat al-Raqqa, April 13, 2015.

48 Guido Steinberg, Die Globale Islamische Medienfront (GIMF) und ihre Nachfolger, in Guido Steinberg (Ed.), Jihadismus und Internet: Eine deutsche Perspektive,in: *SWP*, October 2012, pp. 23–32; Nico Prucha, Die Vermittlung arabischer Jihadisten-Ideologie: Zur Rolle deutscher Aktivisten, in Guido Steinberg (Ed.), Jihadismus und Internet: Eine deutsche Perspektive, in: *SWP*, October 2012, pp. 45–56 (http://www.swp-berlin.org/de/publikationen/swp-studien-de/swp-studien-detail/article/jihadismus_und_internet.html) (accessed May 05, 2018).

49 The verb in Arabic is based on the above reference "dissociation" (*bara'*), lit.: "we are dissociating ourselves from you" (*innana bura'a minkum*).

50 In Arabic the term *dhabh* is used to refer to "slaughter". This term is mainly applied to the ritual *halal* butchering of animals. Slaughter in the sense of combat underlines the notion of cleansing territory from anything or anyone deemed non-Sunni or non-Muslim. Jihadists base this slogan on a statement by prophet Muhammad in the historical circumstance of fighting the Quraysh and has been documented in various hadith collections. For a discussion of this statement as well as an oversight of the hadith collectors referencing it: http://www.ahlalhdeeth.com/vb/showthread.php?t=123429 (accessed May 05, 2018), posted January 8, 2017. This is a slogan used throughout the history of jihadist movements and is a typical repetition used by IS as a nashid and as a title for videos, for example: Patience sahwat of Derna [Libya], we have come to you with nothing other than slaughter, wilayat Barqa, July 12, 2015.

State" is in the making, based on the same theology that had driven Bouyeri to execute Theo van Gogh in broad daylight in Amsterdam.[51]

The title *Salil al-sawarim* is meant to invoke the overall preparedness for battle. Referring to the "clash", the speaker draws a machete from his tactical ammunition vest, augmented by a popular sound effect indicating the readiness to kill by the drawing of a sword or long knife from its shaft, swearing:

> "by God almighty, we will cleanse the [Arab] Peninsula of you, you filth!
> We will liberate Bayt al-Maqdis [Jerusalem] of you, you Jews!
> We are going to conquer Rome,[52] we are like the tribe of Ishaq [Isaac], we will take Rome and al-Andalus,[53] by the will of God, exalted is He."

The crowd responds with *allahu akbar* shouts that collectively approve his furious speech. The foreign fighter from Kosovo holds his passport into the camera and states:

> "this is your passport you tyrants everywhere in the world. By God, we are Muslims, we are Muslims. We are Muslims."

While shouting *allahu akbar*, a number of foreign fighters tear their passports apart and toss them on the ground. The destruction of passports consolidates the pledge of allegiance to the caliph Abu Bakr al-Baghdadi and – most importantly – to God and the full disavowal of any possible loyalty to a non-Islamic state or authority. The underlying concept that is expressed by this action is living out of *al-wala' wa-l bara'*.

The Kosovar Abu 'Abdallah al-Kosovi, who in a later IS video speaks fluent English, has been identified as Lavdrim Muhaxheri by the media.[54] In a non-official IS video published in 2012 or 2013, Lavdrim Muhaxeheri is seen killing a prisoner tied to a pole by firing a rocket-propelled-grenade-7 (RPG) at him.[55] He

---

51 Bouyeri who holds joint Moroccan-Dutch citizenship pledged in court to repeat this act if given the chance (http://news.bbc.co.uk/2/hi/europe/4716909.stm) (accessed May 05, 2018), BBC News, July 26, 2007.
52 The first major threat by IS to conquer Rome was made in a video released by al-Hayyat Media center, showing the execution of several hostages on the shores of the coast of Libya. *Risala mawqi'a bi l-dima' ila ahl al-salib* (Message signed in blood for the people of the cross), Markaz al-hayyat li-l i'lam, February 15, 2015.
53 Andalusia, the southern part of Spain that once belonged to the Umayyad Caliphate, is vowed to be liberated and re-integrated into the caliphate IS claims to have established. On January 30, 2016, a video released by the province of Nineveh (Iraq) features a French speaking foreign fighter executing several alleged spies speaking in French about the importance of reclaiming Andalusia. *Tasfiyyat al-murtaddin* (exterminating the apostates), wilaya Nineveh, January 30, 2016.
54 http://www.warbreaking.com/2015/07/kosovo-cuts-water-supplies-after-isil.html sourcing Aljazeera and Reuters (accessed May 05, 2018).
55 https://www.youtube.com/watch?v=6Ky-j0cENW8, accessed September 27, 2015 (accessed May 05, 2018).

is wanted by Interpol[56] and was named a relevant figure in a possible IS plot to poison water supplies in Kosovo.[57] This echoes a call for waiters serving non-Muslims in Bosnia and Serbia to poison their food and thus participate in the war to restore Islam, as seen in a IS video entitled "Honor in Jihad."[58]

According to sources on Twitter he was last seen in July 2015 in the town of Rutba, in the Iraqi province of Anbar.[59] In addition to native Albanian, he speaks fluent Arabic and English, as he demonstrated in the English-language al-Hayyat production "Rise of the Caliphate and Return of the Gold Dinar."[60]

Speaking first in Arabic then in English, Muhaxeheri praises the gold dinar and promotes the English video nashid "for the sake of allah".

The Clashes of the Swords – Nashid as Pop-Culture

Nashid (pl. *anashid*) are jihad-hymns. These religious songs are exclusively a capella-styled and oftentimes enhanced by sound effects such as the "clash" or "clang" of a sword, a machine-gun, an explosion or the neigh of a horse – suggesting the *Mujahid* embarked on a horse following the historical role models steering into combat.

Since the 1980s, the *nashid* has been a genre of its own, enriching sermons and the videos of jihad in general, conveying elemental and key themes of Sunni extremist theology in a playful style to a wider audience. The use of the Internet was key in popularizing the *nashid*, some of which have entered mainstream pop-culture, such as the song *salil al-sawarim*. Generally, *nashid* acoustically convey rhythmic and easy to comprehend texts featuring religious key words in

---

56 http://www.interpol.int/notice/search/wanted/2014-43350 (accessed May 05, 2018).
57 More than 200 FF http://www.theguardian.com/world/2015/jul/11/kosovo-cuts-pristina-water-supply-over-alleged-isis-plot-to-poison-reservoir (accessed July 11, 2015). http://www.independent.co.uk/news/world/europe/tens-of-thousands-without-water-in-kosovo-after-fears-of-isis-plot-to-poison-reservoir-10383229.html (accessed May 05, 2018).
58 *Honor is in Jihad*, Markaz al-hayyat li-l i'lam, July 4, 2015.
59 https://twitter.com/iraqisuryani1/status/621733495472152576 (accessed May 05, 2018).
60 https://twitter.com/realigazz/status/638374505673531392 (accessed May 05, 2018).

Arabic. This holds true for both Arabic and non-Arabic *nashid*, where likewise Arabic key words full of Sunni extremist meaning are broadcast outlining theological concepts and a general Muslim identity. Such ideological key concepts are enhanced by visual means, either pictures or short video sequences – or the *nashid* serves as the theme for segments within jihadist videos.

The *nashid salil al-sawarim* has become one of the main IS theme songs, often used to enhance videos, including non-jihadist content, such as a video showing a belly dancer with over 1 million views,[61] a "Shiite version" with drums and about 875 000 views,[62] Egyptians mocking IS[63] or a heavily modified "Skrillex" version thereof with over 430 000 views.[64] When searching for this *nashid* in Latin transliteration *salil al-sawarim*, the 'original', unmodified version appears by Abu Yasir with over 640, 000 views and about 4 500 likes.[65] Most of the comments are in English with the seeming majority in favour. Of the nearly 2,000 comments, statements such as "this song rocked so hard the twin tower collapsed" (25 likes) appear as often as references to first-person-shooter games where two teams fight each other to death:

> "Played this over mic in a csgo [Counter Strike Global Offensive, a first-person-shooter] match while yelling Allahu Akbar. Everyone else started yelling with me. The bomb got detonated and we all went totally crazy. 10/10 would jihad again," (742 likes)

or a top comment:

> "My speakers just exploded for like no reason." (957 likes)

Other commentators criticize the popularity of the IS *nashid*, claiming that:

> "Thanks to 4chan & Reddit, metadata won't be able to tell the difference between legit radicalized Westerners and teenagers with really weird senses of humor." (47 likes)

The *nashid* tends to accompany action-related content released by IS, such as in-combat footage or sniper videos, including a video released January 13, 2016 by the *wilaya Halab* ("province of Aleppo"). The 7-minute video entitled "Deadly Arrows" (*sahm al-qatil*) highlights the professional training of IS snipers, with one sniper speaking to the audience about the necessity to fight. Footage showing the shooting of Syrian soldiers through the sniper scope is enhanced by the *nashid Salil al-sawarim*.

As stated, the *nashid* in general is a genre of jihadist media productions that is

---

61 https://www.youtube.com/watch?v=exMS5HkfCFA (accessed May 05, 2018).
62 https://www.youtube.com/watch?v=GZCT6013Skg (accessed May 05, 2018).
63 A news report on mock executions and Egyptians dancing in a funny manner to offend IS, https://www.youtube.com/watch?v=zFR1AUA_RPo (accessed May 05, 2018). About a quarter million views with some strong language in favor of IS in the comments.
64 https://www.youtube.com/watch?v=jg_mZv_SdZw (accessed May 05, 2018).
65 https://www.youtube.com/watch?v=ZQoJvI8XUa0 (accessed May 05, 2018).

meticulously and professionally produced and serves the strategy of conveying ideological parameters and popularizing key words with in-depth meaning to a wide target audience.

A Translation of the nashid Salil al-sawarim

Clashing of the swords,[66] hymn[67] of the reluctant
while the passageway of fighting is the way of life
so amidst an assault, tyranny[68] perishes
the most beautiful echo is silence[69]
concealment of the voice[70] results in the beauty of the echo

By it my religion is exalted[71] and tyranny is laid low
Therefore, my people, awake on the path of the brave
For either being alive delights leaders
Or being dead vexes the enemy

So arise brother get up on the path of salvation
So we may march together, resist the aggressors
Raise our glory and raise the foreheads
That have refused to bow before any besides God

Come on to righteousness
The banner has called us
To brighten the path of destiny
To wage war on the enemy
Whosoever among us dies
In sacrifice for defense
Will enjoy eternity
Mourning will depart
Will enjoy eternity

---

66 *Ṣalīl al-sawārim*.
67 Nashid.
68 This refers to local tyrants (local Arab regimes) and the 'far enemy' (Western nations, supporting regimes in the Arab countries to suppress Islamist and jihadist movements).
69 Lit.: the silencing of the voice is a beautiful echo.
70 Lit.: the silencer is a means of a beautiful resistance [to assassinate enemies in secret].
71 In the meaning of "my religion is honored" (*'izza*), a term frequently used to re-instate lost pride and respect to incite the consumers of jihadist media to get active and participate in an empowering movement. *La 'izza ila bi-l-jihad*, "there is no honor except by jihad" was a popular slogan for the first generation of AQAP and often used within the electronic magazine *The Voice of Jihad*.

Hunt the Rafida – the Killings of Shiites as a Music Video

The *nashid* complements the video sequences of IS fighters undertaking drive by shootings on the Iraqi highway. The targets are unmarked cars that, according to the video, transport Shiite Iraqi soldiers not wearing their uniforms to their bases to report for duty. This part of the movie is entitled as "hunt the *rafida*", a reference made to Shiites who are thus termed as "deviates" or "rejectionists." Any Shiite, in particular those working for the central government in Baghdad are framed as *safavid*, a reference to the Iranian Safavid Empire (1501–1722), whereas IS perceives a war against Sunni Islam because of the interest and de facto presence of contemporary Iran inside of Iraq. In a video released in April 2015 entitled "Hunt the Safavids", IS made it clear that Shi'a Islam is the main threat for the Sunnis in Iraq and that the U.S. occupation served the intent to disempower Sunni Muslims in an attempt to destroy the 'pure Islam'. Thus, in IS perception backed by a wide array of Sunni extremist literature, the Shiites are nothing but *rafida* (pl. *rawafid*), secretly or openly working for Iranian interests and in particular cruel on Sunni civilians.

The SUV's are strain with bullet holes and corpses are seen lying on the motorway – documented by the jihadi camera lens to undermine the effectiveness of such operations and to highlight payback for Sunnis who have been discriminated since the ousting of Sunni ruler Saddam Hussein. Sequences of killing and drive-by shootings in open urban warfare are a frequent element of Sunni extremist videos, however, in this sequence IS shoots to kill, not wasting much ammunition while claiming to thoroughly hunt Shiite Iraqi soldiers, in some cases stopping at cars that crashed as a result of the attack to ensure all the passengers are killed by close up head shots. A caption clarifies "*rafida* hunters – eliminating elements of the *safavid* army on route to their military units."

In one sequence a man walking on the street next to another pedestrian is shot with a Kalashnikov rifle and hit multiple times. A caption in the video explains "eliminating an element of the *Safavid* SWAT forces." The other man who walked next to the victim runs away in horror, apparently unharmed with the camera man making sure to send this message. Taking out members of the Iraqi SWAT team, an elite unit loyal to Iraqi Prime Minister at the time Nuri al-Maliki is part of exercising revenge for the violent breakdown of peaceful Sunni protestors in Hawija, Anbar province, in April 2013, as is later detailed in the film. In one sequence a driver who had managed to escape on foot was caught and executed at close range. The camera pulls the audience into the front seat of the car where the front passenger shoots at the man on foot by leaning out of the window. Below the inside rearview mirror a dreamcatcher dangles while the man runs for his life. The sequence is captioned as "the hungry lions run their prey down." With two shooters aiming at the man, he is hit in the leg and falls into a fence in the Iraqi country side off the motorway. The man shouts in English and apparent disbelief "I am the driver; driver!"

IS projects the message of targeted not indiscriminate killings.

The video halts, the image of the injured man on the ground freezes and turns black and white. Another picture blends in showing the same man in color wearing an Iraqi Army uniform. Invented by IS' Godfather Abu Mus'ab al-Zarqawi to partly justify the execution of Western construction workers contracted by the U.S. Military and thus relying on a decade long history of media work and successful resistance, the injured driver by the photograph is sentenced to death and framed as guilty by association. He is shot in the back at point blank by a *Mujahid* emptying his full clip into the victim. Any allegiance or loyalty, even when an individual is merely the driver for employees of the Iraqi government, is an ultimate death sentence. This loyalty – or proximity – to the defined enemies of the "Islamic State" result in the consequent execution of this individual based on the guilt by association principle and/or a violation of *al-wala' wa-l bara'* if the victim is a Sunni.

Repenting and Recruitment: Inclusion of Sunnis in Conquered Territories

The *nashid* that bears the title of the video series concludes the sequences of the "hunt of the *rafida*" and takes the viewer into the most positive aspect of the "Islamic State", where Sunnis are invited to repent (*tawba*) and coerced to pledge allegiance to Abu Bakr al-Baghdadi. This IS tactic of consolidating power within Sunni majority pockets is part of an overall strategy to project influence and convey that IS seeks to include those who are marginalized and discriminated against by the non-Sunni government of al-Maliki and the Iraqi army.

By sparing the Sunnis in Anbar province who served as policemen or soldiers, IS seeks to include them in its own ranks. The offering of repentance allows the Sunni men to revert to the true *ahl al-Sunna wa-l jama'a*. By denouncing their loyalty to the Shiite-majority government, they renew their loyalty to God in the care of the "Islamic State" that claims to fight for the altruistic cause of all Sunnis. Mosques in Anbar province are used to gather scores of men of various ages who are then offered to repent. This enforces a collective identity of being a Sunni Muslim, with IS-fighters portrayed as avant-gardists and the sole defenders of Sunni Islam. Tribal leaders and subsequently the young and middle-aged men who belong to those families, clans or tribes are summoned to the mosque for collective and public repentance.

The men, exclusively members of Sunni tribes of Iraq, are offered to revert from their state of apostasy (*ridda*) to Sunni Islam through *tawba* and *bay'a* – replacing their loyalty, voluntarily or under coercion, to the Iraqi government for loyalty to God and respectively Abu Bakr al-Baghdadi. This underlines and elevates the core IS tactic of *re-integrating* Sunni Muslims who repent, relinquish loyalty (*wala'*) to the Iraqi government, and hence dissociate (*bara'*) themselves from the influence thereof.

In tactical terms, this *tawba* and re-integration of young men of Sunni tribes aims to destroy the influence of the Iraqi government for years to come. In particular, young men who had been members of the army and police forces in the province of Anbar are shown in the video and called to repent. While their service for the Iraqi government has turned these men into apostates (*murtadd*), IS seeks to reintegrate these men into Sunni Islam and recruit them – without any choice[?] – into the ranks of its army, administration, force, policing units (*al-hisba*) and so on. The sequence of *tawba* by these young men is thus defined as:

> "the apostates of the army, police and *sahwa* councils are summoned publicly to declare their repentance and to dissociate (*bara'*) themselves from *kufr*."

Abu Muhammad al-'Adnani, "the official spokesman of the Islamic State" and a key ideologue narrated the sequence of the repentance in a January 2014 speech:

> "We call on every remaining individual of the *sahwat* without exception, on all the politicians considered to be from the *ahl al-Sunna*, we call on you to repent and declare the end of your war against the *Mujahidin*. Dissociate yourself of supporting and aiding the malicious *rafida*. Whoever *repents before we overpower*[72] will be granted [according

---

72 Emphasis added.

A Milestone for "Islamic State" Propaganda: "The Clanging of the Swords, part 4"   105

The apostates register and issue their repentance speaking into a microphone with their right hand on the Qur'an. Through their repentance, the apostates are re-integrated and greeted as Sunni Muslims by "their brothers, the Mujahidin."

> to extremist interpretation of divine scripture] security. We shall not request anything of him regardless of what he has done in the past; we call on every policeman and all the soldiers, on all agents of the *safavid* security apparatus, clandestine and overt, to the *tawba* and to surrender their weapons and military gear to the Islamic State."[73]

The sequence is concluded by a sermon held by a soldier of the "caliphate" to further instruct the apostates prior to their repentance and subsequent re-version:

> "you have carried your weapons, you stood shoulder on shoulder with these rejectionist Shiites to kill your very own sons [of *ahl Sunna wa-l jama'a*]. We are your sons. We are your very brothers. We have come to protect and preserve your religion and your honour. Today is the day to forgive [and repent] while you are aware that our *shaykh* and *amir* Abu Bakr al-Baghdadi has said: "even if they killed thousands of us; if they killed thousands of you, forgive and pardon them." And we forgive and pardon,[74] isn't that what you ask for? For we are part of the *ahl al-Sunna wa-l jama'a*."

The administered inclusion and re-instatement of Sunni Muslims now under the formalistic rule of the Caliphate is immediately followed by combat footage of IS advancing on enemy positions in urban and rural environments, with scenes of Iraqi soldiers executed on the spot. The audience is therefore encouraged to believe that all those who had been *liberated* and *included* are now partaking in the state project of Sunni Islam.

The coherence of IS messaging matters most in this context. Abu Muhammad al-'Adnani said in his statement that "whoever *repents before we overpower*" will be offered peace and security. This very notion is deeply rooted within jihadist theology since 2010 when Al Qaeda in the Arabian Peninsula (AQAP) re-established itself in Yemen and started fighting for territory.[75] The words of al-'Adnani

---

73 Abu Muhammad al-'Adnani, *wa-l-Ra'id la yukadhib ahlahu*, al-Furqan Media, January 2014.
74 Meaning acceptance of voluntary repentance (tawba), thus not violating the commandment "unless they repent before you overpower them".
75 As discussed in: Nico Prucha, *Online Territories of Terror – How Jihadi Movements Project*

are a direct reference to the Qur'an 5:34 ruling that *tawba* can only be accepted by individuals coming forth on their terms and do not repent in captivity or under duress.

Oftentimes, jihadist videos show captives who are indicted in a kangaroo trial, in which they confess their crimes and violations. Granting these captives mercy would be in violation of the Qur'an 5:34 ("unless they repent before you overpower them – in that case bear in mind that God is forgiving and merciful").[76] Only if one comes forward voluntarily and repents in public can he be forgiven. The *tawba* in captivity before execution is thus only between the individual and God.

By contrast, what IS claims to document in SaS4 in early 2014 is the voluntary and public repentance of scores of Sunni men who served the Iraqi government; IS claims to be 're-instating' them as 'proper' Sunnis into the "Islamic State". These men had been given a 'general amnesty' despite their work for, and affiliation with, the army and police or other Iraqi government bodies, which made them "henchmen", "agents" or simply "dogs" of the Shiites.

After the conquest of territory in the Iraqi province of Anbar, IS moved to consolidate control of those areas and destroy Iraqi government infrastructure. The men who worked for the central government are part of this infrastructure, and IS deals with them as follows: most Sunnis are offered repentance and reintegration. This is not offered to Shiites and high-ranking Sunni officers, in particular those who collaborated with the Americans during the occupation. As a result, these individuals are executed or driven to flee.

After registering at the IS-controlled mosque, the gathered men issue a collective repentance on this day of forgiveness:

> "I dissociate (*bara'*) myself before God of these deeds of disbelief, of which I had been part. And I testify there is no God but God and Muhammad is the messenger of God."

By publicly stating the *shahada*, the Islamic creed, the apostates renounce their mischief and loyalty to anything related to disbelief (*kufr*) and restore their identity as Sunni Muslims professing the oneness of God (*tawhid*).[77]

Strategic Influence on the Internet and the Battlefield and Why it Matters, Dissertation, University of Vienna, June 2014.

76 Ibid.
77 The oneness of God; the fundamental monotheistic principle to not only establish a rule by God's divine commandment, but rather set an identity as a *muwahhid*, who professes the worship and proper rituals for the one God as outlined in the Islamic *shahada* and set by the flag of the 'Islamic State'.

Sunni tribal leaders and elders ('asha'ir) are woven into the power fabric of IS (left) with "common men", former Iraqi non-commissioned policemen and soldiers pledging their allegiance to IS in mosques

Closed Circuit Communication – the Coded Reference of "unless they repent before you overpower them"

The need for rules of engagement in the action radius of jihadist groups extends to answering questions related to their conduct and handling of prisoners, hostages, captured spies, or captives in general. In particular the conflicts in Iraq and subsequently Syria demand the need for more such operational guidelines, in particular within a confessional framework where the jihadist acclaims himself as the only legitimate Sunni representatives in fighting infidels, heretics, hypocrites, rejectionists, and apostates.

This includes, in times of conflict where one must choose an identity for belonging, traitors and spies who must be eradicated and within a punitive legal framework receive a sentence or othr form of punishment. With sectarianism thriving it has become an identity marker for most without many alternatives and is a driving force for the hardliners on all sides. As all of the terms above can be used to describe those who deviate from the jihadist methodology (*manhaj*), jihadist groups may be keen and quick to impose the death sentence. However, operational questions remain uncertain on, for example how to deal with Sunni clerics who gave their services to the enemies? And for whom the alleged spies work, furthermore, when no credible or sufficient proof is found. Is that individual cleric and his closest associates legitimate to execute, despite the scholar's claim to have repented and thus be spared, or shall he be executed just as any alleged spy of lower rank and file or individual of higher social standing within Sunni societies?

This is the essence of a question posted on the interactive Q&A fatwa forum on al-Maqdisi's website by the member *Nusrat al-Sham*, "the Victory for al-

Sham."⁷⁸ His question is entitled whether it is "sufficient for the spy to claim having repented before being overpowered?" The last part of the question, *taba qabla 'l-qidra 'alayhi*, is a direct reference to Qur'an 5:34:

> "unless they repent before you overpower them – in that case bear in mind that God is forgiving and merciful."

The issue is complex, as this spy in particular is a cleric, a *shaykh*, who, in the opinion of the questioner, is an impostor who worked in his religious authoritative role "to tirelessly promote lies." This cleric and his companion have been arrested for their 'swindle'. The *shaykh* was

> "searched and a list of names of Syrian and Lebanese senior officers and high dignitaries was found on him. He confessed spying for the [Syrian] regime but claimed to have repented!"⁷⁹

The core issue at hand is clear: is a Sunni Muslim who claims to have repented in silence before God prior to his arrest to be pardoned? Or is this a violation of Qur'an 5:34, whereas any repentance (*tawba*) under duress or *after* one's arrest is invalid? How can the *tawba* be sincere then?

With both individuals arrested or by whatever means detained, the allegations against the two are further denoted:

> "the *shaykh* had been collecting donations for the poor and spent the money on alcohol and to commit adultery (*zina*), as he confessed. Regarding the companion, there is no proof (*dalil*) for him spying, however, he did confess his desires to be part of the adultery and alcohol consummation with the false *shaykh*."⁸⁰

The question is focused on the practical implementation of *shari'a*-law for both individuals. As he is asking

> "the brothers for a legal decision (*hukm*) on the swindler? And the ruling on his companion?"⁸¹

On behalf of the *"shari'a law council on al-Minbar"*, Abu 'l-Mundhar al-Shanqiti answers online by emphasizing four elements based on the question:

> "He [the cleric] confessed being a spy.
> In his possession was a list of names of senior officers and high-ranking dignitaries [of the Syrian regime].

---

78 Muntada al-Tawhid wa-l-Jihad, *Hal yanfa' al-jasus za'amahu anahu tab qabla l-qidra 'alayhi?*, Question number 6528, http://tawhed.ws/FAQ/display_question?qid=6528 (accessed July 15, 2012).
79 Ibid.
80 Ibid.
81 Ibid.

His relentless self-destructive drive (*inghimas*)[82] into breaking inviolabilities, straying away from the *shari'a* as mentioned in the question regarding the legitimacy of not-recognizing his *tawba*.
Not having rid himself of those names and not having the pertaining numbers cleared from his mobile phone despite the likelihood of his arrest [after confessing]."[83]

Al-Shinqithi sets a general finding as the premises by decreeing the cleric the status of a *muharrib*, who wages war against Muslims. Therefore, he initiates his ruling, and as based

> "on the common understanding for dealing with those who engage in war against Muslims, do not grant them their repentance after you overpower them, this is affirmed and backed by taking His speech – exalted is He – into account: "unless they repent before you overpower them," *al-Ma'ida*: 34. This applies to everyone who is a crude apostate [of Islam], summarizing everything between the warfare [against Muslims] on the one hand while committing apostasy (*ridda*).
> This man had not shown his repentance before his scandalous matter was revealed, therefore claiming to have repented shall not save him then."

In a classical style to back his argument to sentence the cleric determined by al-Shinqithi as an active combatant to death, Ibn Taymiyya's work *al-Sarim al-Maslul* is cited. This citation is out of context, for Ibn Taymiyya (1263–1328 AD), the *Shaykh al-Islam*, had dealt in his – in modern jihadist circles popular – book with those who insulted the prophet and should therefore be sentenced to death. Thus, al-Shinqithi moves further ahead to not only define this particular cleric of being a combatant, but by his deeds on behalf of anti-Islamic forces he is equated to anyone insulting prophet Muhammad. This bears the death sentence as the defined combatant against Islam is, because of his Sunni background, further degraded as a *murtadd*, an apostate.

According to Ibn Taymiyya, in the reading of al-Shinqithi,

> "if the insulter [of the prophet] was also an armed opponent of God and His messenger with the aim to soil the earth with corruption, then he must be punished by one of the mentioned conditions in the verse [5:34]; unless he is to repent before being overpowered (…)."[84]

---

82 In the meaning of plunging carelessly into the rows of his enemies – a reference usually made in a highly positive connotation for *Mujahidin* and in particular suicide-bombers; as there is no return. The wording *inghimas* in this context by al-Shinqithi, however, is quite contrary. Ibn Taymiyya, *Qa'ida fi l-inghimas al-'adu wa-hal yubah?* Riyadh: Adwa' al-salaf 2002.
83 Muntada al-Tawhid wa-l-Jihad, *Hal yanfa' al-jasus za'amahu annahu taba qabla l-qidra 'alayhi?*, Question number 6528, http://tawhed.ws/FAQ/display_question?qid=6528 (accessed July 15, 2012).
84 Ibid., citing Ibn Taymiyya's work *al-Sarim al-maslul 'ala man yushatim al-rusul*.

"Shaykh al-Islam says: If this insulter is a combatant against God and His messenger, causing mischief (*fasad*) to appear in the land[85], then he must be punished by one of the sanctions mentioned in the verse [of the Qur'an]; unless he repented before being overpowered."[86]

The alleged actions, the confession and the names found on the cleric are sufficient for al-Shinqithi to approve the execution. He furthermore refers to two more sources, by al-Nasa'i and Ibn al-Qayyim to back his argument and concludes by responding to the status of the companion of the incriminated cleric, saying:

"he is in the status of doubt, however, his mere presence next to the cleric does not necessarily mean that he is indeed a partner in his espionage against the Muslims. For the matter concerning him, more interrogations must be conducted with the aim of receiving a confession, allowing all tricks and methods of deceit, such as offering him to work as a spy against the regime to assess his relationship status with them."[87]

Reformatting Territory – Consolidating Power and Projecting Influence

The "Islamic State" is driven by a coherent and tightly defined theology, claiming absolute hegemony as the only legitimate representatives of Sunni Islam. The current fight in the Middle East escalated the conflict along sectarian lines as never before in the history of Islam; Syria and Iraq are dominated by a war between Sunni and Shi'a Islam with their respective allies and proxies. IS, like al-Qaeda, considers itself a protection force for Sunni Muslims while denying any space for Shiites, Alawites, Christians, Jews, Druze, Yezidis, homosexuals, seculars or any other group in the region.[88] Two main IS tactics contribute to this denial of space:
1. Military conquest and the immediate destruction or takeover of army outposts, police stations and checkpoints. IS keenly documents the bulldozing of army checkpoints in urban settings as much as storm assaults on remote outposts. These sequences often end with scores of corpses wearing Iraqi

---

85 This can be interpreted as a subtle reference to Qur'an 40:26.
86 Muntada al-Tawhid wa-l-Jihad, *Hal yanfa' al-jasus za'amahu annahu taba qabla l-qidra 'alayhi?*, Question number 6528, http://tawhed.ws/FAQ/display_question?qid=6528 (accessed July 15, 2012).
87 Mantada al-Tawhid wa-l-Jihad, *Hal yanfa' al-jasus za'amahu annahu taba qabla l-qidra 'alayhi?*, Question number 6528, http://tawhed.ws/FAQ/display_question?qid=6528, (accessed July 15, 2012).
88 A vast number of IS videos shows the enforcement of this theology by destroying Yazidi sites of worship or the execution of homosexuals by plunging them to death off high buildings.

army uniforms. IS also documents that the personal items of slain soldiers include Shiite patches, flags, and personal veneration items, all of which is 'proof' of open Shiite warfare against Sunni Islam.[89]

2. As part of consolidating conquered territory after removing government structures, non-Sunni places of worship are systematically destroyed. The annihilation or enslavement of those who attend these sites is part of the consequent implementation of jihadist theology. This constitutes a genocide, in which IS wipes out the cultural heritage sites, mosques, churches, and sites of veneration, including graveyards, tombs of holy men (*awliya'*), and even trees ("tree of Moses")[90] that hold spiritual meaning for local communities. IS systematically cleanses conquered territory of non-Sunni holy sites, destroying not only non-Muslim communities, but anything deemed non-Sunni. Subsequently, Shiite mosques and tombs of holy men or saints (*awliya'*) are demolished and literally blown to obliteration. According to the worldview of IS, the Caliphate can only manifest in its true form when the conquered territory is purged of anyone and anything that violates the "oneness of God," or *tawhid* in Arabic, which is supreme in jihadist theology.

The May 2014 release of *Salil al-Sawarim 4* is the first major media production to 'document' the twofold strategy of winning on the ground while reformatting the landscape to consolidate territory for the "Islamic State." Cleansing (the term *tadhir* is used almost exclusively to describe this) is applied to project this brutal, yet effective, method of building a state. This reformatting of territory in Syria and Iraq, Libya, Yemen, parts of Africa and elsewhere, may be an irreversible destruction of heterogeneous religious communities and the end of pluralism and tolerance in certain areas, particularly within the greater Middle East.

The narrative of waging a without mercy against Shia Islam is important because it incorporates several jihadist ideological core themes. Sunni jihadists regard Shiites as "rejectionists" or *rafida*, but IS includes Shiites when it refers to polytheists, or *mushrikin*. This is intended to convey that Shiites violate the monotheist principle of orthodox Islam – and are therefore legitimate targets.

In *Salil al-Sawarim 4*, footage of scores of men collectively issuing their repentance at a mosque in Anbar province is followed by a fierce armed engagement. The fighting is concluded by the takeover of Iraqi Army barracks in an undisclosed urban environment and the point-blank execution of several cap-

---

89 One of the first major IS videos 'documenting' Iranian involvement in Syria and the presence of Lebanese Hizbullah Mujahidin is the 25th instalment of the 50 video series *Nawafidh 'ala ard al-malahim*, "Protecting the Access Points of Aleppo", Mu'assassat al-I'tisam, November 2013.
90 See for example the video released by the IS-declared province of al-Khayr, August 13, 2015, entitled: izala shajra al-Musa ("uprooting the tree of Moses").

tured soldiers. The soldiers are labelled Shiites and displayed to the audience as henchmen responsible for the misery of Sunnis.

The video shifts to IS fighters looting the conquered outpost and pauses on a *Mujahid* holding a Shiite flag showing Ali and Iraqi Shiite dignitary al-Sistani. One of the Saudi Islamic scholars of the 20th century is cited with the Shiite banner fading into the background to fortify the 'natural' enmity against Shiites:

> "Shaykh Muhammad bin 'Abd al-Latif Al Shaykh[91] – may God have mercy with him – described the *rafida* of his time: "As for now their situation is even more hideous and atrocious having added to their beliefs an absolute exaggeration regarding sainthood (*awliya'*) and the family of prophet Muhammad (*al-salihin min ahl al-bayt*) and others.[92] They believed that this brings about benefit and harm in times of difficulty and ease. They consider this as a means of gaining proximity to God (*qirba*), that brings them closer to God (*taqarrabhum ila l-llah*). This is a central element enforced in their religion.""[93]

Speeches of ideologues such as Abu Muhammad al-'Adnani form the audio track of footage of fighters consolidating territory in the Iraqi province of Anbar. This frames the actions of IS as a direct application of theory and implementation of theological decrees. The "Islamic State" is therefore portrayed as a viable way to bring peace and security to the Sunni Muslims of the Arab World. After all, IS claims to exist only to protect and avenge[94] the Sunni community, the *ahl al-Sunna wa-l jama'a*.

For example, the video plays an audio track of Abu Muammad al-'Adnani alongside footage of bulldozers destroying Iraqi military watchtowers and IS fighters looting American-provided weaponry:

> "We only exist for your defiance and to protect your rights; to halt your enemies by facing them. This is the Islamic State: your only hope and we are sincere by God to

---

91 He is the brother of the former Saudi Great Mufti Muhammad bin Ibrahim (1953–1969) and passed away in 1947. For a relationship of the Saudi scholars with modern al-Qaeda members in the Kingdom: Thomas Hegghammer, *Jihad in Saudi Arabia – Violence and Pan-Islamism since 1979*, Cambridge University Press 2010.
92 Some of the companions (sahaba) of prophet Muhammad.
93 Part of a collection of writings of Muhammad bin 'Abd al-Latif Al Shaykh and essential source for the "ruling on Shiites", chapter 15 of the *al-Gharq* Encyclopedia, http://www.dorar.net/enc/firq/1892 (accessed May 05, 2018). His writings are also reflected in a forum posting "academic articles regarding the strive against the rafida Huthis [in Yemen]", where the exact same passage is cited. *Shabaka Sahab al-Salafiyya*, October 13, 2015, http://www.sahab.net/forums/index.php?showtopic=154946 (accessed May 05, 2018).
94 This notion was broadcast in a video released in November 2014 by the al-Furqan Media Institute entitled wa-lau kariha l-kafirin ("although the disbelievers dislike it"). In this video, the Sunni jihadist 'intervention' coming from Iraq in Syria is contextualized in the overall state of the Middle East since the U.S. occupation of Iraq and the history of Sunni extremist resistance.

escape the unjust heresy in which your [current] leaders have cast you into obliging to those who have aligned themselves with the *rafida*."[95]

The symbolism of the footage is worth noting: after a decade of occupation by the U.S. military and continuous counter-terrorism operations (that at times had been guided by a Shiite confessional agenda against the Sunnis of Fallujah), IS filmed its destruction of the main administration building of the local counter-terrorism unit. Such headquarters or government buildings are used to cooperate with U.S. forces leading the war on terror, including drone warfare and joint military operations.[96] IS exploits such grievances, and together with the reality of 'Shiite boots on the ground' in Syria and Iraq, positions itself as the only reliable protector of Sunnis.

After the building collapses in a detonation, the site is bulldozed. This is portrayed as an attempt to wipe out any memory of the injustices brought upon the Sunni population of Fallujah. One of the *Mujahidin*, claiming to be a local resident, explains:

> "the armoured vehicles are cleansing the earth of the filth of the [Iraqi] government administrators of counter-terrorism in Fallujah. The removal is a salvation for all Muslims, who praise and rise, who have had to endure injustice and tyranny; who have waged war upon the *muwahhidin* and Muslims for so long. These sites that for all this time have [inflicted pain] on our brothers of the Mujahidin and Muslims. All these years of injustice and hostility [are over, citing the Qur'an[97]]: "Their only grievance against them was their faith in God, the Mighty, and the Praiseworthy." All of this is happening with the permission of God and heals the believers chests[98] of the *muwahhidin* and discourage the people of disbelief and hypocrisy."

---

95 Abu Muhammad al-'Adnani, *al-Iraq al-Iraq ya ahl al-Sunna*, Mu'assassat al-Furqan, March 2012.
96 Andrew Cockburn, *Kill Chain, The Rise of the High-Tech Assassins*, New York: Henry Holt and Company 2015. Jeremy Scahill, *Dirty Wars: The World is a Battlefield*, New York: Nation Books 2013, e-book edition.
97 Qur'an 85:8.
98 *Shifa' al-sudur*, healing the believers' chests within the framing of a revenge action-reaction scheme, with a subtle reference to the Qur'an. Shifa'al-sudur is the title of the video showing the killing of the captured Jordanian combat pilot Mu'adh al-Kasasiba, alledgedly an act of revenge for the indiscriminate bombing of Raqqa, Syria. For an analysis of the video and the ideological implications: Nico Prucha/Ali Fisher, Turning up the Volume to 11 is not Enough (part 2), in *Jihadica*, (2015) (http://www.jihadica.com/turning-the-volume-up-to-11-is-not-enough-why-counter-strategies-have-to-target-extremist-clusters/ – art 1) (accessed May 05, 2018); Why counter narratives have to target extremist networks, in *Jihadica*, (2015) (accessed May 05, 2018).

A Foreign Fighter from Bahrain – Citizens of the Islamic State

The scene shifts from sequences of IED attacks to a band of armed *Mujahidin* who hold their passports in their hands. Similar to the opening of the video promoting Abu 'Abdallah al-Kosovi, the foreign fighter from Kosovo, the focus is now set on a foreign fighter from Bahrain. Sympathizers on Twitter identified him two days prior to the video release by his nom de guerre Abu Dharr al-Bahrayni[99] using the Twitter handle @mojahed_bh. He speaks in native Arabic, using a non-colloquial version to boost his standing as an individual with a high degree of religious education.

IS sympathizers and members utilized Twitter before and after the release of SAS4 to popularize the "story of responding to the call of arms by Abu Dhar al-Bahraini in his own words via his Twitter account."[100] In his story, Abu Dharr al-Bahraini claimed his mother had initially begged him to return to Bahrain, but later joined him in Syria. His tweets were then used by media sympathizers to create and disseminate fan content. Abu Dharr al-Bahraini later used the different alias Abu Bara' al-Bahraini and was reportedly killed in Fallujah in July 2015. His real name had been Salman Turki from Riffa, Bahrain, born in 1995.[101]

A screenshot from this sequence is shown above. It contains four elements that exemplify the culture of online fandom for IS:
1. The title of the film in Arabic is shown below the green passport, as well as the then-official Twitter handle of the *al-I'tasimu* Media Foundation. This helps viewers find new official IS content even after accounts are shut down. Although the Twitter account is long gone, non-Arabic speakers are empowered to uncover troves of IS videos and materials online just by using key search terms in Arabic and Latin transcription such as *wa3tasimu*[102].
2. A screenshot of Salman Turki's original tweet emphasizes in Turki's words the initial criticism of his mother who then later joined him in the "Islamic State" project. Under the hashtag "the story of [my] *nafir*" (#نفير_قصة) he tweeted: "As I arrived in Istanbul my mother called me and threatened to kill herself should I not return. She will never allow me to leave. A little while later she came to me in Syria where she adopted the methodology [of IS] and joined the state."
3. Turki's concluding remarks of the movie are shown in the bottom of the frame:
"O you tyrants! Do not think that we tear up your citizenship; we are burning

---
99 Via *jazrawiyya* (@hnun321): https://twitter.com/hnun321/status/467130346765443073 (accessed March 15, 2014).
100 https://justpaste.it/fitu, published on March 19, 2014.
101 Mir'at al-Bahrain, *muqatil al-bahrayni Salman Turki fi sufuf "da'ish"*, July 13, 2015.
102 The number "3" is often used to transliterate the Arabic letter "'ayn" / "3ayn".

it right here, right now. We shall not return to our home countries, no, by God, we are to return, God willing! But not with these [passports], rather by this [petting his Kalashnikov rifle]. By God, we will shred you to pieces, limb by limb, and in doing so we attain the closest proximity to God.[103] By God, we won't rest until we have hammered the last nail into your coffin. You tyrants and worshippers of idols![104] This is your citizenship [holding his passport into the camera]. For I am Muslim! I do not recognize this!"

4. A stamp makes the fan-created picture 'official'. The stamp is a graphic modification of the IS flag that imitates the alleged seal of the prophet. Written below is the "Islamic State in Iraq and Syria," the official name at the time the video was published and before the declaration of the caliphate.

The narrator of *Salil al-Sawarim 4* introduces the men as individuals who heeded to the call to arms (*nafir*) and unity and thus "have the benefit of gathering united in one row (*saff*)[105]."

The men shown are apparently neither Syrian nor Iraqi, but rather Chechens and Arabs from the Gulf States. Continuing the narration, the men are elevated as those who made up

"these convoys (*muwakib*)[106] of migrants (*muhajirun*) to the Islamic State. From every last corner of the earth, unpacking their luggage, to nourish this sacred plant [of the "state"] by their blood."

One of the *Mujahidin* outlines in his own words why he joined IS and what he is fighting for and against – clearly defining his identity as a fighter for Islamic State. This foreign fighter, who claims to be from Bahrain, holds his red passport in his left hand and a microphone in his right hand. Symmetrically aligned, he is flanked by two *Mujahidin* of exact height who are both holding green Saudi Arabian passports in their hands. The symmetry is further enhanced by two erected flagpoles in the background, each with a black banner of the "State" framing the men.

First, he praises Prophet Muhammad, using a violent image:

"peace and blessing upon who has come slaughtering with laughter (*al-duhuk al-qital*)[107] Muhammad, son of 'Abdallah."

---

103 In Arabic: *taqarrub*.
104 Hence the branding as 'polytheists' or *mushrikin* in Arabic.
105 The Arabic term *saff* for row, refers to the rows obligatorily kept in order during prayer.
106 Often the reference for "caravans" is the Arabic term *qafila*, used in the meaning of a popular theme penned by the Godfather of Jihad 'Abdallah 'Azzam, *Ilhaq bi-l qafila* ("Join the Caravan"), Peshawar 1987.
107 The statement *duhuk al-qital* is based on a transmission by Ibn Faris and Ibn 'Abbas, both companions of Muhammad, which is not conveyed in the hadith collections but rather

He repeatedly uses this imagery while neglecting any description of the prophet not related to time of war.

This image of prophet Muhammad enjoying combat and laughing into his enemy's faces gives jihadists 'license' to express joy when applying hard power (beheadings, general combat) for their cause. In their view, this justifies the content of the IS video "And Kill them Wherever you Find them", which shows perpetrators of the November 13, 2015 Paris attack beheading hostages in Syria and Iraq, holding the severed heads into the camera, and smiling.

IS video justifying the November 13, 2015 Paris attacks in the words of nine alleged assailants. Multilingual propaganda for a diverse target audience; German (left), Arabic original (right).

This is the kind of role model some Sunni extremists seek to popularize, while neglecting the intellectual and philosophical sources that have been the backbone of over 1,400 years of Islamic history.

The foreign fighter from Bahrain then issues

> "a warning to the tyrants Al Khalifa, the rulers of Bahrain, the henchmen of the Al Salul[108] and obedient dogs for the Americans."

---

conveyed by historical writer and scholar Ibn Taymiyya. This is according to a question posed by Abu Yusuf al-Sabi'i, asking for the source of Muhammad's statement, "I slaughter laughing," which he read in Ibn Taymiyya's book "The Whip of Shari'a", Multaqa Ahl al-Hadeeth Forum (http://www.ahlalhdeeth.com/vb/showthread.php?t=12210) (accessed May 05, 2018), September 11, 2003.

108 In jihadist slang, a reference for the Al Sa'ud, the ruling Saudi family. Salul is a repeated insult for the Saudi government as well as the Saudi mainstream media. The historical figure

Given that Bahrain has threatened to revoke the citizenship of those who have left the country and joined IS, Salman Turki continues:

> "The Bahraini government has issued an ultimatum to the *Mujahidin*, who profess the oneness of God (*muwahhiddin*), who have responded to the call (*nafir*) to join the battlefields of jihad.[109] If they do not return to Bahrain within two weeks, they will have their citizenship revoked."

"Citizenship" is paired with extremist identity in jihadist media, for a "true" Sunni Muslim should never hold state-issued citizenship from an un-Islamic government and thus belong to a society that is not governed by the full set of "rules of God" (*hukm allah*), which are – ironically – interpreted and applied by humans. However, IS claims to consist of the "soldiers of God" (*jund allah*) who are hence in God's closest proximity, decreeing who is a Muslim and who is not. As Indonesian Kyai Haji Hodri Ariev puts it:

> "In reality, the extremists are nothing but petty dictators, who seek to deceive Muslims by wearing masks that conceal their human fallibility, while presenting themselves as God's chosen spokesmen."[110]

The Bahraini government's threat to revoke an IS *Mujahid*'s citizenship is the final phase in consolidating individual commitment to a new identity: being a citizen of the "Islamic State" and pledging full loyalty and allegiance to this project. There is also hardly a way out of the group from this point on.[111]

---

of 'Abdallah b. Ubay b. Salul was used in the speech "A Muslim Bomb" by Osama bin Laden in December 1998 after the East Africa embassy bombings. The ruling family of Sa'ud are considered as traitors as much as 'Abdallah b. Ubay b. Salul. He became a Muslim in Medina at the time of prophet Muhammad and later lost a great deal of influence when the majority of the population of Medina accepted Islam. Apparently he was never a passionate Muslim and betrayed Muhammad twice, leading to allegations against him of lacking belief and commitment to God. The term salul today is used in Arabic for traitors and hypocrites, even more so in reference to the Saudis.

109 In the understanding of IS and AQ, the "battlefields of jihad" (sahat al-jihad) are online as much as offline. Media guidelines and strategies, advice for active fighting jihadi groups was, for example, set in late 2013 by Mu'assasat al-Ma'sada al-I'lamiyya / Fursan al-Balagh al-I'lam, *Bayan nusrat al-ansar li-ikhwanihim al-Mujahidin al-abrar* (https://shamikh1.info/vb/showthread.php?t=21520) (accessed May 05, 2018), October 10, 2013. This statement is signed by the most influential contemporary jihadi media key figures. For an analysis: Nico Prucha, *Online Territories of Terror: How Jihadi Movements Project Strategic Influence on the Internet and the Battlefied and Why it Matters Offline*, manuscript of forthcoming book, 2016.
110 Kyai Haji Hodri Ariev, *The Theology and Agenda of Extremist Movements in Indonesia*, in Kyai Haji Abdurrahman Wahid (ed.), *The Illusion of an Islamic State*, LibForAll Foundation Press, 2009. E-book version.
111 Former German gangster rapper Denis Cuspert a.k.a. Abu Talha al-Almani gave a similar sentiment in a video message to his followers and fans in Germany: "why I gave my citizenship to the Islamic State; meaning why I gave up my German citizenship, giving the bay'a deliberately to the Islamic State of Iraq and al-Sham? Because for me as a Muslim [it is

The conviction is further elevated by the individuals' firm posture to fight, bleed, kill, and die for this identity and frame of reference, as the Bahraini foreign fighter Salman Turki declares:

> "Let me tell the government of Bahrain from this blessed place; o you intellectually depraved ones, aren't you fully aware that we are the soldiers of IS in Iraq and in al-Sham? We do not give a damn for your citizenship! Don't you get it? We renounced our loyalty to you. Don't you realize that you and your citizenship, worldly laws (*qawanin*), constitutions, and your threats are all under our feet [with us tramping on your values and structures of power]?
> Haven't you coped with the fact that our *amir* is the *amir al-mu'minin* ["the leader of all believers"]? He is the scholar Abu Bakr al-Baghdadi who tears down walls and erodes the borders [between Muslims], who crushes the disbelievers. Aren't you aware that our commander ordered us to not recognize the borders of the despicable Sykes-Pikot [agreement]; for the lands of the Muslims are one!"

When Turki Salman rejects the borders created by the Sykes-Picot-Agreement, he is echoing AQ-inspired literature. For over three decades, these writings aspired to spark a 'jihadist renaissance' in the Islamic world, in particular in the Middle East and North Africa.

IS is therefore acting on the writings of famed scholars of jihad and attempting to implement their ideas, notably eroding the border between Syria and Iraq. Similarly, it claims to be a movement leading the Islamic world into a golden age. The jihadist writings, furthermore, act as proclaimed theological and ideological authoritative sources, purporting that the historic Caliphate ceased to exist because of a conspiracy against Muslims – hence the Islamic world is divided by the Sykes-Picot-Agreement and in parts occupied. The "Islamic State" not only projects the image of being an avant-garde in understanding and therefore restoring "Islam", but also *an actor actively succeeding in the fight* for statehood.

The root-cause for the misery of division and occupation is perceived to be an unholy alliance. 'Abd al-Majiid 'Abd al-Maajid, an Afghanistan-based AQ ideologue and prolific writer, outlined this line of thought in the Arabic-language *Tala'i al-Khurasan* electronic magazine. He writes that the misery:

> "is repeating the catastrophes for the Muslims over and over again. It is but the hand of the Jews and Christians, which is clearly involved [in the fate of the Islamic world]. And the final confirmation is the dismemberment or the assault of the great Islamic State [the Caliphate and its subsequent division] into tiny state-entities.[112] These states are so tiny that they hardly can be found on a map. Consequently, the tyrannical Crusader

---

obligatory] to join an Islamic State, ruled by the Qur'an and Sunna; in which the shari'a is implemented." *Mein Treueid an den islamischen Staat* (http://alplatformmedia.com/vb/showthread.php?p=201868#post201868) (accessed May 05, 2018), April 12, 2014.

112 Usually this is a reference to the Sykes-Picot arrangement, which led to the creation of the modern-day Arabic states.

hostilities began against the Muslim countries of Afghanistan and Iraq after Bosnia, the Philippines, Somalia, Sudan and the occupation of the land of the al-Aqsa Mosque [Palestine] by the Jews in accordance with the pledge to their Crusader-brothers [to wage war on Islam].[113] They have risen by killing women and children there. And when the Islamic *Sahwa*[114] began to become more widely known in the 20th century, they turned against it by any means possible."[115]

The foreign fighter from Bahrain concludes:

"Don't you understand that al-Baghdadi ordered us if we are to return to our home countries, we are not to arrive with your filthy citizenship. Rather, will spread and grow (*tamaddud*)[116] by the will of God and by Him granting us victory (*bi-nasr minhu*); then, we will come for you!
We are the soldiers of IS in Iraq and al-Sham and our state will expand, expand, and expand (*tamaddud*) until you are forced to get out of your thrones for which you have sold your religion for."

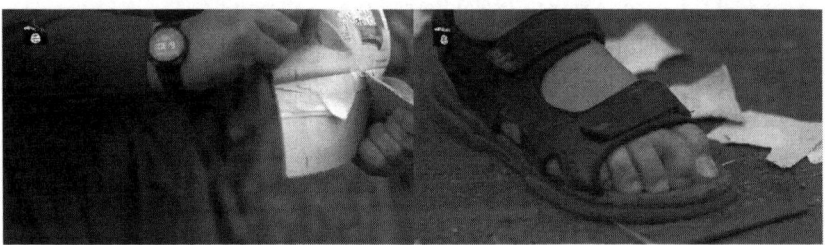

Consolidating one's conviction by renouncing any belonging to the nation state of origin.

The gathered men start tearing up their passports and throw them to the ground. This is the final step of renouncing all ties and loyalty to their countries of origin and pledging allegiance to the project "Islamic State", of which they now claim to be citizens.

---

113 A footnote states that "it is well known that the first phase in establishing a Crusader-Zionist state in Palestine was the Balfour agreement." Since this historical agreement, al-Maajid argues, further phases have come into effect to secure the creation of such a state that would manifest the final stage of the assumed war against Islam and Muslims alike. Furthermore, the pledge contains "active help and support by the British to the Jews to [first of all] proclaim the state of Israel on Palestinian territory and assist to seek recognition of this state on an international level."
114 A term describing awakening or recovery of consciousness – al-Maajid refers to it as the beginning and the rise of a militant-jihadist struggle against perceived enemies and vassal regimes that developed into a global network. Parallel to active insurgencies and attacks, ideological parameters and rulings have been established and disseminated by the Internet.
115 'Abd al-Majiid 'Abd al-Maajid, *Manhaj al-ghuraba' fi muwajihat al-jahiliyya*, Tala'i al-Khurasan, 7th edition, August 2006, p. 45.
116 Dawlatu l-Islam baqiyya wa-tammadud, "the "Islamic State" will remain and expand" is one of the earliest slogans.

Guilt by association: IS reasoning for executions at checkpoints

As stated, the documentary-style movie is intended to project a state-building process. Following the furious speech by the Bahraini foreign fighter, the film takes viewers to the plains of Anbar province, where IS is building a checkpoint on a remote desert highway. Jihadist videos often show soldiers on patrols, search and destroy missions or maintaining checkpoints to single out individuals such as government workers, plain-clothes army members, foreigners, etc.

As these groups often operate within their home territory, they know whom to look for. The video intends to convey that IS has mastered this tactic, as the checkpoint seems professionally established, with several cars, including several Toyota pick-ups mounted with .50 caliber heavy machine guns. The "intelligence" branch of IS is part of the checkpoint. A *Mujahid* fully dressed in black has a laptop with an apparent database on it where he compares the names of the identity cards given to IS-soldiers at the checkpoint.

The theme of this part of the film is defined as "singling out the apostates for extermination, based on inquiry and cross checking with a digital database of men wanted by the *Mujahidin*."

Checkpoints and background checking.

Some of those stopped are rightfully confused; the IS checkpoint resembles an Iraqi army checkpoint and IS fighters are wearing army-issued uniforms; no IS-symbols, icons and no black flag are seen at the checkpoint. Rather, IS fighters wear the insignia of the Iraqi army, badges with the Iraqi flag on their arm, and in some cases the "Anti-Terror-Unit, Special Forces" badge. The film describes these sequences as fighters "singling out one of the local [Iraqi] government criminals in [the province of] Salah al-Din."[117]

The use of checkpoints such as these and the targeted execution of government employees, Iraqi army soldiers/policemen, and non-Sunnis, especially Shiites (often identified by their names), has enabled IS to drastically root out key figures of the Iraqi government. The film is documenting a phase of terri-

---

117 The official English name is "Saladin Governorate."

torial consolidation prior to IS' conquest of large Iraqi cities, especially Mosul in June 2014.

Identifying a high ranking Iraqi governmental official and justifying his subsequent execution. The IS-fighter on the left wears official Iraqi Army Special Forces badges.

Two men are taken out of their SUV. One is identified as a student, as he had claimed, and released, while the other is a high ranking Iraqi government official and taken aside. He is seen in the following scene sitting on the ground in front of an open grave and shot in the back of his head. Like previously, the film justifies these actions by citing a historical scholar, in this case Imam al-Bukhari, the most important collector of the sayings and doings (*hadith*) of the prophet Muhammad as described by his companions:

> "Imam al-Bukhari – may God have mercy with him – said about the *rafida*:
> "I do not differentiate between praying behind a Jew, a Christian, or a *rafidi*. Do not eat the meat they slaughter. Do not observe their funeral processions and do not tend to their sick.""[118]

The victim is guilty by association. First and foremost, he is executed for being a Shiite. Second, as he is Shiite and a member of the Iraqi government, the reasoning for IS to execute him is clear: (i) as a Shiite member of the Iraqi government, he is directly responsible for the marginalization of Iraqi Sunnites, (ii) he bears the guilt of having collaborated with American forces during the occupation of the country, (iii) he must pay a personal price for the massacre of Sunnis in April 2013 in Hawija, Anbar province. Immediately after the citation of Imam al-Bukhari, both a civilian Iraqi government employee and a plain-clothes Iraqi soldier captured at the checkpoint are executed.

The men, one of them identified by his ID card as Mash'al Khalif Shaghir, are forced to sit on the desert ground before a dug out grave with their hands tied

---

118 The quote by Imam al-Bukhari, a renowned hadith collector, is the essence of many anti-Shiite writings and sentiments, as discussed on the al-Burhan website ("The Ruling of the Scholars of Islam and their Fatwas in regard of Shiism"), http://alburhan.com/main/articles.aspx?article_no=3992#.VsTk6VLLecQ (accessed May 05, 2018). Likewise, Islamport.com offers a collection of citations on why it should be forbidden to pray with or behind Shiites: http://islamport.com/w/aqd/Web/3689/211.htm (accessed May 05, 2018).

behind their back. They fall into their graves when shot in the back of the head. Next to the executioner a stands a *Mujahid* holding the IS-flag.

The execution of Mash'al Khalif Shaghir – an Iraqi soldier and hence an "enemy of Islam."

"Entering a New Stage"

The video switches to a new subchapter, visualizing the greater context of the "Islamic State", showing sequences of earlier published jihad videos. The sequences show IS during the phase of military conquest of key zones in the Iraqi province al-Anbar, most notably the city of Fallujah.[119] The execution of sixteen Iraqi army soldiers captured by IS in an abandoned house after being forced to videotape their statements for the central government, is among the blend of jihad video meshes, with a clear visualized reference to the time of U.S occupation and the "Godfather" Abu Mus'ab al-Zarqawi.[120]

This scene is special as it shows how dedicated IS deploys camera-men to the frontlines, producing and using images consistently for their media productions. The short sequence of the execution of several Iraqi soldiers follows after IS proudly parades captured tanks in the city of Fallujah, Humvees, heavy artillery and anti-aircraft weaponry mounted on trucks and Toyota pick-ups project IS as an army in the making, having evolved from the guerilla war.

The sequence on the right that appears in *Salil al-sawarim* was released in February 2014 in a major video production with the title *Malahim al-Anbar al-*

---

119 Al-)Qaeda force captures Fallujah amid rise of violence in Iraq, in *The Washington Post*, January 3, 2014 (https://www.washingtonpost.com/world/al-qaeda-force-captures-fallujah-amid-rise-in-violence-in-iraq/2014/01/03/8abaeb2a-74aa-11e3-8def-a33011492df2_story.html (accessed October 9, 2015).

120 This modus operandi is very much a repetition of the "days of Abu Mus'ab al-Zarqawi", the founder of the predecessor of IS who is held in honors by his nickname *amir al-dhubbah*, the "leader of slaughter." Al-Zarqawi videotaped the beheading of American radio entrepreneur Nick Berg in 2003 and used the online media as his main tool of communication throughout his operations. Throughout the years, al-Furqan media, the same media institute used today by IS, published a variety of online videos showing the execution of captured Iraqi soldiers, police men, and ministry employees in a similar to identical style as of today's videos.

Victory parades and executions – part of the consolidation of territory strategy

kubra, part 2 ("Epic Battle of greater al-Anbar [province], part 2"). The men had been captured in a rural area of al-Anbar province, not far from Fallujah, when their unit succumbed to IS after a fierce firefight. Some are covered in blood and wounded. Much like the later videos, especially the *'Ala minhaj al-nubuwwa* ("Upon the Prophetic Methodology"), released end of July 2014, the soldiers are lined up, beaten, and rushed off. A speech by Abu Muhammad al-'Adnani praising the "days of Abu Mus'ab al-Zarqawi" is played while the viewer sees the captures soldiers leaning against a wall bearing two IS flags. The soldiers are coerced to confirm that they have been sent "to kill Sunnites" and are reporting at the time to Iraqi Prime Minister Nuri al-Maliki. In the following scene, the 16 men are kneeling on the ground with their hands tied behind their backs and executed ("implementation of the rule of God on the *Safavid* soldiers"). The scene is filmed from two angles whereas in the February 2014 video the killing is only shown from one angle, while in the May 2014 *Salil al-sawarim, part 4* video the second angle is used.

The February video is concluded by IS driving a U.S. provided Humvee through the streets of Fallujah showing off their flag – a precursor for IS videos of later 2014 and throughout 2015.

In an hour-long video released on October 9, 2015, entitled *Ramadi Malham al-Jihad* ("Ramadi, the slaughterhouse of jihad"), the martyred IS-commander Abu Muhannad al-Swaydawi is eulogized at length. New footage of the February 2015 video is shown here, depicting the executions of the 16 captured Iraqi soldiers and others from yet another camera angle. Al-Swaydawi addresses the viewers as a military commander and as a deeply pious individual. He is seen unmasked and his role as a lead executioner of the above described site is elaborated. He is projected posthumous as a true leader of men, "who knew his soldiers before him under his command."[121]

This sequence of *Salil al-sawarim* is narrated by Abu Muhammad al-'Adnani,

---

121 Lit.: in the rows (sufuf) before him, referencing the order and conduct of orthodox prayer rites. *Al-Ramadi malhamat al-Jihad*, wilayat al-Anbar, October 9, 2015.

strengthening the theme of entering a new phase of consolidating power in the Iraqi heartlands of Sunni tribal areas:

> "Soldiers of the state, know that today you have entered a new phase in the stages of conflict. For you have returned to the cities and taken hold of the territory. Anyone of you is ready to be killed one thousand times before of even thinking of taking one step back. The cities and areas are under your control. First and foremost, Fallujah, which will not be ruled by anything other than the rule of God (*shari'a allah*) – with the permission of God. There is no space for secularists, for Fallujah belongs to the *Mujahidin*.[The province of] al-Anbar belongs to the *Mujahidin*; [the provinces of] Nineveh, Kirkuk, Salah al-Din belong to the *muwahhidin*. Diyala, the north and south of Baghdad, belong to the people of the *Sunna*."

Al-'Adnani's audio speech is concluded by a short order implemented immediately in the video: "kill, use silencers and sniper rifles." The audience assumes the viewpoint of a sniper, watching unaware Iraqi soldiers manning checkpoints in an urban environment. As al-'Adnani stated, the jihad has been taken back into the hearts of Iraqi cities with snipers and assassins conducting surgical strikes against the remnants of the Iraqi central government to open and then effectively claim territory. The anthem *Salil al-Sawarim* is played to the footage of unaware soldiers being shot by snipers from the viewpoint of the audience of the video.

Uniting the Sunni tribes of al-Anbar

The 'cleansing' of Iraq's al-Anbar province is enhanced by the IS claim to be the sons of the very people they are fighting for. Like in the era of Saddam, IS is obliged to work with the Sunni Arab tribal elders to maintain and consolidate their power. As IS is fighting for the inclusion and the restoration of honor of all Sunnis and because many of the IS fighters in Iraq are fighting at home, in their home turf, the role of tribal elders pledging allegiance to al-Baghdadi is a central theme for IS videos in Syria[122] but in particular in Iraq.[123] The tribal elders, the leaders of the respective Sunni tribes in Fallujah, are summoned in a mosque where a IS fighter gives a speech on the motifs of IS to fight for the Sunnis and

---

122 Halab November 2013 pledge.
123 Example / killing of Shiite soldier to consolidate bay'a 'asha'ir In a video published by the IS provincial media department of Fallujah, June 7, 2015, entitled "the Tribes of Fallujah are the Thorne in the Eyes of the Enemies", the tribal elders are assembled. The elders read out a statement acknowledging the "Islamic State", the reestablishment of the Caliphate and the leadership of Abu Bakr al-Baghdadi as the "leader of the faithful" (*amir al-mu'minin*). The alliance of the tribesmen of Fallujah and of the al-Anbar province with IS is consolidated by the execution of an Iraqi soldier who had exhibited during the speech of the tribal leader. Wilayat al-Fallujah, *al-Mu'tamar al-'asha'iri al-awwal bi-'anwan 'asha'ir al-Fallujah shawka fi 'uyun al-'a'da'*, June 7, 2015.

calls on the loyalty of the Arab Sunni tribes: "the sons of the "Islamic State of Iraq and Sham" are in the midst of their tribes in the province of al-Anbar."

In his speech, grievances and the Iraqi reality since 2003 is reflected and summarized. The statements given by Abu Mus'ab al-Zarqawi and his successors are clearly reflected in this speech. The main fear phrased by this IS fighter was coined by al-Zarqawi in the video of the beheading of American Jack Armstrong, who was abducted and killed in 2004 as a conspiracy of disbelieving outside forces wishing to (re-) colonize Iraq. This implies a direct attack on Sunni Islam and a tearing apart of Islamic territories, as internalized in the trauma of having lost Palestine.[124] The loss of any Islamic territory is a direct assault on the Islamic identity.

The fighter having morphed into a preacher, thus bearing weight by his actions to his words, calls out to continue the tradition of fighting the U.S. since 2003 in Iraq and to target the remaining henchmen. These are considered as agents of an attack on the core identity of Islam from within, with the greatest threat being secular forces.

> "The past colonization, my beloved brothers, has led to the creation of secular parties. These [political] parties stand between a [united] Islamic nation and the return to religion. The new occupation is more complex and harmful. In order to dissolve Islam [as a political force] the religion is disfigured by the creation of so-called Islamic parties. This allows the slaughtering of our youth in the name of acting against terrorism and extremism. This is a major catastrophe and we need to be aware of this. We have to assume responsibilities [with the tribal Sunni elders present]. My brothers, by God, what is termed as an election is nothing other than a new conspiracy dressed in filthy clothes to re-subject our [Sunni] Islamic community under the [Shiite] rule of al-Maliki and his soldiers. What have we received of whom we elected? Anything other than war and slaughter with the rivers of blood our precious youth (...). By God, our honor! Who has surrendered us to the crusaders and *safavids*? Those we voted for."

Legitimate sorrow and grievances existing in the Iraqi context since 2003 and before, having endured decades of the Saddam regime, are effectively exploited in religious disguise for political gains – building and capitalizing on a real sectarian war within that framework.

Referring to the sectarian agenda and doings of Shiite militias, the preacher equates these Shiite militias to the Iraq army as a whole:

> "Militias are what we refer to as "the army" (*al-jaysh*), the police, the *sahwat* – the traitors and apostates[125] – are eating away the best of our youth and hand them over to the al-Maliki regime."

---

124 As outlined in: Hazim al-Amin, *Al-Salafiyyat al-yatim – Al-Wajha al-filastiniyya li-"l-jihad al-alami" wa-"l-Qa'ida"*, Beirut: Dar al-Saqi 2011.
125 Apostasy (*al-ridda*) carries the death sentence and hence any Sunni Muslim who has joined forces with the Sahwat forces is a legal target for IS to capture and kill.

> That is not all. They [the *safavids*, the Shiites and others siding with the Maliki regime] are disrupting and rewriting the everyday lives of Muslims. Don't allow the handing over of the honor (*'ird*[126]) of Muslims over to our enemies, who are the ones that have called for these elections and political operations [to consolidate their power and continue the politics of exclusion of Sunnis].
> My beloved [brothers], do we return to the phase of this betrayal? Will we once again turn in our beards and turbans, our intellects, our honor and dignity and hand it all over on a golden plate to al-Maliki?"

The sequence concludes with an important socializing element: sharing food together insider the mosque after the sermon of the IS-representative. During the speech in the mosque the mainly elder men, Sunni tribal leaders and men of influence from segments of local society, had been served tea and water. The meeting room of the mosque where the speech is held with the technical support of what appears to be a state of the art sound system is furthermore well equipped with 0.5 liter water bottles for the audience. Eating together at the end of the talk in a mosque, a sermon comprising mainly political elements and the notion of shared Sunni identity, the breaking of the bread also serves to nourish the ties and the alliance crafted that became integral for the steep rise and success of the "Islamic State"; co-opting the tribal leaders (*'asha'ir*) as brothers into the local Sunni "statehood" in the making.

The Mujahidin on a Mission

Throughout the video, IS presents itself as a highly pragmatic and militarily capable organization. The words of an IS preacher are put into action as the camera films four battle-ready *Mujahidin* wearing Kevlar vests, cartridge belts, and desert camouflage uniforms, most likely looted from the Iraqi Army.

The IS fighters resemble professional soldiers in their U.S.-provided uniforms complete with combat gear and helmets with attached flashlights. All four enter a Kia Sorento SUV that will be part of a larger operation, and a cameraman approaches the passengers for some final words of encouragement:

> "Let's go my brothers! I ask mighty God, Lord of the Mighty Throne[127], that God may enable you to overcome your enemies."

---

126 On the term "honor" in Islamic context: Frank Stewart, *Honor*, Chicago: The University of Chicago, 1994. For a description of "honor" in the context of Sunni extremism and in general for women: Madawi Al-Rasheed, *Contesting the Saudi State – Islamic Voices from a New Generation*, Cambridge University Press: Cambridge 2007, pp. 166–168.

127 *Rabb al-'arsh* implies mighty power, as referenced in the Qur'an, for example Sura al-Tawba, Verse 129: "If they turn away, [Prophet], say, 'God is enough for me: there is no God but Him; I put my trust in Him; He is the Lord of the Mighty Throne.'"

The video shifts to night-time in a rural part of Iraq, where isolated bungalow-styled houses are standing far apart from one another. The sequence is titled "Hunting the *Sahwa*, storming the house of a filthy *Sahwa* commander."

The IS soldiers are dressed as Iraqi Army Special Forces, wearing no IS-insignia or other identifying elements. They detain a man in his twenties and an older man, presumably his father. As the older man is pushed outside his house, he shouts "take it easy, let me call the Army so I can verify [who I am]", believing he is dealing with an Iraqi Army unit out on a search-and-destroy mission. This is intended to evoke memories of the height of the counter-insurgency campaign, when the homes of Sunnis were targeted in storm and search raids.

The idea that Shiites sought power to crush the Sunnis appeared frequently in the videos of Al Qaeda in Iraq and its successor, the "Islamic State in Iraq". The *Sahwat*, or awakening councils, later became an integral part of American strategy to quell the Sunni jihadist insurgency. Following the withdrawal of U.S. combat troops in December 2011, the Sunni jihadi forces immediately resumed their operations. Three years later, *Salil al-Sawarim 4* showed the capture, interrogation and subsequent execution of *Sahwa* members and leaders. By then, IS had become emboldened by recent victories and well-equipped by looting modern weapons from the Iraqi Army.

This sequence was filmed during the stages of IS conquest and consolidation. As such, the motto "hunt the *Sahwa*" is about rooting out potential resistance and (counter-) insurgency within the nascent "Islamic State".

Two *Mujahidin* take the captured *Sahwa* leader away and ask him, "Sir, sir, where are the terrorists, where?" Realizing his fate and that of his son and family he replies: "I fear you are da'ish!"

The next sequence is in daylight: the captured *Sahwa* leader and two of his sons are digging their own graves. The *Sahwa* leader is presented as a broken and disillusioned man, collapsing in his own grave. One IS fighter asks one of his sons, referred to as "*sahuji*", a mock term for *Sahwa* members:

Mujahid: "where do you work, you are a member of which division?"
The captive replies: "12th Division."
Mujahid: "Where is al-Maliki's army and why haven't you been freed?"
The young man replies: "al-Maliki's army is a failure"
A subtitle says, "they are digging their graves by their very own hands".
Mujahid: "What got into you to join this failure of an army?"
Prisoner: "I got involved by my own choice and because of my father" [pointing to his collapsed father].
Mujahid: "Who is your father [in the Iraqi Army]?"
Prisoner: "My dad is a *Sahwa* commander."

Mujahid: "A *Sahwa* commander. Set up to fight the *Mujahidin*, the defenders of your honor (*'ird*)."
Prisoner: "Yes. Against the *Mujahidin*."

The next sequence shows the father barely able to continue digging his grave. One of the Mujahidin lectures him: "Getting tired? Dig! Are you out of energy? Unlike when you became a Sahwa elder clinging on power."

In shock and exhausted, the father utters his final words, advising and deterring his Sahwa comrades:

"I advise everyone in the *Sahwa* forces to exercise repentance (*tawba*) and to stop their work. That is what has brought me [and my sons] here, digging our own grave."

Digging their graves. An interrogated son and a disillusioned father.

An older photo of the *Sahwa* commander flashes on the screen, with the word 'yesterday'. He is dressed in traditional white Arabian cloth, sitting at a desk with the Iraqi flag in the background, as an apparently high-ranking Iraqi governmental official. A photo of 'today' then appears; he is worn out, digging his own grave. "They came to my house to snatch me. From my house![128] They cannot be stopped." The picture freezes, turns to black and white and the Arabic word "slaughter" (*dhabh*) appears, sealing their fate.

Nashid: Fight for Ramadi

As part of the "operation shield for the Sunnis" in Ramadi the video continues by taking the audience into the heat of battle.

> Nashid
> "Oh soldiers of truth let's go, let the tunes of resistance ring out/
> Indeed Sham is illuminated, for assemble every soldier/
> The Islamic State has been established, so wipe out every existing border/
> Wherever we roam, the Rabbis of the Jews are humiliated/

---

128 Private and sacred space; payback after a decade of non-Sunnis violating the same sacrosanct space.

We break the crosses and wipe out the grandchildren of the apes/
The state of *tawhid* will remain, despite the trembling of those who are full of hate/"

The visual layer is filled with advancing IS-fighters in what appears to be an urban area. The viewer is taken into the battle siding with gunmen pointing and firing their M-16 assault rifles into houses, while others run to the front line to toss grenades into the last manned strongholds of the Iraqi Army. Abandoned tanks are set on fire, blue colored Iraqi police Humvees are taken as loot and the highlight of shooting down an Iraqi Army helicopter by a shoulder-launched anti-aircraft missile concludes the action of the battle for Ramadi.

Killed Iraqi soldiers are shown up close. The dead soldiers are framed as Safavids and as such as Shiites. The "operation shield for the Sunnis" is underlined by a citation of the historical scholar Imam al-Sam'ani:

"The Islamic community reached a consensus on the excommunication (takfir) of the Shiites due to their opinion that the *sahaba*[129] are misguided. [Furthermore,] they neglect the consensus of the Islamic community and accredit the *sahaba* in inappropriate[130] terms."

From the slain Iraqi soldiers the camera moves to the loot of the Mujahidin, the *ghanima*, focusing on one fighter:

"we have taken cars, equipment and the heads of apostates. And: our meeting place is Jerusalem, God willing."

"Today is the day of retribution"

The viewer is taken into the desert at night. Illuminated by night vision, the *Mujahidin*, "the *sahwa* hunters", march to their next target, "to terrorize the heads of the disbelievers in their own homes." The scenario resembles prior sequences: platoons of IS *Mujahidin* conduct raids and execute officers of the Iraqi Army, particularly those belonging to the Sahwa Councils, who are mostly Sunni, and therefore accused of apostasy.

Sunni Sahwa Council members are an integral part of the *insider threat* described in SAS4. In this case, the Sunni Sahwa Council member is accused of having converted from Sunni to Shia Islam – strengthening the IS narrative that the attack from within is the most dangerous threat, and that IS is the only defender of Sunni Islam. According to this narrative, any Sunni tribal leader working for the Shiite dominated government of Nuri al-Maliki is per definition

---

129 The companions of prophet Muhammad.
130 *Yansibuna*, lit.: offend, insult.

an apostate. Any Sunni, however, perceived as moving to Shiism is considered the ultimate apostate, a traitor to his tribe, lineage, and heritage.

The *Mujahidin* are again wearing regular Iraqi Army uniforms with no insignia of the "Islamic State". One of the *Mujahidin* defines this as "today, today is the day of retribution!" Retribution, in Arabic *qisas*, engulfs the theological concept often expressed as "an eye for an eye". The *shari'a* council of IS uses it to apply a clear ruling against its enemies, justifying subsequent executions as retribution, the deserved payback after a decade of humiliation. The foundation of *qisas*, or retribution, is set on the Qur'anic reading of Surat *al-baqara* (The Cow), verse 179:

> "Fair retribution saves life for you, people of understanding, so that you may guard yourselves against what is wrong."

Furthermore, the notion is supported by Qur'an 5:45, stating in the *words of God* (*kalimat allah*):

> "In the Torah We prescribed for them a life for a life, an eye for an eye, a nose for a nose, an ear for an ear, a tooth for a tooth, an equal wound for a wound."

This basic interpretation is in line with what al-Qaeda's main ideologue Abu Mus'ab al-Suri prescribed:

> "aggression against Muslims necessitates retaliation in the same manner (*'amaliyat bi-l-mithl*) or operations that deter aggression (*rad' al-'adwan*)."[131]

Jihadists frequently refer to the principle of "an eye for an eye". The 'classical' Al Qaeda school of thought uses this sentiment to primarily justify attacks in the West[132] that avenge interference with, and occupation of, Islamic territory. However, "Islamic State" uses this logic to justify its actions toward local enemies in Syria and Iraq.

Another Qur'anic concept introduced is that of "giving full measure" (*qistas*) to enemies or transgressors to repay them in full for their offenses against Sunni communities.

---

131 Citing Philipp Holtmann, *The Concept of Deterrence in Arab and Muslim Thought*, Manuscript 2012.For further reading: Philipp Holtmannn, *Abu Musab al-Suri's Jihad Concept*, Tel Aviv, Dayan Center, 2009, chapters 8–9; Also: Abu Mus'ab al-Suri, *Da'wat al-Muqawama al-Islamiyya al-Alamiyya*, published on the Internet, 2004: http://archive.org/details/Dawaaah (accessed June 24, 2012).

132 For example, the German language video by the Islamic Movement of Uzbekistan, featuring Mounir Chouka, who asks the audience: "what would you do, if somebody where to ignite explosives on German soil following the example of the Bundeswehr airstrike on September 4, 2009 in Kunduz, killing scores of people?" Böses Vaterland, Islamic Movement of Uzbekistan, Jund allah Media, February 2012.

"Give full measure when you measure, and weigh with accurate scales: that is better and fairer in the end." 17:35

IS uses the concept of "giving full measure" to justify its preoccupation with old grievances and guilt by association in times of war within Arab countries. Their extremist interpretation of religious sources[133] and the corresponding audio-visual output offers theological validation for IS and its behaviour as a "state". In their view, the same theological guidelines apply to anyone acting on behalf of jihadist theology worldwide, including self-motivated individuals.[134] As recent jihadist videos from Egypt show, other jihadist groups and movements have emulated this ideological current.[135]

Banging on the door, the *Mujahidin* behave similarly to the Iraqi Army, claiming that this is a random search and ordering the inhabitants "to move, we are the army!" The film then shows a man in the custody of the *Mujahidin*, a caption in the video clarifies: "a filthy Sahwa leader arrested by the Sahwat hunters."

The detainee is brought into a neighbouring house in a complex that is most likely the home of the greater family of this Sahwa leader. He demands, "where is the arrest warrant? I am a tribal leader.[136]" Believing to be in the custody of the Iraq Army, he seeks to clarify by saying "I have fought terrorism."

A split screen appears, with a series of videos showing the captive in traditional tribal dress receiving members of the Iraqi central government. The video is overlaid with the original footage of the interrogation. One picture shown in the overlay depicts the IS prisoner with three American soldiers in full combat gear, suggesting he had fought with the U.S. Army.

---

133 For example the extremist analysis of selected hadith, statements by Prophet Muhammad, by Abu 'l-Hasan al-Azdi, *al-Qistas al-'adl fi jawwaz qatl atfal wa-nisa' al-kuffar mu'aqiba bi l-mithl*, Ansar al-Mujahideen forum, 1432 a.H.
134 The discourse following the killing and attempted beheading of a British soldier in Woolwich, London, was set in the words of the two assailants by the logic of an eye for an eye. This attack in early 2013 was credited in the English-language Inspire magazine, 11th Edition (2013), 24–25. For a practical[?] discourse of al-mithl bi l-mithl, justifying operations against Western targets for the sake of "defending Muslim countries": Abu Mus'ab al-Suri, *Da'wa al-muqawama al-Islamiyya al-'alamiyya*, 933. Al-Suri references *al-mu'amala bi l-mithl*, to imitate the acts of the enemies, thus exercising the principle of retribution in full.
135 Al-Qisas al-hayyat, Ajnad Masr, https://twitter.com/ajnad_misr_am/status/456777846598283264, published May 18, 2014. This twenty-minute long video equates police brutality and military state repression against the Muslim Brotherhood members protesting to support ousted MB Muhammad Mursi to the targeted killing and attacks on individuals and high-ranking officers of the "security organs." The film follows two media strategies: (i) showcasing targeted assassinations of key players of the Egyptian security establishment while (ii) avoiding any civilian, any Sunni, casualties, a lesson learned from past mistakes of Egyptian jihadist movements.
136 Ana shaykh 'ashira.

The videos and the pictures were most likely taken from the mobile device or desktop computer of the detained Sahwa leader.[137] As more pictures and short video sequences are shown, the IS media operatives highlight a sequence taken from a local Iraqi news station years ago, where the captive received a high ranking Iraqi Army delegation, stating:

> "we are honoured by your visit[138], even when the [Iraqi] state has not given us everything. Nevertheless, we are very happy to receive the governor of [the Iraqi province of] Diyala – may God protect him."

The main video resumes in colour, and the detainee repeats his statement, "I have fought terrorists." One of the *Mujahidin* replies: "You have supported armed insurgents, isn't that the case?"

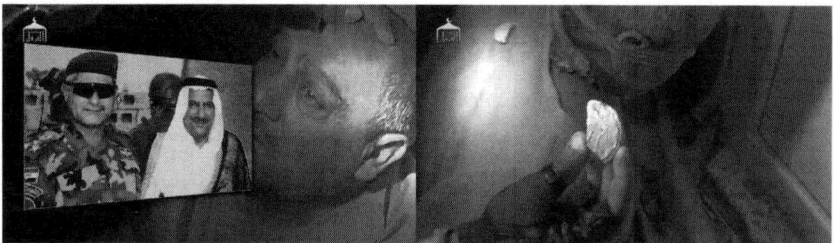

A collaborator and convert to Shiism as proven by the "stone" of clay used by Shiites for prayer rituals.

Another *Mujahid* smashes four pieces of clay on the *sahwa* leader's head, who by now is blindfolded and facing the wall while remaining squatting on the ground. The Shia use palm-sized clay coins or tablets for their prayer rituals, placing them on prayer rugs and touching them with their foreheads during ritual prayers (*sujud*). For orthodox Sunnis, this is an evident and clear practice of *shirk* (polytheism). The prayer stones are the ultimate reason for passing a death sentence. As one *Mujahid* shouts, calling the target not only a *sahwa* leader, but a key driver in the propagated sectarian war against the Sunnis of Iraq, as a result of Shiite support for the U.S. occupation:

> "he chose to be a Shiite. He puts down his head on the stone and prays on it, because he has become Shiite."

---

137 In the video a desktop personal computer is seen next to the detained Sahwa leader forced to squat on the ground.
138 Since he is a Sunni tribal leader, this implies Sunnis in his region have accepted and submitted to the Shiite central government rule of al-Maliki.

Praying on the stone underlines a deviation of the practice of *tawhid*, claiming the prayer on the stone is directed to figures such as 'Ali, diminishing the role of God who should be worshipped alone without distraction.

The IS-fighters then head to the neighbouring building, where the son of the *sahwa* leader lives. The fighters, dressed in Iraqi Army uniforms with no indication of their true identity, knock on the door and call for Nuri. He is led outside. A caption in the video clarifies:

> "The son of the *sahwa* leader who is a despicable source of information for the *Safavid* army intelligence."

The viewer is taken back inside the house where the father is restrained. One of the *Mujahidin* readied his sidearm with a huge silencer mounted. Before shooting him in the back of the head he asks "do you know who we are? We are the Islamic State." The tribal leader falls on his back and lies on a carpet where he is shot multiple times at close proximity in the head. The movie takes the viewers to his son, neither blindfolded nor shackled, lying on the floor on a carpet. He, too, is shot multiple times at close range with a [silencer-]suppressed side arm, soaking the carpet and the wall with his blood and brain tissue. One of the combatants steps over his body and says:

> "May God curse you, traitor! This revenge is for our brothers!"

Both men were shot in the head point blank in the father's house, spilling their blood over the carpets. This is part of the payback, as carpets are sacred objects; out of respect, visitors take off their shoes before stepping on them, and stepping on prayer rugs is to be avoided by all means.

The payback on behalf of Sunnis consists (i) of storming private houses in a similar fashion as Sunnis endured during and after the occupation by American and Shiite-majority forces; (ii) and the point-blank execution on carpets, which is perhaps comparable to the Mafia practice of shooting victims in the face, thus denying their families an open-casket farewell ceremony.

Reverting to the ahl al-Sunna wa-l jama'a – collective repentance

After the assassination of the senior *sahwa* leader and his son, the viewer is taken to witness the mass repentance of former Iraqi army, police and *sahwa* units in the Sunni majority province of Anbar. IS presents itself as a liberator, returning to serve the Sunni community united against the Shia.

The inclusion of the common Sunni population is key in the attempt to consolidate power and territory. The systematic hunt for and execution of important officials who worked for the central government ("*sahwa*" and "*rafida* hunters") in Baghdad is a strategy that seemed to work well for IS in the early months of 2014.

As we have seen, IS maintained Iraqi army-style checkpoints following an intelligence operational procedure to single out and execute government officials and off-duty army and police personnel, while also humiliating and shooting them inside their homes. In this manner, IS rooted out and exterminated the network and framework of the Iraqi central government, destroying key infrastructure, liberating imprisoned jihadists, and systematically executing government workers throughout the hierarchy.

By contrast, the offer of "repentance" or *tawba* serves as a framework of Islamic jurisprudence for former Sunni soldiers and other Sunnis not deemed guilty of any inexcusable crimes. The public *tawba* is part of the state-appeal of IS, fighting for territory on behalf of the local Sunni population. The inclusion of the "*ahl al-Sunna in Iraq*" is the backbone of this project of statehood, and a recurring narrative in IS videos after *Salil al-Sawarim 4*.

After showing IS' outreach and communication work with tribal elders, the film shows how IS engages with "common" Sunnis, first and foremost, the Sunni soldiers and policemen who lost their network and hierarchy when the central government lost control of the area.

The men are called to a local neighbourhood mosque where a fighter fulfils the role of a preacher. As the unarmed men, some in traditional garb others in Western-style clothes, enter the mosque, a caption clarifies, "members of the army, police and *sahwa* come in scores to the repentance centers (*marakiz al-istitaba*) in Anbar."

These centres serve as nodes in the IS network to fulfil the deeper meaning of *istitab*: "to call on someone to repent." As IS made gains and consolidated territory throughout 2014 and 2015, it published videos showing the repentance of former soldiers and government employees, showcasing the application of *tawba* as institutionalized within "offices to call on people to repent."[139] Throughout the footage in *Salil al-Sawarim 4*, an audio track of IS spokesman Abu Muhammad al-'Adnani guides the audience:

> "Sunnis of Iraq, we cannot bear seeing your sons as slaves of the rejectionist Shiites (*rafida*), as servants and henchmen for them; we cannot remain silent on their behalf. We cannot stand witnessing your sons continue on the path to hell; therefore, we must call and reach out to them. We want nothing but [restore] power and dignity in this world, salvation and happiness in the afterlife. You will not see anything other but mercy and compassion for your sons coming from us. Don't you see that we offer and accept repentance (*tawba*) of your sons, even if they have killed thousands of us? Don't

---

139 *Ta'ibun a'ibun*, wilayat al-Furat, July 28, 2015.

you perceive that all we ask your son to lower his weapon from our faces and cease supporting the *rafida*, the tyrants, and return to his religion?"[140]

The speech underlines the sequence of men gathering at the mosque, guarded by multiple fully-equipped masked IS fighters, some with handcuffs on their ammunition vests. The viewer is taken inside the mosque, where an IS preacher talks into a microphone to a large crowd of men, sitting on the ground, as is custom for Sunni Muslims during the Friday prayers when listening to the *khutba*. Similar to Islamic clerics and authoritative figures, the preacher, uses modern day, non-dialectic Arabic:

> "May God preserve your life, I swear by God, your presence here is blessed and fills our hearts with the outmost joy. Our lord, exalted is He, says: "unless they repent, make amends, and declare the truth. I will certainly accept their repentance: I am the Ever Relenting, the Most Merciful.""[141]

> "We do not wish of you to come to this place to repent in fear of us. There is no good in this, we want of you to return to yourself, repent fearing God. Return, repent and return to your lord, fearing God, exalted and mighty is he. Do not fear the swords of the *Mujahidin*, for we are your brothers and your sons."

The crowd of men repent following the guidance of the IS preacher, collectively issuing the *tawba* by his lead:

> "I dissociate myself before God[142] before God from the deeds of the disbelievers of which I took part in. And I bear witness there is no God but God and Muhammad is the messenger of God."

---

140 Speech by Abu Muhammad al-'Adnani, "the official spokesman for the Islamic State in Iraq and Syria": wa-layumakinanna lahum dinahumu l-ladha artada, released by al-Furqan Media.
141 This summarizes the above cited IS video ta'ibun a'ibun: those who repent (ta'ibun) and in doing so declare their repentance by speaking the truth, detailing their actions and allegiance before IS and in some cases issue their repentance after being arrested by IS, in others claiming voluntary repentance.
142 The collective repentance is enforced by personally vowing: "I dissociate myself" and thus, following the return to the concept of *ahl al-sunna wa-l jama'a*, giving the individuals no way out but to subject themselves as loyal worshippers under the command of IS. This is an instrument in practice on the foundation of the concept of *al-wala' wa-l bara'*, as outlined in the report. "Loyalty and dissociation" which often is used in the framing of *muwalat*, "loyalty" for God and Muslims and dissociation or renunciation to the disbelievers in general. The concept of *al-wala'* equates "loyalty" with love for a group of Muslims who are perceived as proper believers in their rites, conduct of life and actions for God. The ultimate distance, or dissociation, *al-bara'* to those defined as disbelievers, including nominal Muslims who are considered as not sincere in their faith. Madawi Al Rasheed, in citing Saudi head cleric bin Baz in his *Majmu'a fatawa* (vol. V, 149), outlining the concept of *al-wala' wa-l bara'* as: "Hatred and enmity mean to hate them in your heart, never to take them as friends. Muslims should not hurt them. If they greet you, you should return the greeting. You should also preach to them and guide them to the Good. Jews and Christians are people of

According to the IS preacher this concludes the repentance:

> "I ask God to protect you, God willing, and that he may accept your repentance which is God willing a sincere one, your repentance is only before God.
> However, *ya shabab*[143], recently a group repented and afterwards joined the new *sahwa*. And by God, there is no other but him, we have their names.[144] They have been apostates, they came to us declaring their repentance here to only recommit apostasy and sign up for the new *sahwa*. Now there is not another chance to repent. I swear by God, there is not another chance to repent. Anyone we get a hold of, by the permission of God, exalted and mighty he is, we will bring before the elders and folks of his tribe and we will carry out the punishment (*hadd*) in public. Anyone who choses this path will meet the same fate."

The sequence ends, and the viewer is taken into the heat of battle, described in a caption as, "wiping out a convoy of the *Safavid* army after assaulting their base." The shift from a scene of repentance to footage of a battle suggests the consolidation of the 'liberated' Sunni hinterland, as well as the inclusion of those who repented into the fighting ranks – with the immediate military assault on the "*Safavids*", "Shiites", and any non-Sunni in Iraq.

"My brother, if I die, join me, for a life of humiliation is no life at all"

The combat sequence from an immersive first-person perspective is enriched by a *nashid*. The first thing the viewers see is an abandoned Humvee and a Toyota jeep with visible bullet holes all over the windshield suggesting the driver was killed leaving the vehicle otherwise operational. Through the constant gun fire a Mujahid, perhaps the camera man, shouts, "*allahu akbar*, the apostates abandoned the vehicles and fled!" Concluded by perhaps the same man saying "oh god, take our blood until you are satisfied my lord." A *nashid* starts to play, while several Humvees taking fire by heavy machineguns speed off. During one sequence, enriched by the *nashid* chanting "the smoke of my bomb is like the smell

---

the book. They should be given *aman* [peace], unless they do injustice, then they should be punished. One can also give them charity."

143 The term *shabab*, "youth", needs to be understood within Arab-Islamic social framework. It has a positive connotation whereas the "youth" is often addressed as the new generation tasked to bring pride and honour to their predecessors and families, respecting Islamic values and customs. The literature of jihad often refers to the *shabab* and also uses the specific *shabab al-Islam* reference that was made popular by Osama bin Laden and others in their call to arms and to get active for the Islamic community (*umma*). The "Islamic State" in the Arab Sunni heartlands in Syria and Iraq implements bin Laden's rhetorical expectation.

144 As demonstrated in this video, IS works effectively with military graded intelligence to hunt dissenters and 'high valuable targets' to root out resistance and create facts on the ground such as Sunni-only neighbourhoods, etc.

of musk[145] while the scent from my grenades is like ambergris", a Mujahid throws a Molotov cocktail on a disabled Humvee from a close distance. This *nashid*, bearing different titles such "Akhi Abligh" or "brother inform my companions" is found on YouTube. On one channel this *nashid* has been listened to over 46,000 times. Published by the user "ruhalamin" the *nashid* is visually enhanced by a picture from the computer game "Tom Clancy's Division"[146] and has 226 "likes" and 40 comments as of this writing.[147] The comments are mainly in English and Arabic and cover a rich blend of approving IS, calling for the final meeting at Dabiq, or simply asking what game the picture is taken from. Comments from a neo-Nazi spectrum are also present calling for a nuclear response in general.

---

145 See also Eli Alsheech who states that the texts of Hamas "commonly state that the martyrs' corpses, gravesites, and personal belonging emit the scent of musk, a fragrance that the Qur'ān associates with Paradise and that the Islamic tradition (hadith) considers a proof that a martyr was accepted by God." Egoistic Martyrdom and Hamas' Success in the 2005 Municipal Elections: A Study of Hamas Martyrs' Ethical Wills, Biographies and Eulogies, in *Die Welt des Islams* 48 (2008), pp. 35–36. In reference the hadith was related: "No-one is wounded in the Path of God, and God knows best who is wounded in His Path, except that he will come on the Day of Resurrection with his wounds spurting blood. Its colour will be like the color of blood and its smell will be that of musk" (al-Bukhari, Book 7, No. 441). 'Azzam narrates this very same story in a *khutba* ("The Sword is the Solution") in Afghanistan. In this sermon 'Azzam provides more details on the death of al-Kurdi, who "asked to attain the shahada as well that his brothers may seal their life with it." 'Azzam then relates that the "pleasant smell of musk was spread, when he left" this world. Usood 2, published by the Ansar al-Mujahidin in 2007 who include besides *khutbas* by 'Azzam contemporary training sequences and speeches by Osama bin Laden, Abu Yahya al-Libi and Abu 'l-Layth al-Libi (who was killed in a drone strike in early 2009). 'Abdallah 'Azzam, *al-Jihad bayna Kabul wa-Bayt al-Maqdis*, video, Seattle, USA., 1988. Another example is the opening of the grave of Osama al-Shurbshi, a Palestinian shahid. His grave was opened to place his deceased father (d. 2007) next to his son, who died for the cause of al-Fatah (1982). As his corpse is uncovered, the smell of musk is predominant, such an unnatural state is claimed being *karamat al-shuhada*': http://www.youtube.com/watch?v=69Vgx4vIKuY (22.10.2010). The video has more than 600,000 hits For more information: http://moneer1976.maktoobblog.com/578717/م-الشوربجي-أسامه-الشهيد-جثث-حقيقية-قصة/ (next to musk, "something like smoke exited the grave and a strong (perfume like) scent was smelled. One of the brothers passed out due to this strong and beautiful aroma." In this example (1.7 million hits) a karama is accredited to a Palestinian boy before he died. Lying in a coma in a hospital bed, only his left index finger is moving (and interpreted as confessing the shahada); http://www.youtube.com/watch?v=z9ZrPn3rDe8. Pictures of the shuhada' appear regularly in various jihadist videos and in some cases *karamat*, such as the sprawled right index finger of deceased (confessing the unity of God (*tawhid*)) or – what is interpreted as – a smile on the face of the dead are to 'proof' that the shahid has confessed to the last and now has gained entry to Paradise.
146 Announced for release by Ubisoft in 2016, https://tomclancy-thedivision.ubi.com/game/en-us/home/ (accessed May 05,2018).
147 https://www.youtube.com/watch?v=Yg604vLbaWg (January 11, 2016) (accessed May 05, 2018).

Towards the end of the *nashid* in the *Salil al-sawarim 4* video most of the vehicles are at blaze in the dark of night.

> "My brother, tell my companions here I am moving forward /
> I will leave the glitter of the worldly life and won't say where I'm going /
> To the most benevolent and the most merciful[148] in ease once I am buried /
> I am blowing up the enemy's barracks[149]; how perfidious and what deceiving traitors they are /
> Don't you see what I see in the fruits of the palm trees[150] in the gardens /
> Do you hear the sounds of the enemies artillery beating the drums of the wedding ceremony[151] /
> The smoke of my bomb is like the smell of musk while the scent from my grenades is like ambergris /
> My brother, if I die, join me, for a life of humiliation is no life at all."

From Battle to Historical Scholar Ibn Kathir – the Rationale for the Fight

As often is the case in IS videos showcasing firefights and attacks, the audience is taken to a calm setting after the fighting has ended, with IS fighters sweeping the 'liberated' areas. A killed Iraqi soldier, illuminated by flashlights, introduces this sequence. The video freezes and a body of text appears on the screen:

> "Ibn Kathir, may God have mercy with him, said in regards of the *rafida* insulting the companions of the prophet – peace and blessing upon him: "and whoever thinks about the companions – may God be pleased with them – [in an offensive manner] has indeed insulted them all by claiming they are immoral and opposed the prophet; opposing him in his rule and in his opinions. Whoever takes this posture (...) is a disbeliever according to the consensus of the noble Imams. Shedding his blood is most *halal*.""

The following sequence shows several IS fighters entering a house in search of a high-ranking officer of the counter-terrorism unit. As usual throughout the film, the fighters are wearing Iraqi army uniforms. The victim believes he is dealing with a government unit and cooperates in hope of ending this "misunderstanding". Unlike the other victims, he seems to be alone at home and fights back in despair when he realizes his mistake.

---

148 Al-Rahman, referring to God.
149 *thakna:* residence, compound.
150 This is a reference to the palm trees in the gardens of paradise, as described in several verses of the Qur'an, i.e. 23:17–21.
151 For the Sunni martyr in the afterlife, where among his rewards he will be married to the Hur al-Ayn, the paradise maidens, as outlined in an early "Islamic State in Iraq" document: 'Abd al-'Aziz bin Muhammad (Abu Osama al-Iraqi), *Mushawiq al-arwah ila nisa' bilad al-afrah*, Global Islamic Media Front, Dhu l-Hujja 1427 (2007).

A Milestone for "Islamic State" Propaganda: "The Clanging of the Swords, part 4"   139

Selective reading of Ibn Kathir to foster hatred against Shiites (left); handing out of IS pamphlets explaining "the creed and methodology of the Islamic State" (right) in the streets of Fallujah.

Raiding the homes of counter-terrorism units

The IS fighters enter the man's house at night who later identifies himself as Makki Mahmud 'Abid. He is sitting on the floor and is interrogated:

> Mujahid: "Are you a [regular] soldier?"
> 'Abid: "No. I am an officer."
> Muhajid: "Where do you work?"
> 'Abid: "For the police, special counter-terrorism unit in the city of Samara', Salah al-Din [province]."

The picture freezes and splits in two parts a *modus operandi* used throughout the movie. He is seen wearing his Iraqi Special Forces uniform on the right hand and shackled sitting on the floor on the left hand. The interrogation continues:

> 'Abid: "I work as the director of the counter-terrorism unit in Salah al-Din and am commissioned for the branch in Samarra'."

'Abid is blindfolded and led into his bedroom where the IS-fighters begun searching the room. Several of his Special Forces uniforms on the bed and one *mujahid* pulls out a knife saying "we do not forget and we do not stay idle in the light of your injustice." However, the attempt to behead 'Abid fails and the camera stops when at least two *mujahidin* are trying to wrestle him to the ground. 'Abid is blindfolded and shackled. The next scene shows the severed head resting on his back as often in jihadi videos with executions scenes. The scene is narrated again by IS-spokesman Abu Muhammad al-'Adnani:

> "I swear by God, our minds won't be at ease, we won't rest, life will not be pleasant for us, as long as there remains a single Muslim in the prisons of the disbelievers. We pledge to God and pledge to you we will do everything we can to free you; we will give all our possessions and our lives to this cause. We won't spare any efforts to cut off the heads of those butchering you; the investigators and judges [of the regime of al-Maliki]."

The Islamic State will Remain

The video ends with a lengthy sequence showing a series of IED attacks on various Iraqi army and governmental vehicles. In some cases, the explosion is so massive that the vehicles are shredded to pieces.

Distribution on Twitter – the Jihadist Dissemination Highway

In the first twenty-four hours after publication on *YouTube*, the video was viewed 56,998 times on the *Mu'assassat al-I'tasimu YouTube* channel. The average user watched a little over 17 minutes of the hour-long film. Collectively, *YouTube* users spent the equivalent of 686 days watching this one video. In other words, for each hour that passed, users spent 28 days watching the video.

YouTube removed the most prominent video files, as they were deemed "to be in violation of *YouTube*'s policy on shocking and disgusting content". However, duplicates of the video file have been posted on *YouTube* and are also available via *archive.org* and *justpaste.it*.

On March 19, 2014 (left) the video had been watched over 117,000 times; on March 19 (right) close to 150,000 times.

Awareness of the video release spread on Twitter with two distinct peaks in tweeting. These occurred on the day of release (17 May) and the following day (18 May).

Between 17 May and 8am on 19 May 2015, we observed a total of 32,313 tweets carrying the name of the video. There were an average of 807.825 tweets per hour, the median being 736.5. Tweets contained a range of #tags in addition to the title of the video, the most common of which are shown below.

The #tags used most frequently were Arabic references to *Salil_al-sawarim_ four*, followed by *The_Islamic_State_in_Iraq_and al-Sham*, and the al-Furqan Media department.

Although all the prominent tags were in Arabic, Twitter's automatic coding did not classify all tweets as being in Arabic. This demonstrates the reach of the

A Milestone for "Islamic State" Propaganda: "The Clanging of the Swords, part 4"

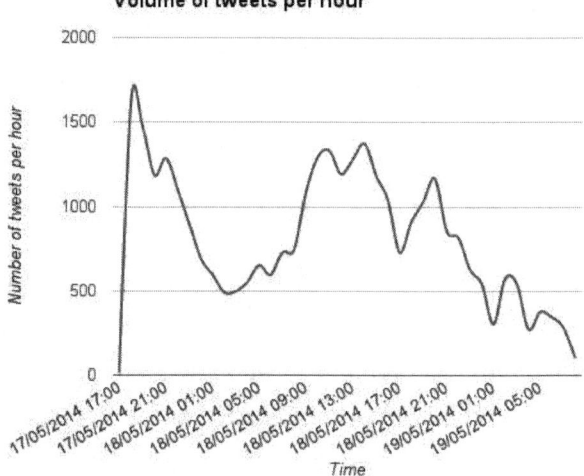

Volume of tweets containing the title of the video صليل الصوارم between 17th and 19th May

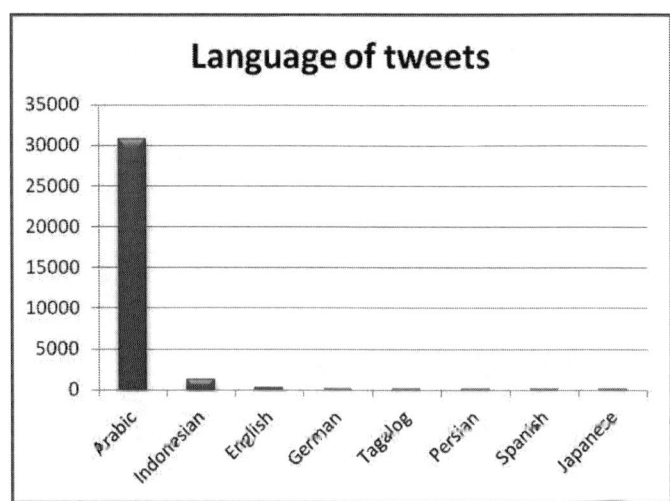

video and shows that some multilingual users were proactively translating content and helping users access the information in a range of languages.

Analysis of user locations also suggests users who can bridge between languages or physical communities are important. The map and graph below reflect the time zones users selected when setting up their profiles.

Although they lack the pinpoint accuracy of geocoding, time zones provide a useful indication of the region where users are likely to be – and users are far more likely to choose a time zone than enable geocoding. However, it does also

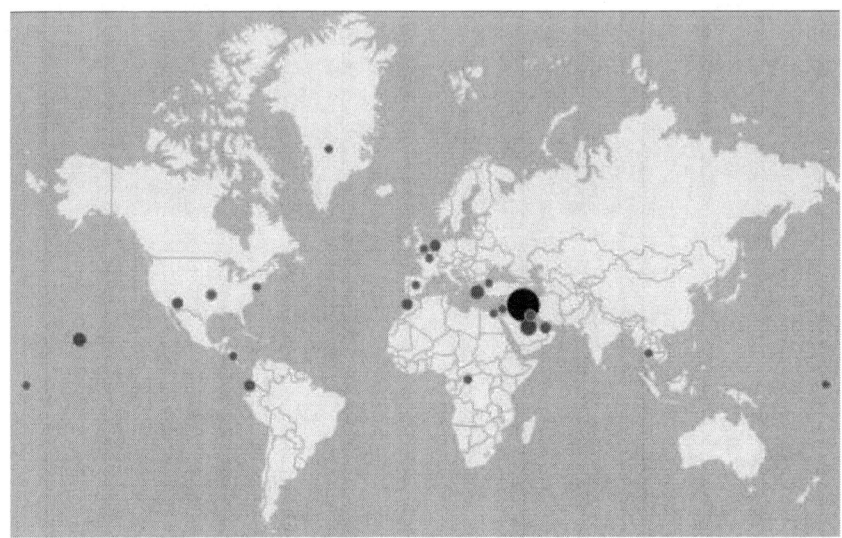

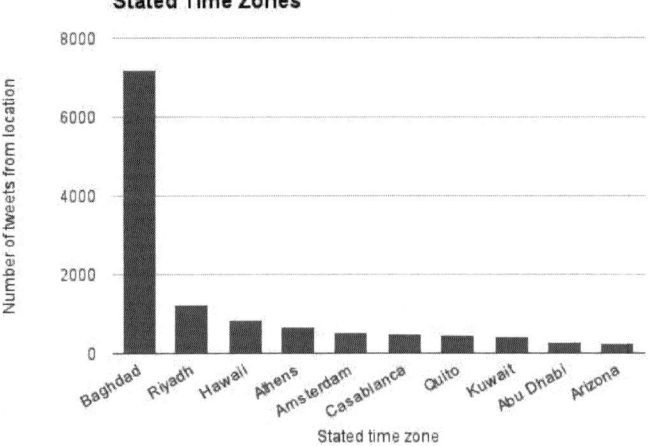

mean groups of users are erroneously shown in Greenland and the middle of the ocean given the time zone they selected – such as the International Date Line.

These limitations aside, analysis of the large sample size helped improve the probable accuracy of most time zones selected, and demonstrates that they provide a useful indication of users' likely location.

Users used a range of different devices to tweet, but mobile technologies, and particularly phones, were dominant. The most common ways users tweeted about the video was an app on an Android mobile phone, (*Twitter for Android*) followed by an iPhone app, (*Twitter for iPhone*). These were followed by the classical web interface – logging into *Twitter* via a browser on either a desktop or laptop computer ("the web"). Tablets, including the iPad and Android-operated devices, were also used, but to a lesser extent.

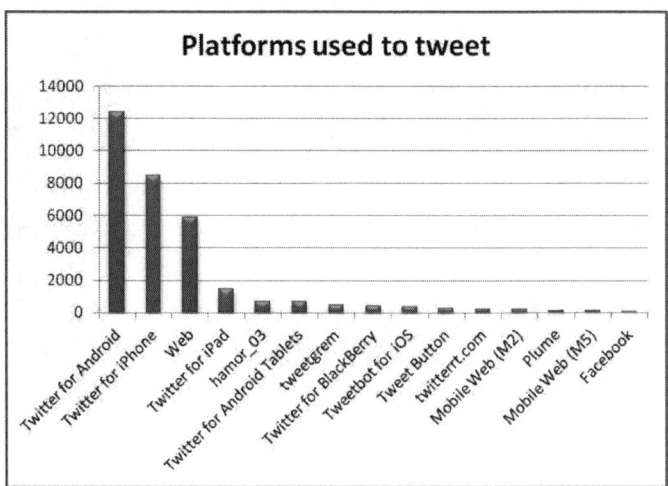

As the graph above shows, awareness of the video on *YouTube* and archive.org was spread using a range of digital technologies. This last case emphasises the importance of understanding the jihadist social media phenomenon as a cross-platform trend, as users were using *Facebook* to promote tweets about a video posted on *YouTube*.[152]

The video was also highlighted by sympathizers on tumblr, with one user posting a picture of the title of the video on a big flat screen while holding a Dutch-labelled popcorn bag in front of the camera. The act was intended to confirm the validity of the user's claim to be "just one of your beloved brothers from The Netherlands."[153]

The use of multiple means of distribution is highlighted by the range of links embedded in tweets about 4 صليل الصوارم (*Salil al-sawarim 4*). The top 50 links are included in an appendix.

Tweets often display an abbreviated version of the link or a t.co link, but the metadata of each tweet also contains the 'expanded URL' – the original URL entered by the user. While *YouTube* is the most frequently referenced platform,

---

152 Nico Prucha/Ali Fisher, Tweeting for the Caliphate: Twitter as the New Frontier for Jihadist Propaganda, in *CTC Sentinel*, June 25, 2013: (http://bit.ly/17Aqej9) (accessed May 05, 2018).
153 The Clanging of the Swords, part 4 was made available with Dutch subtitles on YouTube, as well (link defunct).

"Just one of your beloved brothers from The Netherlands"- SAS4 on a big flat screen with Dutch popcorn.

the appearance of *justpaste.it* and *archive.org* near the top of the list emphasizes the cross platform nature of the distribution.

In addition to *Twitter*, other services are used to construct the cross-platform *zeitgeist*. For example, the most linked-to *justpaste.it* page contains links to jihadist material on *archive.org*, *gulfup.com*, *YouTube*, and even *Twitter* accounts to follow, such as @wa3tasimu.

The use of a cross-platform zeitgeist enables users to locate the video content even when some *Twitter* accounts are suspended and the original video files posted to *YouTube* have been removed.

Jihadist groups frequently advocate that supporters share their media content with others. As a result, viewers who use all available means to spread videos like SAS4 can feel like active participants and consider themselves media-*Mujahidin*.

When SAS4 was released, it immediately engaged a wide group of users. However, accounts charged with countering jihadist social media content stayed surprisingly quiet. For example, the Twitter account run by the U.S. State Department intended to engage jihadist accounts in Arabic (@dsdotar) was silent on Saturday, 17 May and Sunday, 18 May, 2015.

As the Twitter stream shows, *@dsdotar* did not produce a single tweet between 16 and 19 May. By the time *@dsdotar* burst into action again on Monday, 19 May, SAS4 had been viewed over 100,000 times. The following section assesses the roles played by key Twitter users in propagating a range of links to this video on 17 and 18 May.

بسم الله الرحمن الرحيم
مؤسسة الفرقان للإنتاج الإعلامي
تقدم
(صليل الصوارم 4)

لتحميل الملف كاملا:
https://archive.org/download/al_saleel_4/SaleelSawarim.mp4
https://archive.org/download/as_sawarim_4/SaleelSawarim.mp4
http://www.gulfup.com/?Cl0r1d

صفحات الأرشيف:
https://archive.org/details/al_saleel_4

Important Users on the SAS 4 Twitter Network

The information shared concerning the video release of SAS4 created a network of 6,428 Twitter users and 19,601 edges, with some users mentioned frequently. The graph below shows the frequency with which prominent users were mentioned.

To extend the analysis of prominent members of the network, we created a representation of the network sharing the video via Twitter. It contains 6,428 Twitter users and 19,601 edges. The network had an average path length of 5.7 and a diameter of 15.

From the visual representation it is evident that a number of different users

A Milestone for "Islamic State" Propaganda: "The Clanging of the Swords, part 4"   147

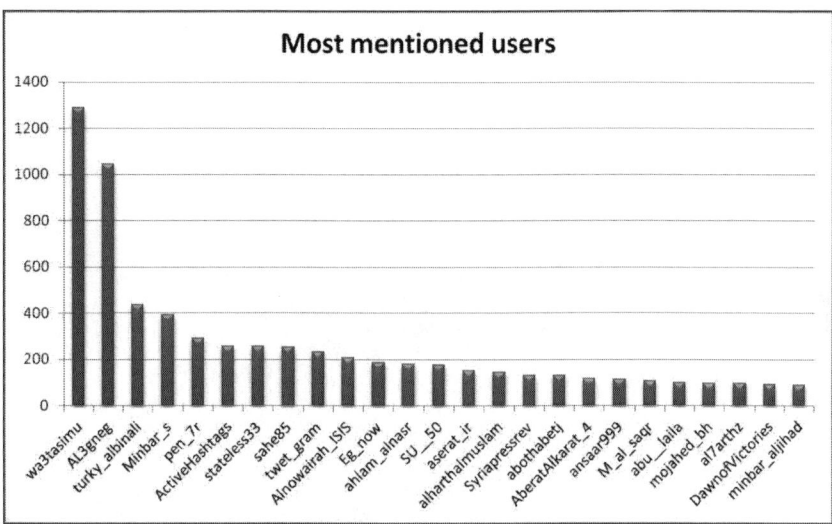

were prominent in different sections of the network. Rather than the majority of the network orbiting one of a few influential accounts, in a series of hub and spoke structures, this network has multiple interconnected hubs through which information flows in multiple directions.

This provides the network a degree of resilience that allows information to continue flowing in the event of Twitter account suspensions. The interconnected hubs provide a level of redundancy so that there are a number of other pathways through which information can flow. As Paul Baran's calculations showed, distributed communications systems need a relatively low level of redundancy for the majority of the network to maintain communication in the event of major network disruption.[154]

Viewing the network map in greater detail can show which users communicated with each other, which reached the same communities, and which were a bridge to specific communities. For example, in the network representation, nodes of the same colour are within the same interconnected community. This means they are more likely to interact with other members of that community than the rest of the network. These can be assessed in greater detail in a more detailed version of the network map where connections between specific nodes can be examined.

Through a refinement of the network image, a core group of users becomes visible. The image below shows only those users who have at least one mutual

---

[154] Paul Baran, *On Distributed Communications: I. Introduction to Distributed Communications Networks*, RAND August 1964 (http://www.rand.org/pubs/research_memoranda/RM 3420.html) (accessed May 05, 2018).

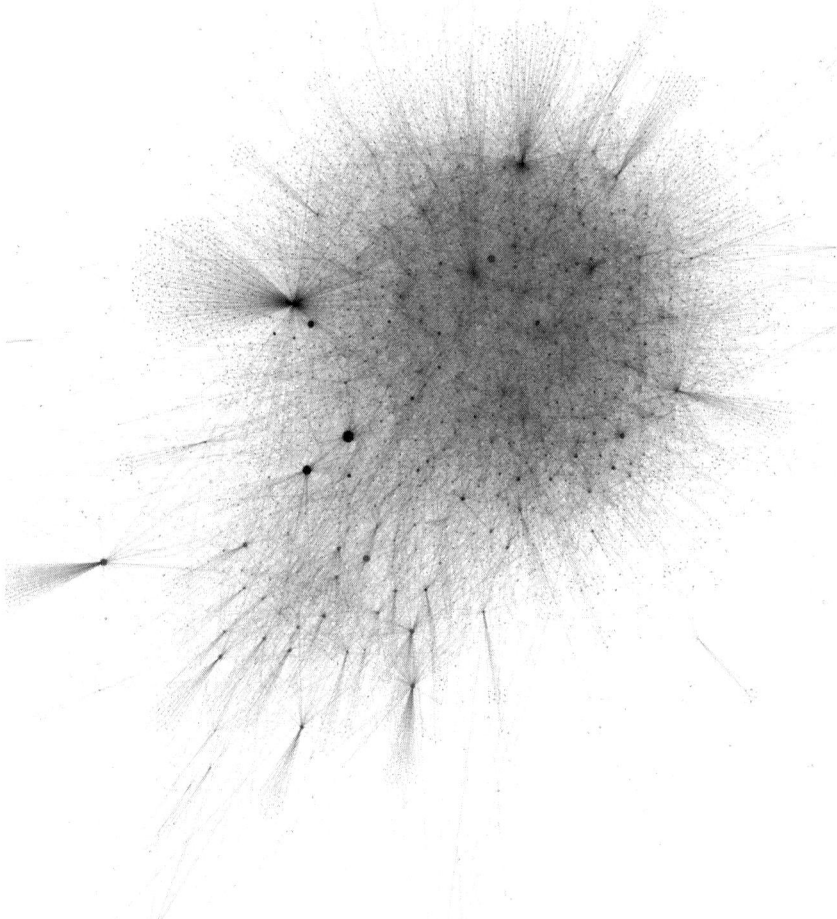

connection – meaning they have mentioned someone who has also mentioned them.

This network of mutual connections contains 165 Twitter accounts (2.5 % of the total network), including all of the top twenty-five most mentioned users. On average, a node in this core group has slightly more than five connections to other accounts in this group. This means the network has a density of 0.031–3 % of all possible connections exist. This is sufficient to provide the network with a level of resilience.

Resilience in this context is shown by the way a network limits the impact of losing important nodes, in this case in the form of account suspensions. For example, with the loss of the five most connected nodes (ranked by times men-

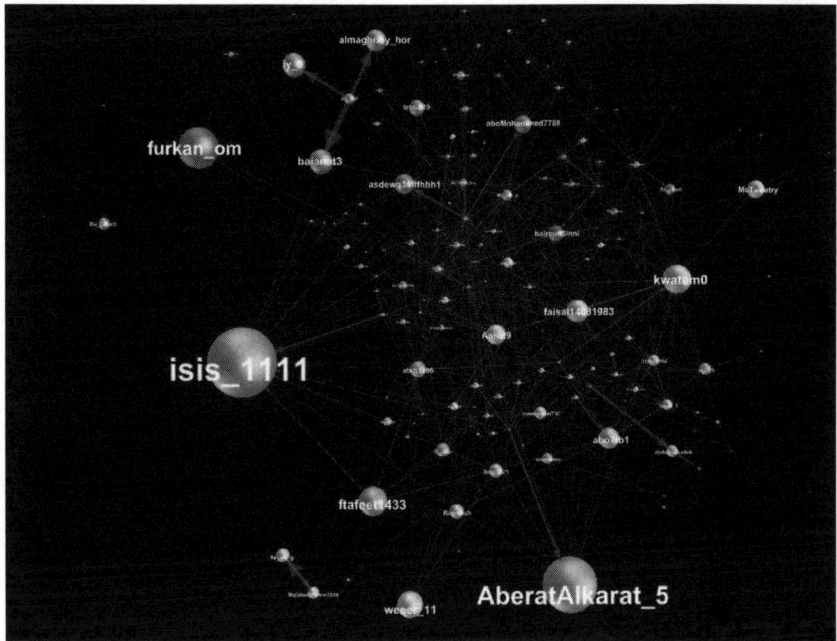

tioned by others) every remaining node would still be connected to this network, with only a slight reduction in graph density to 0.027.

Similarly, the removal of the five most important nodes (ranked by Pagerank) leaves the graph density unchanged at 0.031 and again, every remaining node would still be connected to the network. This means that the current occasional account suspensions on Twitter are unlikely to have any practical impact on the ability of users to share information and propagate content.

As of 2018, with the migration to Telegram since early 2016, the effects of account-suspension on Twitter have become even more of a whack-a-mole game. IS organizes "media raids" on Telegram, in channels and groups that are access-only by invitation and end-to-end encrypted to then inspire supporters to ensure their media is placed on the internet where a wider audience is reached – including targeting those, who are Arabic illiterates.

The identification of key actors in the network can provide greater insight into the way information travelled. For example, this analysis can differentiate between those users that are important for reaching specific communities, and those users that are part of the core of the network. This type of analysis is important, as not all users are influential in the same way. For example, some users will be influential within the core of the network, while others are important as they form a bridge to wider communities.

Position on the scatter plot below is based on two network metrics: 'pagerank' and 'betweenness'. The size of the nodes reflects the number of times the account was retweeted or mentioned. Nodes with the same colour are in the same statistical community.

- Users in the bottom left of the graph tend to have no particular role and can be thought of as general users, although they may have high value to an often small and very specific group.
- Those in the top left of the graph tend to be in the core (or one of the cores) of the network. This indicates they are often those most invested in the network and have access to privileged information.
- Those in the bottom right of the graph fulfil the role of bridging between the core content producers and a specific community. The value of this role often comes from tailoring information to a specific 'audience' and as such these users are more valuable to that group but less important to everyone else.
- Users in the top right are rare. They have a dual function, as they have the same trusted status as those in the top left of the graph. They also fulfil the same 'bridge' role as users in the bottom right of the graph, reaching areas of the network which others do not.

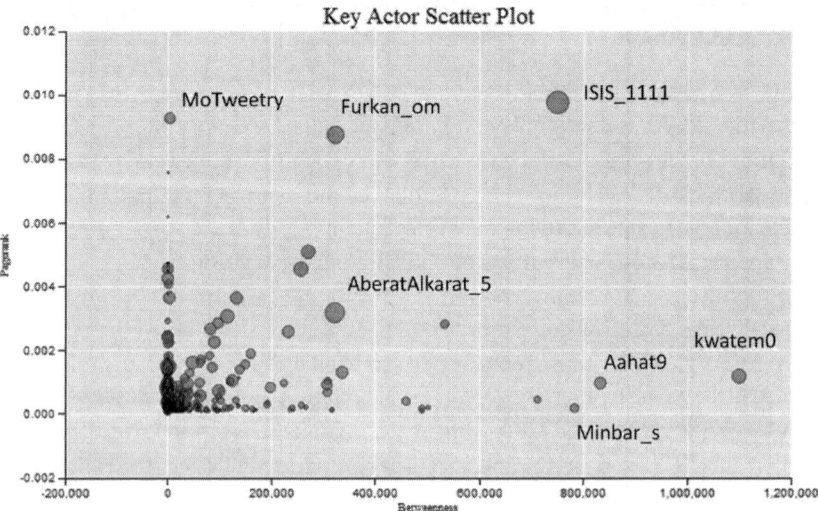

In the case of the network disseminating information about the release of SAS4, the 'pagerank' scores are particularly low, which backs the earlier visual observation that the network is dispersed and has multiple interconnected hubs. The graph shows that @Minbar_s, @Aahat9, and @kwatem0 were important conduits for the spread of information to communities that other accounts could not reach. Conversely, @furkan_om and @MoTweetry were most important nodes in the networks to share the video. Most importantly, @ISIS_1111 was the single node that was able to fulfil both core and bridging functions simultaneously, with other accounts such as @AberatAlkarat_5 fulfilling a similar role to a lesser degree.

In addition to the roles users played in the network, the time at which they were influential is also an important aspect of the analysis. This is known as their engagement profile, the extent to which other Twitter users engaged with them over a given time period.

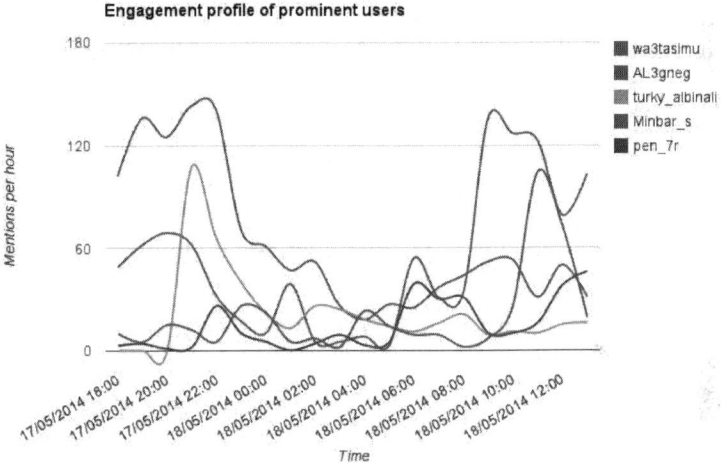

The engagement profiles of the top five most mentioned users in the network shows two periods of particularly intense activity. It also shows that different accounts were prominent at different times. For example, *@wa3tasimu* and *@turky_albinali* were prominent in the first peak but not the second, while *@AL3gneg* and *@Minbar_S* were prominent during the second peak.

This analysis demonstrates the need for agile counter-strategies, as accounts become important at different times during the dissemination of content. In addition, it provides additional context to the key actor graph; for example, illustrating that *@Minbar_s* was an important conduit for information to a particular community.

Summary of Findings

- Jihadist groups have become increasingly sophisticated in their use of social media and mobile technologies.
- The "Islamic State", in particular, has not only mastered the use of the Internet and social media, but also produces and publishes a large amount of coherent

visual content in Full HD video. This is quite evident in SAS4, which set the standard for subsequent IS videos, showing a coherent application of theology (=ideology) on conquered territory.
- SAS4 popularised foreign fighters Lavdrim Muxaheri (Kosovo) and Salmān Turkī (Bahrain), who gained their own online fan cultures within wider IS fandom. Salmān Turkī is idolized as a martyr and 'kept alive' by fan-created content, whereas Lavdrim Muxaheri has been featured in other IS videos.
- IS pitches SAS4 as one of the first videos to show the 'Reconquista' of Iraq by IS soldiers following the 2011 withdrawal of U.S. combat troops. Furthermore, it is also one of the first videos to show a high degree of applied theology on retaken/conquered areas in Iraq.
- The concept of "repentance" (*tawba*) features prominently among the applied theology, and IS "weaponises" it to replenish its ranks and consolidate Sunni tribal areas, as well as cities in Iraq. A strong point of the SAS4 video shows the "Muslim identity", as preached by AQ and now IS, put into practice as a uniting identity marker to fight for the establishment of an "Islamic State" and subsequently as "the caliphate".
- Arabic was the language most associated with the initial release of SAS4, and the majority of users stated a location in the Middle East, more specifically Baghdad. However, European and North American locations were not uncommon.
- The release of SAS4 was announced through a resilient and dispersed network on Twitter, backed and interlinked to jihadist online forums, blogs, and a rich blend of file-hosting sites such as archive.org. This network had sufficient interconnection and redundancy to continue to operate indefinitely in spite of the current level of account suspensions or blog, forum, file-hosting link shut downs.
- On each platform, especially on social media platforms, there are clusters of mutually reinforcing accounts, which create a level of resilience that allows jihadists to have a persistent presence on the platform. The release of SAS4 highlights the multiplatform zeitgeist, which has become a feature of the jihadist social media phenomenon. Accounts on one social media platform are used to reinforce the content on other social media platforms, creating mutually reinforcing connections across platforms. This means users could turn to *Facebook* or *Google+* if a specific Twitter account is suspended to locate the replacement Twitter account – or use the Arabic hashtags to find new accounts on Twitter instantly.
- Most jihadists that take the propagation element (*da'wa*) of their activity seriously have back-up accounts already set up and users following their primary account are directed to also follow the back-up, in case of an account suspension. This gives the networks further resilience and makes it easier for

users to stay up to date with 'trusted' accounts that are verified by other IS accounts not effected by account suspensions.
- The Twitter account run by the US State Department engaging jihadist accounts in Arabic (*@dsdotar*) was silent on the day SAS4 was released, Saturday, 17 May, as well as Sunday, 18 May. By the time *@dsdotar* burst into action again on Monday, 19 May, the video had been viewed over 150,000 times, with users collectively spending the equivalent of over 680 days watching this one video.

Recommendations for Analysis

The online dissemination of video content such as الصوارم صليل 4 (SAS4) is rapid. This is a network-based phenomenon, which requires an appreciation of the relational aspects of digital technologies and social media. The complex nature of these networks provides jihadist groups with a degree of resilience, meaning the network is largely unaffected by current approaches and account suspensions.

Approaches to analysis could be more effective if focused on identifying groups of users rather than individual accounts. Those charged with running programs to challenge jihadist groups have the opportunity to increase their impact by focusing on network disruption in addition to the current attempts to counter specific content and individual accounts. In addition, there is a need for agile counter-strategies, as accounts become important at different times during the dissemination of content.

Jihadists do not restrict themselves to office hours. The release of the video on a Saturday may have been a tactical decision, seeing as those employed to challenge or disrupt the propagation of jihadist media are less likely to be active over the weekend. This was ultimately illustrated by the two-day break in activity from *@dsdotar*.

Appendix 1: Top time zones

Location	Frequency
Baghdad	7196
Riyadh	1213
Hawaii	827
Athens	660
Amsterdam	533
Casablanca	501
Quito	446
Kuwait	412
Abu Dhabi	293
Arizona	253
Pacific Time (US, Canada	215
London	168
Cairo	100
Jerusalem	46
Greenland	41
Bangkok	39
International Date Line West	36
Istanbul	34
West Central Africa	34
Eastern Time (US, Canada	29
Paris	28
Madrid	28
Central America	27
Mid-Atlantic	23
Vilnius	22
Kyiv	20
Hong Kong	20
Mumbai	18
Kabul	16
Atlantic Time (Canada	16
Stockholm	16
Central Time (US, Canada	16
Beijing	14
Dublin	14
Ljubljana	13
Nairobi	13

A Milestone for "Islamic State" Propaganda: "The Clanging of the Swords, part 4"

(Continued)

Location	Frequency
Helsinki	12
Mexico City	12
Rome	11
Tokyo	9
Mountain Time (US, Canada)	8
Kuala Lumpur	8
Adelaide	8
Sarajevo	8
Moscow	7
Berlin	7
Islamabad	7
Dhaka	7

Appendix 2: Top 50 links

URL	Frequency
https://www.youtube.com/watch?v=rwop8h6htQQ	1451
http://youtu.be/95r4gugiubw	1451
http://justpaste.it/Saleel_As_Sawarim4	625
https://archive.org/download/al_saleel_4/SaleelSawarim.mp4	455
http://www.youtube.com/watch?v=MKaaTM9WSG0	407
http://www.youtube.com/watch?v=DsHRTNG-vcs	406
http://www.youtube.com/watch?v=4vJcsjuE62E	404
https://www.youtube.com/watch?v=95r4gugiubw&feature=youtu.be	340
http://www.youtube.com/watch?v=95r4gugiubw&feature=youtube_gdata_player	327
http://youtu.be/FHhlq1oOeo8	235
https://www.youtube.com/watch?v=95r4gugiubw	221
https://www.youtube.com/watch?v=95r4gugiubw&feature=youtube_gdata_player	195
https://www.youtube.com/watch?v=rwop8h6htQQ&feature=youtube_gdata_player	146
http://youtu.be/rwop8h6htQQ	133
http://justpaste.it/swarim4	111
http://www.youtube.com/watch?v=95r4gugiubw&feature=youtu.be	103
http://m.youtube.com/watch?feature=youtu.be&v=95r4gugiubw	90

(Continued)

URL	Frequency
http://youtube.com/watch?v=rwop8h	74
http://roayaeyecenter.com	71
http://justpaste.it/ekgt	58
http://www.gulfup.com/?yFDqse	55
https://www.youtube.com/watch?v=XCmT7FrNoAA	50
https://www.youtube.com/watch?v=rFI7lLnoUyY	47
http://Layans.com	45
http://youtu.be/qDcwIGItiyk	44
https://www.youtube.com/watch?feature=player_detailpage&v=rwop8h6htQQ#t=2622	44
http://youtu.be/Sbr2NXSNalE	40
http://youtu.be/ujU5YHu3PlM	39
http://justpaste.it/fi2z	34
http://justpaste.it/fiby	33
http://safeshare.tv/w/BYiAzmPafE	32
http://www.youtube.com/watch?v=rwop8h6htQQ&sns=tw	28
https://youtu.be/rwop8h6htQQ	27
http://justpaste.it/fi6e	26
http://www.youtube.com/watch?v=95r4gugiubw	24
http://justpaste.it/fib0	24
http://www.youtube.com/watch?v=SbkrrXrX_cY	23
https://www.youtube.com/watch?v=95r4gugiubw&feature=yo	21
http://a9d2.com/11857.html	21
https://archive.org/download/Swarim-4/Swarim4-3.3gp	21
http://justpaste.it/fi8h	21
https://www.youtube.com/watch?v=rwop8h6htQQ&feature=youtu.be	21
http://youtu.be/Sk_MDa92T9U	20
https://youtu.be/95r4gugiubw	17
https://m.youtube.com/watch?v=rwop8h6htQQ	17
http://www.youtube.com/watch?v=ujU5YHu3PlM&feature=youtu.be	16
https://www.youtube.com/watch?v=kwNFE9lvdmA&feature=youtube_gdata_player	15

Clemens Holzgruber

"Now You See Me – Now You Don't": Analysing Jihadists' Online Privacy-Enhancing and Counter-Surveillance Strategies

> They want to know what you send, when you send it, to whom you send it to, why, and how to use it against you. They monitor your social media. [...] The United States government, the government of the United Kingdom, France, and elsewhere, want to jail you. They want you to suffer. And they aren't playing games.[1]

Introduction and Content

New media and communication technologies and their role as powerful instruments of transnational terrorism have been subject to fierce academic and political debate in recent years, not least since the Islamic State's (IS)[2] apparently sudden rise in 2014. Sunni extremist groups such as Al-Qaeda and IS, in particular, have adapted quickly to our age of digital dependence and paranoia and make extensive use of various online platforms to broadcast their message and project their narrative.[3] Platforms most commonly used are online social networks (OSNs) such as Twitter and Facebook, video-hosting websites like YouTube, online content-sharing web services such as Justpaste.it and Archive.org, as well as private messaging services such as Telegram.[4] There are several reasons why migrating to the online sphere is considered a fruitful endeavor for terrorist

---

1 *Remaining Anonymous Online*, uploaded August 20, 2014, (https://justpaste.it/anonlyne) (accessed September 3, 2017).
2 There has been confusion on how to name the Islamic State, as the group has changed its name several times in the past years. In this chapter, I will refer to the group either as the Islamic State or IS, which is the most recent name adopted after the declaration of the caliphate on June 29, 2014. For a chronology of the different names of IS, see: Aaron Y. Zelin, The War between ISIS and al-Qaeda for Supremacy of the Global Jihadist Movement, *The Washington Institute for Near East Policy*, Research Note 20, June 2014, p. 1.
3 See for example: Gabriel Weimann, *Terrorism in Cyberspace. The Next Generation*, New York: Columbia University Press 2015, p. 23 ff.
4 Gabriel Weimann, Why do terrorists migrate to social media?, in Anne Aly/Stuart Macdonald/Lee Jarvis/Thomas Chen (Eds.), *Violent Extremism Online. New perspectives on terrorism and the Internet*, London: Routledge 2016, pp. 46 ff.

organizations; among other things, the simplicity of using the Internet and its global reach, the low cost of accessing new technologies, and the generally lacking ability of total government control. Hence, new media technologies and the rise of OSNs have broadened the publicity of jihadi groups, increased the speed of their information distribution, and widened the networks and audience reached.[5] While the majority of cyberterrorism researchers argue that terrorist movements are among the primary beneficiaries of the Internet,[6] there are some who claim that the actual effects of new communication technologies are more complex. In their view, the payoff for terrorist groups using these technologies may not be as big as suggested, as new weaknesses may balance the benefits arising from their online activities.[7]

One of the main threats jihadi movements face is that their enemies in general and adversary governments in particular are likewise exploiting new technological tools for counter-terrorism measures. Since OSNs are built upon visibility, enabling users to share personal information about their locations, ideas, affiliations, and networks, they can also be considered to function as social surveillance technologies.[8] Although the visibility on OSNs allows terrorist groups to exchange and share information on a broad scale, to reach new audiences, and to organize in a faster and more efficient manner, it is very likely that the information distributed online is also obtained by third – and often opposing – parties. Governments can benefit from the plethora of new data available on the Internet to gain intelligence about sensitive information, such as the location of terrorist leaders, military strategies, plans concerning new terrorist attacks, the group's internal workings, and so forth.[9] In using new communication technology, jihadists are thus confronted with an inevitable trade-off dilemma: on the one hand, they became heavily dependent on Internet-based media for communication and recruitment purposes, a field in which they have proliferated ever since. Maintaining a strong online presence has therefore become an essential aspect of the groups' organizational structure, capabilities, and long-term survival. On the other hand, governments have simultaneously increased their ability to acquire sensitive information about these movements.

---

5 Weimann, *Terrorism in Cyberspace*, pp. 25 ff.
6 See for example: Ibid., p. 25; Imran Awan, Cyber-Extremism: Isis and the Power of Social Media, in *Society* 54ii (April 2017), pp. 140 ff (accessed May 05, 2018). Martin Rudner, 'Electronic Jihad': The Internet as Al Qaeda's Catalyst for Global Terror, in *Studies in Conflict and Terrorism* 40i (March 2016), pp. 14 ff. (accessed May 05, 2018).
7 Manuel R. Torres Soriano, The Vulnerabilities of Online Terrorism, in *Studies in Conflict & Terrorism* 35iv (March 2012), p. 264 (accessed May 05, 2018).
8 Daniel Trottier, *Social Media as Surveillance. Rethinking Visibility in a Converging World*, Surrey: Ashgate 2012, p. 11.
9 Ken Menkhaus, Al-Shabaab and Social Media: A Double-Edged Sword, in *Brown Journal of World Affairs* 20ii (Spring 2014), pp. 322 f. (accessed May 05, 2018).

Online data leakage can have severe consequences for jihadists, thwart their plans, and endanger members and group leaders, who are often subject to incarceration and targeted killings, which in turn can threaten the movement as a whole.[10] From their perspective, finding practical solutions to this dilemma is vital for the future trajectory of jihadi movements and hence has been discussed intensively within jihadi circles.

Although some research institutes have addressed and reported on how jihadists try to counter government monitoring and to remain anonymous when operating online,[11] there is only limited and fragmentary academic research on their counter-surveillance strategies. Brantly (2017) highlights how widespread jihadi discussions about online operational security are, but only briefly examines the means and technology used for privacy-enhancing purposes. He only mentions central issues such as the discussions regarding virtual private networks (VPN) in passing and omits other important strategies such as encryption tools used, the subject of smartphone confidentiality, and cryptocurrencies. Moreover, the article focuses solely on safety and privacy aspects and does not address the steps to balance the trade-off dilemma discussed above.[12] This provides a useful starting point, but the issue requires deeper inquiry. Sinai (2015) describes the innovation and adoption curves of jihadi movements, focusing on several cases in which jihadists have successfully as well as unsuccessfully evaded government surveillance when committing and plotting terror attacks, rather than analyzing online counter-surveillance strategies in particular.[13] To my knowledge, apart from these two contributions, the academic literature only peripherally touches upon the issue of jihadi online operational security.

Academic studies of the methods through which jihadists try to solve their dual interest of maintaining a strong online presence and a broad audience reach while trying to remain anonymous online are largely absent. The purpose of this chapter is to fill parts of this research gap by synthesizing knowledge, providing an evaluation of the privacy-enhancing tools used and the discussion among

---

10 Ibid., p. 323.
11 There are several institutes that track and report on jihadi online activities. These include the Middle Eastern Media Research Institute (MEMRI), which runs the Cyber & Jihad Lab monitoring project specializing in tracking and translating jihadi online content, and the Flashpoint Institute, which provides business risk intelligence and has written several articles on technologies used by jihadi movements with a focus on Big Data Analysis of Arabic-language sources.
12 Aaron Brantly, Innovation and Adaptation in Jihadist Digital Security, in *Survival. Global Politics and Strategy* 59i (January 2017) (accessed May 05, 2018).
13 Joshua Sinai, Innovation in terrorists' counter-surveillance: The case of al-Qaeda and its affiliates, in Magnus Ranstorp/Magnus Normark (Eds.), *Understanding Terrorism Innovation and Learning: Al-Qaeda and beyond*, New York: Routledge 2015.

jihadists, focusing on the period until the end of 2017. This contribution will set the stage for further research on this matter. To provide the necessary context, this chapter first discusses the evolution and different phases of jihadi media activities and illustrates the importance of new communication platforms, as well as the general perception of new media technologies by Al-Qaeda and IS. Subsequently, an overview of the groups, organizations, and media outlets publishing on the issue of online operational security is given. Next, it highlights the steps taken to ensure the best ways for jihadists to mitigate monitoring by adversary governments and institutions. This section outlines how jihadi privacy-enhancing strategies have evolved, as well as the current state of internal jihadi discussions. Following this, the steps IS and Al-Qaeda have taken to solve the trade-off dilemma of maintaining a strong online presence while simultaneously avoiding government surveillance are demonstrated. Finally, the findings are summarized and conclusions about jihadi online operational security are drawn.

The chapter is based on a qualitative reading of primary and secondary sources. The section on the general media strategy by IS and Al-Qaeda is mostly a secondary analysis of existing literature. The main part of this contribution, dealing with jihadists' online operational security and the measures applied to solve the online trade-off dilemma, predominantly relies on primary sources found online and on the Darknet, as well as articles published by research institutes reporting on jihadi online activities. Although numerous jihadi manuals provide offline counter-surveillance advice, this chapter only concentrates on the suggestions and methods used to hide their traffic online. As an analysis of the activities of all groups that can be labeled as jihadi would go beyond the scope of this contribution, the focus is on IS and Al-Qaeda, as well as some affiliated groups and organizations.[14] There are several reasons for this selection. IS and Al-Qaeda have attracted the greatest interest from academics and journalists worldwide and have been vanguard groups when it comes to the dissemination of propaganda and publications concerning the safe use of the Internet. In addition, there is a complex network of technical groups affiliated with IS and Al-Qaeda that write and share advice about the latest online technologies and privacy features.

---

14 The issue of how to label actors and different currents within the spectrum of Islamist movements has been discussed intensively among researchers. In this chapter, I will refer to the Islamic States and Al-Qaeda as jihadi groups. For a more detailed discussion, see: Thomas Hegghammer, Jihadi-Salafis or Revolutionaries? On Religion and Politics in the Study of Militant Islamism, in Roel Meijer (Ed.), *Global Salafism: Islam's new religious movement*, London: Hurst & Company 2009. For a critical evaluation of Hegghammer's categorization, see Rüdiger Lohlker, The Forgotten Swamp Revisited, in Rüdiger Lohlker (Ed.), *New Approaches to the Analysis of Jihadism: Online and Offline*, Göttingen: Vienna University Press 2012.

Jihadists' strategic use of online media

Since the turn of the millennium, the Internet and other computer-mediated forms of communication have impacted on and transformed Muslims' religious perception and conduct. By increasingly transferring religious debates and practice to the online sphere, the Internet has led to the development of new methods of configuration and organization within Islamic networks. As more Muslims seek religious guidance and advice online, new hierarchies and ways in which knowledge is accessed and transmitted have emerged.[15] This applies in particular to jihadi groups, who in the early 1990s were among the first to take advantage of the opportunities created by the proliferation of new communication technologies. Ever since, they have steadily relocated more resources to the Internet.[16] As a consequence, the professional promotion and marketing of their theology via the World Wide Web has become one of the central foundations of jihadi movements.[17] Over the past two decades, several shifts in their Internet usage have taken place. According to Zelin (2013), the development of jihadi media activities can be divided into four phases.[18]

The first phase started in the 1980s and consisted mostly of the distribution of essays, magazines, newsletters, audiotapes of sermons, and videos of lectures and battle scenes. The communication strategy was not online but rather relied on the dissemination of physical material. The second phase took place in the 1990s when top-down websites formed the core element of jihadi communication. Individuals running the sites could exert full control of the information spread, as audiences were not able to actively engage in discussions. This changed in the third phase, beginning in the 2000s, when interactive forums became more widespread. Although users were now able to participate in online discussions and post material themselves, the content of the forums was strictly administered and posts as well as users who ran counter the intended ideas of the forum were deleted or banned so that the discussion would remain ideologically homogenous. In the fourth stage, which started in recent years, OSNs replaced forums and became the central hub for the dissemination of jihadi content.[19] These new communication platforms lowered the barriers for involvement in the global jihadi movement and enabled low-level members and online supporters

---

15 Gary R. Bunt, *iMuslims: Rewiring the House of Islam*, Chapel Hill: University of Carolina Press 2009, pp. 7 ff.
16 Weimann, *Terrorism in Cyberspace*, pp. 38 ff.
17 Bunt, *iMuslims*, pp. 184 f.
18 Aaron Y. Zelin, The State of Global Jihad Online. A Qualitative, Quantitative, and Cross-Lingual Analysis, *New America Foundation*, January 4, 2013 (https://www.newamerica.org/international-security/policy-papers/the-state-of-global-jihad-online/).
19 Ibid., p. 4.

who do not have a direct link to jihadi organizations to become active and a mouthpiece for the movement's goals.[20] In general, the changes within jihadi communication can be described as: "a clear shift away from the highly organization-centric model advanced by Al-Qaeda, towards one where unaffiliated sympathizers can interact with and, to some extent, shape propaganda content in real-time by actively participating in its further dissemination, thus contributing to the organisation(s) whose message they convey."[21]

Online, practically everyone can join this movement at any time and become a virtual warrior fighting for the aspired global Islamic revolution. Ali Fisher (2015) describes the strategies applied by the jihadists groups to maintain a persistent online presence and to benefit from OSNs despite current steps taken by governments and social-media providers to counter these activities. He draws from netwar concepts and describes how the media mujāhidīn[22] operate "through a dispersed network of accounts which constantly reconfigures much like the way a swarm of bees or flock of birds constantly reorganizes in mid-flight."[23] Fisher defines this phenomenon as a Swarmcast because, in contrast to traditional means of communication, it does not operate through a clear distribution hierarchy where the content producer is in full control of the message broadcast to the respective audience. Instead, a loosely affiliated network of media mujāhidīn download and save the content on their servers, which they can then again republish via their accounts and through different online channels. This network provides a vast and efficient distributing system, making it very difficult for authorities and network providers to censor jihadi publications online.[24]

In tandem with the spread of new information technologies, jihadi movements also added a new concept to their understanding of jihad: the term media jihad. According to this doctrine, the duty of jihad may be performed not only through combat engagement and acts of violence but also by actively participating in the perceived "media war".[25] This media jihad is considered part of the *jihād bi-l-lisān* (jihad with the tongue),[26] which is deemed to be a central aspect of

---

20 Yannick Veilleux-Lepage, Paradigmatic Shifts in Jihadism in Cyberspace: The Emerging Role of Unaffiliated Sympathizers in Islamic State's Social Media Strategy, in *Journal of Terrorism Research* 7i (February 2016), p. 44 (accessed May 05, 2018).
21 Ibid., p. 37.
22 The term mujāhid (Pl. mujāhidīn) denotes a person who engages in Jihad (see the other chapters).
23 Ali Fisher, Swarmcast: How Jihadist Networks Maintain a Persistent Online Presence, in *Perspectives on Terrorism* 9iii (2015), p. 4 (accessed May 05, 2018).
24 Ibid., pp. 8–16.
25 Nico Prucha, Jihadist innovation and learning by adapting to the 'new' and 'social media' Zeitgeist, in Magnus Ranstorp/Magnus Normark (Eds.), *Understanding Terrorism Innovation and Learning. Al-Qaeda and beyond*, New York: Routledge 2015, pp. 118ff.
26 Often also referred to as *jihād bi-l-qalam* (jihad with the pen).

what jihadists perceive to be their religious duty of engaging in jihad.²⁷ According to this conviction, *jihād bi-l-lisān* includes activities such as inspiring (*taḥrīḍ*) the respective audience, providing counter-arguments to the traditional media outlets, disseminating the movement's ideas, reaching new adherents, calling them to submit to its theology, join its fight, as well as to threaten and intimidate their enemies.²⁸

Image featured in the fourth edition of Al-Qaeda's Al-Risalah magazine

Given the vital role online communication has for jihadi movements, groups such as IS and Al-Qaeda have raised the media mujāhidīn on the same level as regular mujāhidīn fighting on the battlefield.²⁹ The category of the media mu-

---

27 For more on the discussion on *jihād bi-l-lisān* see: Philip Holtmann, Virtual Leadership: A Study of Communicative Guidance Patterns in Online Jihad, Diss. Phil. University of Vienna 2013, pp. 120 ff.
28 See for example: Maktabat al-Himma, *Mujāhid anta aiyuhā al-iʻlāmī*, June 2015, pp. 13 ff. and 23 ff. (https://archive.org/details/mojahed_ilamee_is) (accessed August 3, 2017).
29 Ibid., pp. 20 f.; Holtmann, Virtual Leadership, p. 119.

jāhidīn is very inclusive and encompasses media operatives engaged in producing recordings and reports from the frontlines and online supporters distributing jihadi content at the same time.³⁰ The conviction that the engagement in the media mujāhidīn is equal to military service is echoed in an IS publication titled "Media Operative, You are a Mujāhid Too", where it says:

> "The media is a jihad in the path of Allah. [...] And the media jihad against the enemy is of no less importance than engaging in fighting the enemy."³¹

Besides publishing and disseminating propaganda in support of jihadi groups, the media mujāhidīn are also obliged to stay informed about current affairs, government monitoring capabilities, the latest technological trends, and counter-surveillance methods. Several jihadi publications on this matter have called on online activists to adapt, learn, and improve their technical skills.

> "It is incumbent upon the media mujāhid to be seriously concerned with his security [...] because the enemy is lurking and will not waste any chance to attack if the opportunity arises. [...] It is incumbent upon the media mujāhid to monitor the responses and comments of the enemy about his work [...] And the media jihad is one of the most important fronts which needs adaptation to the particular circumstances."³²

To emphasize the existential necessity of adequate counter-surveillance measures jihadi ideologues often invoke Islamic traditions and sources.³³ One of the most frequently quoted traditions in this context is the Quranic verse 4:71. It reads: "O believers, take your precautions; then move forward in companies, or move forward all together."³⁴ By referring to such sources, they stress that finding the safest ways to operate online is not just a strategic gimmick but a divine command and a clear obligation upon every mujāhid. The following section shows how and through what means jihadists are trying to fulfill what they perceive as their religious duty to apply the best online operational security means possible.

---

30 Charlie Winter, 'Media Jihad': The Islamic State's Doctrine for Information Warfare, in *The International Centre for the Study of Radicalisation and Political Violence*, February 13, 2017, p. 9 (http://icsr.info/2017/02/icsr-report-media-jihad-islamic-states-doctrine-information-warfare/) (accessed May 05, 2018).
31 Maktabat al-Himma, *Mujāhid anta aiyuhā al-iʿlāmī*, p. 9. Translated by the author.
32 Muʾassasat al-Qayrawān, *Al-Mujāhid al-iʿlāmī. Al-Khuṭawāt al-ʾūlā, li-iḥtirāf al-jihād al-iʿlāmī*, March 2012, pp. 8f. (https://ia800300.us.archive.org/16/items/mars2012/9irawan_jihed-i3lami.pdf) (accessed August 21, 2017). Translated by the author.
33 See for example: Abu Ubayda Abdullah al-Adm, Safety and Security Guidelines for Lone Wolf Mujahideen and Small Cells, in *Al-Fajr Media Center*, (January 2016), pp. 7f. (https://cryptome.org/2016/01/lone-wolf-safe-sec.pdf) (accessed July 30, 2017).
34 Ibid., p. 11. Translation by: A.J. Arberry, *The Koran Interpreted*, New York: Touchstone 1996, p. 110. Other Quranic verses quoted in this context are 8:60 and 4:83.

Tech-savvy jihadism

While jihadists have recognized the need to overcome government surveillance measures throughout their existence, the techniques applied have changed over the time. Determining the exact time at which jihadist debates over operational security started is difficult. One of the earliest public statements in this respect can be traced back to 2007, when the Global Islamic Media Front (GIMF) published its first encryption tool, *Asrar al-Mujahideen*. However, the discussion about the right online behavior was still limited at that time, as it took place in password-protected forums with limited audience reach or consisted of articles in Al-Qaeda's *Inspire* dealing primarily with encryption technologies.[35] In recent years, public jihadist debates on online operational security and the means applied have steadily increased and become more sophisticated. Many have attributed this to the leaks by Edward Snowden, the former NSA contractor who published classified information regarding the operational scope and technical capabilities used by intelligence agencies. They claim that since the Snowden leaks revealed massive surveillance of citizens by government institutions on an unprecedented scale, this significantly raised the level of concern within jihadi circles.[36] Evaluating the exact influence the Snowden leaks had on jihadist movements is difficult, as political interests often bias the results presented. Having faced severe setbacks due to the interception of satphone and e-mail communications, tech-savvy jihadists were well-aware of the extent to which governments spy on ordinary citizens long before Snowden leaked any documents.[37] His leaks have frequently been referenced in jihadist publications aiming to raise awareness for operational security online.[38] Additionally,

---

35 Steven Stalinsky/R. Sosnow, Al-Qaeda's Embrace of Encryption Technology, Part I: 2011–2014, in *MEMRI Cyber and Jihad Lab*, April 28, 2014 (http://cjlab.memri.org/uncategorized/al-qaedas-embrace-of-encryption-technology-2007-2011/) (accessed May 05, 2018).
36 Steven Stalinsky/R. Sosnow, Al-Qaeda's Embrace of Encryption Technology, Part II: 2011–2014, And the Impact of Edward Snowden, in *MEMRI Cyber and Jihad Lab*, April 28, 2014 (http://cjlab.memri.org/lab-projects/tracking-jihadi-terrorist-use-of-social-media/al-qaedas-embrace-of-encryption-technology-part-ii-2011-2014-and-the-impact-of-edward-snowden/) (accessed May 05, 2018).
37 Flashpoint Partners, Measuring the Impact of the Snowden Leaks on the Use of Encryption by Online Jihadists, in *Flashpoint*, September 16, 2014 (https://fpjintel.com/public-reports/measuring-the-impact-of-the-snowden-leaks-on-the-use-of-encryption-by-online-jihadists/) (accessed May 05, 2018).
38 See for example: Stalinsky/Sosnow, Al-Qaeda Encryption Technology, Part II.; Snowden is also mentioned in numerous publications by the EHF, see for example: Electronic Horizons Foundation, *Khadamāt al-VPN*, uploaded August 18, 2017 (https://pastethis.at/5SiW2ZfR) (accessed September 6, 2017); Electronic Horizons Foundation, *Taqrīr amnī 'an Windows 10 wa-sharikat Microsoft*, uploaded August 17, 2017 (https://pastethis.at/C0Ahy31f) (accessed September 7).

Snowden's revelations triggered privacy activists and tech-companies concerned with online anonymity to develop new tools to limit the government's reach.[39] Jihadists, in turn, began to use the very same technologies for their extremist agendas, turning technologies developed for benign privacy purposes into essential terrorist assets. It is thus clear that although Snowden alone cannot be credited with the advance in jihadists' operational security, his leaks have at least partly shaped their perception of privacy-enhancing technologies.[40] Over recent years, an extensive library of jihadi literature exclusively about the issue of operational security has been built up. As it is becoming increasingly difficult to keep track of the numerous jihadist authors who publish on new technologies and counter-surveillance measures online, the following section will highlight the main channels, organizations, and contributors dealing with these matters.

Who is writing about online security strategies?

In recent years, jihadists have stepped up their efforts to provide their counterparts with sophisticated technical knowledge and training. As of today, there is a complex nexus of different organizations and outlets dealing with new media technology and teaching the necessary skills to avoid government scrutiny. This nexus operates through various channels, publishes in numerous languages and tries to reach as many supporters as possible. While most publications found online are in Arabic, more and more literature in other languages is becoming available, mostly in English and French, but also in German and Dutch.

The main originators of jihadi-inspired information on privacy-enhancing measures are technical groups writing in support of jihadi movements online. Several technical departments affiliated with IS and Al-Qaeda specialize in up-to-date knowledge about current technological trends and threats, raising awareness about the importance of appropriate online-behavior, informing supporters about steps to be taken in order to remain anonymous, providing followers with guidelines on how to maintain an online presence in social networks, and in some cases even in developing tools and apps to protect the communication of their fellow jihadists. In researching this topic, one faces difficulties in establishing direct links between the jihadi groups themselves and

---

39 Robert Hackett, Snowden Leaks Advanced Encryption by 7 Years, U.S. Spy Chief Says, in *Fortune*, April 25, 2016 (http://fortune.com/2016/04/25/snowden-encryption-james-clapper/) (accessed May 05, 2018).
40 Rowan Scarborough, Islamic State, al Qaeda are big fans of Edward Snowden's tweets, in *The Washington Times*, October 16, 2015 (http://www.washingtontimes.com/news/2015/oct/16/islamic-state-al-qaeda-are-big-fans-edward-snowden/) (accessed May 05, 2018).

the organizations distributing associated online content, and their actual relationship often remains obscure.

One of the most prominent organizations is the technical department of the Global Islamic Media Front (GIMF),[41] an independent media project that disseminates propaganda material on jihadi activities. It used to operate via websites and is now mostly present on Twitter and Telegram.[42] As it primarily distributes publications in support of Al-Qaeda, a tangible affiliation between the GIMF and the latter's nucleus is likely.[43] Apart from ideological propaganda, the GIMF also has a technical department that mainly focuses on creating several encryption technologies and publishes on emerging technologies as well as counter-surveillance methods.[44] From having been one of the first organizations dealing with the issue of encryption and secure communication programs, its outreach and role regarding online operational security have quietened down recently.

Since its rapid rise, which culminated in the declaration of its caliphate in mid-2014, IS has launched what many describe as the most successful jihadi media campaign so far, moving its propaganda to OSNs and new online platforms. At the same time, IS-affiliated groups also started to deal with issues related to online operational security and have led the internal jihadi discussion on privacy-enhancing methods ever since. While the GIMF's concentrates on encryption technology, IS-affiliated tech-companies have addressed a broad number of topics, many of which will be discussed later on. Currently, one of the central and most active IS-affiliated groups concerned with the dissemination of technological knowledge is the Electronic Horizons Foundation (EHF). This is a pro-IS organization that provides online supporters with technical expertise. According to several reports, it is a collective project of various IS-affiliated groups such as the The Technical Department of the Islamic State as well as several Telegram channels and Twitter accounts focused on technical advice.[45] The EHF regularly publishes articles and technical manuals and administrates archives on Justpaste.it and Pastethis.at, where it collects all its previous items and publications. Moreover, the EHF also operates a library-bot on Telegram that

---

41 For a detailed discussion on the GIMF, see Manuel R. Torres Soriano, 'Between the Pen and the Sword': The Global Islamic Media Front in the West, in *Terrorism and Political Violence* 24v (November 2012) (accessed May 05, 2018).
42 https://t.me/GIMF_Tech (accessed September 5, 2017).
43 https://t.me/GIMF_Sub2 (accessed September 5, 2017).
44 https://www.gimfmedia.com/tech/en/ (accessed August 5, 2017).
45 The Middle East Media Research Institute, Jihadi 'Help-Desk,' Tech Channels On Telegram and Twitter offer Tech support, Tutorials, Up-To-Date Cyber Security Info, in *MEMRI Cyber and Jihad Lab*, February 8, 2016 (http://cjlab.memri.org/lab-projects/tracking-jihadi-terrorist-use-of-social-media/jihadi-help-desk-tech-channels-on-telegram-and-twitter-offer-tech-support-tutorials-up-to-date-cyber-security-info/) (accessed May 05, 2018).

serves as an archive of articles, videos, and banners published by the EHF.[46] While most EHF publications are distributed in Arabic, it has recently started translating its articles into other languages. So far, these include Arabic, English, French, and Dutch.[47]

In addition to the organizations mentioned above, a significant amount of information about operational online security is shared on jihadi online forums, blogs, individual Telegram channels, and file-sharing sites such as Justpaste.it, as well as in social media accounts of supporters or members or IS and Al-Qaeda. Moreover, numerous articles published in jihadi online magazines deal with the issue of online operational security. Such magazines include IS's weekly Arabic magazine *Al-Nabāʾ* and its French-language magazine *Dār al-Islām*. Al-Qaeda also operates several foreign-language magazines that regularly address issues related to online operational security, including the English-language *Inspire* and *al-Risalah*. In December 2015, the first edition of a German-language tech magazine called *Kybernetiq* was published, which concentrates on instructing jihadi supporters about how to operate securely online. Currently, there are two online editions of *Kybernetiq* as well as an additional website on the Darknet, through which jihadist propaganda and privacy updates are distributed.[48] While most journalists have attributed *Kybernetiq* to IS, there is some evidence that it is in fact run by Al-Qaeda supporters.[49]

Counter-surveillance measures and technologies applied

From their inception, jihadi groups took the issue of counter-surveillance seriously and tried to educate their followers about the importance of hiding information from adversary governments. The early methods were rather simple,

---

46 https://t.me/change_log (accessed September 01, 2017); https://justpaste.it/EHF (last accessed August 01, 2017). The website was removed in August, 2017. Afterwards the EHF moved its online archive to pastethis.at https://pastethis.at/f2EEpd41 (accessed September 14, 2017); Telegram.me/@HorizonsLibbot (accessed September 14, 2017).
47 https://pastethis.at/E48vQVv5 (accessed September 23, 2017).
48 http://kybrntqae2ceoele.onion/index.html (accessed September 14, 2017).
49 In the second edition of *Kybernetiq*, the editors make fun of reports that link the magazine to IS, stating that after the first edition was published "it was circulated that we were members of the Islamic State. Our denials even increased their speculations." *Kybernetiq* 2nd edition, November 2016, p. 1. (http://kybrntqae2ceoele.onion/2016/11/12/Vorwort-Kybernetiq-Ausgabe-002.html) (accessed September 14, 2017). Translated by the author. Shortly afterwards, an English version of an article featured in the second edition of *Kybernetiq* was re-published in the 4th edition of Al-Qaeda's *Al-Risala*h magazine and featured on the *Kybernetiq* homepage. Although this does not explicitly prove that the editors of *Kybernetiq* are actually affiliated to Al-Qaeda, it makes it likely.

such as avoiding unnecessary suspicion or using dead drop e-mail accounts.[50] Over time, jihadists' discussions of various privacy-enhancing methods have become more advanced and have addressed various new technologies. Today, anyone seeking to stay anonymous online can choose from a number of user-friendly applications and programs that are not only easy to obtain and handle but also claim to offer the latest privacy-enhancing technology. It therefore often seems as if taking the necessary precautions to avoid transmitting sensitive information is straightforward and does not require advanced technical skills. Jihadi tech organizations are well aware that the situation is much more complicated and frequently stress the importance for online supporters to be well-informed on the technologies available and the capabilities of government surveillance, as shown in the following example:

> "The carelessness of the supporters (*anṣār*) regarding the security aspect will make them easy prey for the regional and international intelligence agencies. [...] Indeed, the mujāhidīn are the primary target, and the intelligence agencies seek to collect information about them using all means possible [...] The issue is dangerous and should not be underestimated."[51]

Being cognizant of their enemies' capabilities, IS and Al-Qaeda now intensively discuss the effects of using technologies such as smartphones and cryptocurrencies and heavily rely on encryption technologies, VPNs, particular browsers, and live operating systems.

Encryption Technologies

The employment of encryption technologies is one of the earliest and essential aspects of the jihadi strategies to mitigate adversarial online surveillance.[52] In general, the use of encryption technology by jihadists can be separated into two periods. During the first period, jihadi movements pre-eminently focused on developing their own tools, an endeavor, which was spearheaded by the technical

---

50 Magnus Ranstorp, The virtual sanctuary of al-Qaeda and terrorism in an age of globalization, in Johan Eriksson/Giampiero Giacomella (Eds.), *International Relations and Security in the Digital Age*, New York: Routledge 2007, pp. 51 f. A dead drop account is a way to conceal one's e-mail traffic. Rather than sending the e-mails, the written message is saved in the draft folder, which then can be read by anyone who has access to the e-mail account.
51 Electronic Horizons Foundation, *Maqālāt amniyya. Amnuka ʿalā Twitter*, uploaded January 11, 2016 (justpaste.it/twittersec) (accessed July 11, 2017). Translated by the author.
52 Several articles published in jihadi magazines emphasize the importance of encryption technology and provide general introductions to this matter. See: *Al-Nabaʾ* 61st edition, December 2016, p. 8 (http://jihadology.net/2016/12/29/new-issue-of-the-islamic-states-newsletter-al-naba-61/) (accessed September 14, 2017).

department of the GIMF. But in recent years, jihadists have shifted to external encryption services developed by privacy activists, a practice that proliferated especially in the aftermath of the Snowden leaks.

In 2007, the GIMF launched its encryption software called *Asrar al-Mujahideen* (Secrets of the Mujāhidīn), which was the first jihadi self-made encryption software. According to the GIMF, the *Asrar al-Mujahideen* software was created based on the assumption that programs developed by non-jihadi specialists cannot be trusted and in the belief that intelligence agencies may be planting such programs to monitor their communication more thoroughly. Hence, the GIMF urged jihadi supporters to trust only their own software, claiming that it guaranteed the highest level of privacy.[53] The software was updated in 2008 and the new version launched as *Asrar al-Mujahideen 2.0*. This could be used to send encrypted messages through a process similar to PGP (Pretty Good Privacy), using asymmetric encryption keys of 2048-bit length.[54] Several high-ranking jihadi figures have lauded the confidentiality provided by *Asrar al-Mujahideen 2.0* and have endorsed its use.[55]

In 2013, the GIMF added another program to its toolbox, this time an encryption feature that could be utilized as an add-on to several instant messaging programs. Called *Asrar al-Dardarshah* (Secrets of Chatting) it was described as the "first Islamic encryption plugin."[56] When launching the *Asrar al-Dardarsh* software, the GIMF bragged about the up-to-date technology used, noting that "Asrar al-Dardarshah offers the highest levels of encryption for secure communication through instant messaging. [...] It [...] secures communications with the greatest degree of secrecy and is based on the highest standards reached by cryptography and digital telecommunications engineering."[57] Reflecting a general shift from e-mail services to messaging apps and OSNs, the creation of *Asrar al-Dardashah* reveals the GIMF's efforts to keep jihadist networks up to date and adapt associated communities to emerging online trends. The most recent encryption program developed by GIMF is *Tashfeer al-Jawwal* (mobile encryption program), which was released in September 2013 and quickly re-

---

53 Global Islamic Media Front, *Download Asrar al-Mujahideen* (https://www.gimfmedia.com/tech/en/asrar-al-mujahideen) (accessed August 5, 2017).
54 Ibid.
55 Al-Qaeda in the Arabian Peninsula especially has promoted *Asrar al-Mujahideen* and has dedicated two articles in the first and second edition of its *Inspire* magazine to the program. *Inspire* 1st edition, June 2010, pp. 41–43 (https://azelin.files.wordpress.com/2010/06/aqap-inspire-magazine-volume-1-uncorrupted.pdf) (accessed September 14, 2017); Inspire 2nd edition, Fall 2010, pp. 58–60 (https://azelin.files.wordpress.com/2010/10/inspire-magazine-2.pdf) (accessed August 9, 2017).
56 Global Islamic Media Front, *Download Asrar al-Dardarshah* (https://www.gimfmedia.com/tech/en/asrar-al-dardashah/) (accessed August 5, 2017).
57 Ibid.

placed by an improved version.⁵⁸ *Tashfeer al-Jawwal* runs on Android or Symbian smartphones, employs asymmetrical encryption and enables encoding messages and files as well as sending and receiving 400-letter messages. Additionally, it uses the Twofish encryption algorithm with cipher block chaining and claims to have the same strength as advanced encryption standards (AES).⁵⁹

Up until 2013, the GIMF was virtually the only jihadi tech organization creating encryption. In December that year, however, the Al-Fajr Technical Committee (FTC), an organization whose members and group affiliation is unknown, released its asymmetric encryption program *Amn al-Mujahid* (Security of the Mujāhid).⁶⁰ A second version specifically for Android systems followed suit. The program relies heavily on previous encryption tools and does not significantly differ from previous technology developed by the GIMF.⁶¹

IS has also taken to developing encryption programs, launching its own *Asrar al-Ghurabaa* (Secrets of the Strangers) in 2013 after splitting from Al-Qaeda.⁶² Little is known about *Asrar al-Ghurabaa*, which is likely due to a lack of trust in this program. Shortly after the release of *Asrar al-Ghurabaa*, the GIMF published a statement in which they advised against using the app, stating that "the program is suspicious and its source is not trusted."⁶³

While the programs mentioned above used to be state-of-the-art instruments in jihadi encryption activities, several recent publications have sharply criticized and advised against the use of self-made jihadi encryption software. An example of this is an article published in the first edition of the German-language jihadi tech magazine *Kybernetiq* examining the *Asrar al-Mujahideen* software.⁶⁴ The author warns supporters against using any encryption software with a mujāhid branding, as they have several weaknesses. First, he argues that the software has not been updated since 2008 and that intelligence agencies have deciphered the

---

58 Global Islamic Media Front, *Download Mobile Encryption (V 1.1)* (https://www.gimfmedia.com/tech/en/download-mobile-encryption/) (accessed August 5, 2017).
59 Ibid.
60 The announcement text for *Amn al-Mujahid* was published on the Jihadi forum Shumukh al-Islam and is retrievable online via Jihadology.net: Al-Fajr Media Technical Committee, 'Surprise'-Program (Security of the Mujāhid) – For Safe Encrypted Communication, December 10, 2013 (http://jihadology.net/2013/12/10/new-statement-from-al-fajr-medias-technical-committee-surprise-program-security-of-the-mujahid-for-safe-encrypted-communication/) (accessed September 06, 2017).
61 Ibid.
62 Stalinsky/Sosnow, Al-Qaeda Encryption Technology, Part II.
63 Global Islamic Media Front, *Warning About the Use of the Program Asrār al-Ghurabā'*, December 4, 2013 (http://jihadology.net/2013/12/04/new-statement-from-the-global-islamic-media-front-warning-about-the-use-of-the-program-asrar-al-ghuraba/) (accessed September 6, 2017).
64 *Kybernetiq* 1st edition, December 2015, pp. 4f (http://kybrntqae2ceoele.onion/download/kybernetiq_001.pdf) (accessed July 30, 2017).

algorithms and technology used. Second, the 2048-bit key employed by *Asrar al-Mujahideen* is not up to date, as there are several programs available which use more secure encryption keys.⁶⁵ Third, and most critically, if using a program that has a jihadi label and is used only by jihadists one quickly becomes "branded [as if one were wearing] a stamp on one's forehead saying 'Look Intelligence Agencies, I am using a jihadi encryption program'."⁶⁶ He concludes that using jihadi software such as *Asrar al-Mujahideen* can be a severe security risk and attract the attention of the intelligence apparatus.⁶⁷

While it is likely that many still use the programs discussed above, the focus of most currently active tech-savvy jihadi groups has increasingly shifted from developing their own security tools to finding, evaluating, and explaining the best programs available. The Signal, Threema, and Pidgin applications are mentioned particularly often.⁶⁸ Recent jihadi publications describe Signal as the most secure and advanced encrypted messaging tool.⁶⁹ The EHF, for example, has published an article about Signal, claiming that it was not only created by the developer of PGP encryption Philipp Zimmermann but has also been used and recommended by Edward Snowden, a fact which they view as a clear proof of its quality. In contrast to other encrypted messaging tools, Signal is an open-source software program and thus continuously improved by encryption experts. Its software is therefore always equipped with the latest encryption technology.⁷⁰

Other, slightly different apps are critically evaluated and advised against by jihadi technological departments. Threema, an application that claims to provide the most advanced encryption technology, for example, is regularly described as being insecure, not only because it is closed-source software, but also because it does not support essential encryption features, among others Forward Security.⁷¹ Forward Security is a popular cryptography tool that creates random keys based on an unpredictable algorithm for each new session. This means that

---

65 Ibid., p. 5.
66 Ibid., p. 5. Translated by the author.
67 Ibid., p. 7.
68 Electronic Horizons Foundation, *Al-Dalīl al-shāmil li-taṭbīq Signal. Al-Tawāṣul al-mushaffar*, uploaded August 16, 2017 (https://pastethis.at/M5EE6CUM) (accessed September 6, 2017); Electronic Horizons Foundation, *Al-Dars al-thālith 'ashara min silsilat amn al-hawātif al-dhakiyya: Threema Gmbh*, uploaded August 16, 2017 (https://pastethis.at/x18O4s WI) (accessed September 6, 2017); Electronic Horizons Foundation, *Sharḥ istikhdām taṭbīq Pidgin. Li-l-muḥādathāt al-mushaffara maʿ brūtūkūl 'OTR' 'alā niẓām Windows*, uploaded August 16, 2017 (https://pastethis.at/v9n9gJdB) (accessed September 6, 2017). Other programs discussed include Gajim, Conversations and WhatsApp.
69 Electronic Horizons Foundation, *Al-Dalīl al-shāmil Signal*.
70 Ibid.
71 Electronic Horizons Foundation, *Al-Dars al-thālith 'ashara Threema Gmbh*.

even if a person's key has been compromised once it does not threaten previous or future communication.[72]

With regard to encrypted e-mail services, most jihadi tech-groups dealing with the privacy of e-mail servers advise against using the most widely used providers, such as Gmail, Yahoo, and Outlook, since these demand and pass on a lot of private and sensitive information and do not provide high security measures to protect one's privacy.[73] Instead, it is recommended using e-mail services that apply PGP encryption, such as ProtonMail, Tutanota, and Hush-Mail.[74]

Finally, encryption is not limited only to messaging. It can also be used to protect documents and data, which is considered an absolute necessity among jihadists. The most-praised software for this purpose is Veracrypt. It is a free, open-source software used to encrypt files and documents that is regularly mentioned in connection to Live Operating systems such as Linux and Tails.[75]

Encryption is one of the most important technologies used by jihadists to protect their messages and hide data transferred via networks, the Internet, mobile phones, and so forth. They have long made use of and are well informed about current developments in encryption technology. According to recent publications, several jihadi tech experts have grown skeptical of technology with a mujāhid label and advise supporters to rely on non-jihadi programs, which are viewed as more advanced, less conspicuous, and providing better privacy online. Although the GIMF has lately gone silent on this matter, it is likely that the developers still believe that their programs are more secure and that software created by non-mujāhidīn are precarious. This may indicate a disagreement among different jihadi tech-groups over which software can be deemed trustworthy.

VPN Services

Another major measure by jihadists to obscure their online footprint are VPN services. Jihadists have been using VPNs extensively, and much of the literature at hand directly or indirectly deals with VPNs. According to a report by the Flashpoint institute, jihadists have been using VPNs since 2012, when they

---

72 Ibid.
73 Electronic Horizons Foundation, *Khadamāt al-barīd al-iliktrūnī al-mushaffar*, uploaded August 21, 2017 (https://pastethis.at/QG8SKj0d) (accessed September 6, 2017).
74 Ibid.
75 Electronic Horizons Foundation, *Sharḥ mufaṣṣal istikhdām barnāmaj Veracrypt li-tashfīr al-milaffāt*, uploaded August 18, 2017 (https://pastethis.at/g96xZoH2n) (accessed September 6, 2017).

started applying Cyber Ghost VPN.[76] Their VPN use has since become more advanced, not only providing basic recommendations and suggestions but, with the availability of many different VPN services, jihadists started publishing detailed manuals on how to use VPNs and critically assess the strength and weaknesses of various services. Today, there is a large jihadi library dealing with all issues related to VPNs.

There are several services recommended by jihadi movements, some of the most popular are NordVPN, OpenVPN, HideMeVPN, F-Secure Freedom.[77] In an article dealing with VPN services for Android systems, the EHF provides several guidelines on how to use them and compares different programs. According to the article, NordVPN "is considered one of the best private virtual services."[78] The article explains that NordVPN uses a double encryption method to protect the users' data, as well as two layers of VPN by running all traffic through the "The Onion Router" (TOR) network. Moreover, NordVPN is recommended due to its robust protocols and several features supported by the application, such as the ability to use bitcoin. One of the additional functions that distinguish NordVPN from other services is that it forces users always to use VPN when surfing online.[79]

However, the article notes that not all VPN services guarantee online anonymity and are not as secure as often claimed. One of the VPN services criticized by the EHF is the Chinese software PureVPN. Its general evaluation is very critical stating that "we do not recommend depending on PureVPN."[80] PureVPN, as well as other weaker VPN services, should be therefore avoided and only be used if it is impossible to access stronger software.[81] When using more vulnerable services, the EHF states, one always risks leaking data and the IP address. Moreover, the article warns that there many VPN services are in fact scams used by governments to make it easy to spy on those seeking anonymity online. It states:

> "Many VPN services do not provide the best security demands on the Internet. [...] These VPN services invade your privacy and sell your information to companies [...] as well as intelligence agencies."[82]

---

76 Laith Alkhouri/Alex Kassirer, Tech for Jihad: Dissecting Jihadists' Digitial Toolbox, *Flashpoint*, July 2016, p. 3 (https://www.flashpoint-intel.com/wp-content/uploads/2016/08/TechforJihad.pdf) (accessed May 05, 2018).
77 Electronic Horizons Foundation, *Al-Khadamāt al-iftirāḍiyya VPN fī anẓimat Android*, uploaded August 16, 2017 (https://pastethis.at/K8T25rr5) (accessed September 6, 2017).
78 Ibid.
79 Electronic Horizons Foundation, *Al-Khadamāt al-iftirāḍiyya*.
80 Ibid., Translated by the author.
81 Ibid.
82 Ibid., Translated by the author.

Statements like this demonstrate that jihadi tech organizations recommend supporters to proceed very carefully when choosing a VPN service, arguing that intelligence agencies are always trying to deceive them by creating new and fake programs.

These are just some examples of the broad range of jihadi publications on VPN services. The literature available on this issue demonstrates that jihadists take the matter of masking IP addresses very seriously and view VPN services as one of the pillars of counter-surveillance. Moreover, it shows that tech-savvy jihadists have a good understanding and overview of the services available as well as the benefits and disadvantages of each service. Their sophisticated understanding of VPN services has evolved over the years and jihadi tech groups regularly publish on this issue so that online supporters stay up-to-date on the latest VPN technologies available.

Browsers

Using the right web browser to hide one's identity online is another widely discussed topic among jihadists, who urge their supporters to stay away from browsers which they believe to be unsafe and monitor their online behavior. The TOR (The Onion Router) network is the favored and most often mentioned browser in jihadi literature. Early on, jihadists endorsed the TOR network and started using it when operating online. It is often described as "one of the most important instruments in our defensive weapons stockpile. It veils and anonymizes our sources. It basically makes us invisible from controllers, bypasses Firewalls and provides uncensored Internet-access."[83]

Although TOR is generally considered to be the preferred choice among jihadists, in a publication in Al-Qaeda's *Al-Risalah* magazine written by the *Kybernetiq* editors titled "The Dark Side of the Onion" the author cautions supporters that improper use of TOR can void the security provided by the browser. The article states that today several intelligence services and individual hacking groups are actively trying to attack and infiltrate TOR, exposing the network's users to new security threats.[84]

The TOR network consists of three different nodes, the Entry Guard, which encrypts the data and sends it to the second node called the Relay Server, where the data is encrypted a second time. Eventually, the connection to a website is

---

83 *Al-Risalah* 4th edition, January 2017, p. 41. (http://jihadology.net/2017/01/10/new-issue-of-the-magazine-al-risalah-4/) (accessed September 6, 2017). A longer version of the article was first published in the 2nd edition of *Kybernetiq*. Later, an English translation by the *Kybernetiq* editors was re-published in the 4th edition of Al-Qaeda's *Al-Risalah* magazine.
84 Ibid., pp. 41 ff.

Image featured in the fourth edition of Al-Qaeda's Al-Risalah magazine

finalized via an exit node, which can be described as the gateway where the data leaves the TOR network and is transferred to the Internet. The encryption technology and relays mask the user's IP address by making it seem as if the traffic originated from the exit relay, which can be located anywhere in the world. According to the *Kybernetiq* article, exit nodes can be a security threat for jihadists, as the article states:

> "Although your IP-Address is masked, the person in control of the traffic in between the Exit-Node and the Website you are entering is the one who controls all the traffic that goes through it. The attacker can now actively manipulate and remove the encryptions applied to your network traffic and even passively switch off security protocols (that mask) what you do within the Tor network".[85]

In the second edition of *Kybernetiq*, the editors also provide a sample case to demonstrate that "operating your own *TOR Exit Node* is a cakewalk"[86] and that it is relatively straightforward to manipulate the exit node to obtain private data of users browsing via the TOR network.[87] To avoid this kind of leakage, the author advises taking several measures, such as regularly updating the TOR browser, preventing unnecessary plugins and add-ons, always using end-to-end en-

---

85 Ibid., p. 41.
86 *Kybernetiq* 2nd edition, p. 11. Translated by the author. [Emphasis in original]
87 Ibid., pp. 11 f.

"Now You See Me – Now You Don't"   177

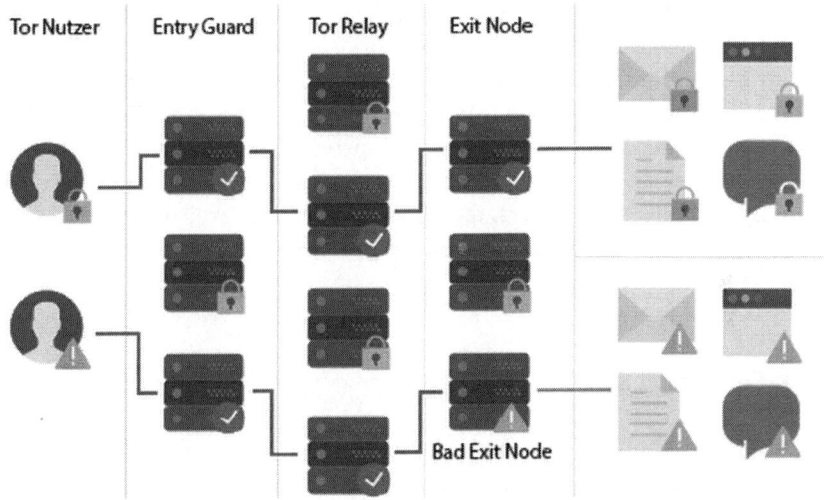

Image published in the 2nd edition of the German-language magazine Kybernetiq showing the structure of the TOR network and warning about the dangers of unsafe exit-nodes

cryption software, and rejecting any new SSL certificates.[88] Although the author still views TOR as the securest browser available, he concludes "that we should not rely solely on TOR. It is important to know how TOR should be used. [...] Intelligence agencies such as the NSA and GCHQ are also operating exit nodes and are trying [...] to control and monitor the TOR network."[89]

Other jihadi-approved browser applications are Orbot or Orfox. Orbot provides a browser that enables TOR on Android systems.[90] Orfox also works in a similar way, with some minor modifications, which makes it possible to enter the TOR network with an Android operating system and the Mozilla Firefox browser.[91] For other browsers such as Google Chrome and Opera, which are perceived as being unsafe, jihadi tech organizations always advise using them in combination with VPNs.[92]

TOR is one example that shows that when it comes to obscuring their online

---

88 Ibid., p. 9. SSL stands for secure sockets layer. It is a protocol which creates a secure connection between a client and the server over which to send information. However, SSLs might end up having the opposite effect when using TOR.
89 Ibid., p. 14. Translated by the author.
90 *Dār al-Islām* 10th edition, August 2016, pp. 40 f. (http://jihadology.net/category/dar-al-islam-magazine/) (accessed September 8, 2017).
91 Electronic Horizons Foundation, *Al-Dalīl al-shāmil li-TOR 'Orbot' Android*, uploaded August 16, 2017 (https://pastethis.at/KHf2HB5y) (accessed September 6, 2017).
92 Electronic Horizons Foundation, *Sharḥ al-tasjīl fī mawqiʿ Twitter, bidūn raqm hātif min khilāl mutaṣaffiḥ Opera wa-iḍāfat Surfeasy*, uploaded March 15, 2017, (https://ln.sync.com/dl/0c9c91700/jqeexwbx-d6hqnjs5-2remrjw3-juwijgnv) (accessed September 6, 2017).

traffic jihadists make extensive use of western technology developed for well-intended privacy purposes. The TOR network is very popular and used in many countries to avoid censorship regimes, which can make it a useful tool for countering political oppression. However, jihadists have seized TOR for their own agenda and consider it the essential browser for their online undertakings. While the jihadi literature on browsers has increased over time and today deals with several different browsers, the majority of sources available still focus on TOR. Despite the current doubts about the actual privacy provided, jihadists have yet to find a better alternative.

Live Operating Systems

An increasing number of jihadi publications dealing with privacy-enhancing techniques address the issue of live operating systems (LOS). Jihadi tech groups regularly warn their supporters that most operating systems are not safe. A recent example is an EHF article dealing with Windows 10, which was exposed to criticism due to privacy concerns.[93] According to the article, Windows is well known for monitoring and selling information about its users and with Windows 10, they "developed a system that infiltrates the privacy of its user rigorously."[94] As a consequence, most OS, such as Windows 10, should not be trusted and are best avoided. Instead, jihadi supporters should shift towards more secure LOS, with Linux[95] and Tails as the preferred systems.[96]

Linux provides a well-established open-source operating system, as well as a variety of software options which can be customized by the user. In the second edition of *Kybernetiq*, the author addresses Linux, stating: "Windows is not an open-source operating system. [...] Most malware, such as viruses, worms, and trojans, target Windows users. [...] We therefore only use open-source operating systems such as [...] Linux."[97] The article also highlights that Linux is easy to use,

---

93 Conner Forrest, Windows 10 violates your privacy by default, here's how you can protect yourself, in *TechRepublic*, August 4, 2015 (http://www.techrepublic.com/article/windows-10-violates-your-privacy-by-default-heres-how-you-can-protect-yourself/) (accessed May 05, 2018).
94 Electronic Horizons Foundation, *Taqrīr amnī 'an Windows 10*. Translated by the author.
95 Linux refers to the Linux kernel, as well as several programs, tools, and services. The program is therefore also often referred to as GNU/Linux because many of the programs used are actually GNU tools. For the purpose of this chapter and to increase readability, I will refer to the different programs and services simply as Linux.
96 Ibid. Another OS discussed by the EHF is the security-focused Qubes OS, see: Electronic Horizons Foundation, *Madkhal ilā niẓām Qubes OS*, uploaded August 18, 2017 (https://pastethis.at/M9i6T99W) (accessed September 13, 2017).
97 *Kybernetiq* 2nd edition, p. 21. Translated by the author.

does not need a high-end computer but runs even on older models, and is a very safe way to operate online.[98] The EHF has published a whole series of articles on Linux, giving a step-by-step introduction on how to download and use the LOS most effectively.[99] It argues that the strong kernel of the Linux system and its continuous development makes it more independent than other OS.[100] Moreover, since Linux enables users to control and choose several system configurations and the software applied, users should not be afraid of programs or updates that make it easy to hack the computer. Hence, the EHF views Linux as an easy to use and fast OS, which can be used in combination with other privacy-enhancing programs, such as most VPN services, encryption software, and the TOR network.[101]

While Linux is considered to provide a good level of privacy, most jihadi publications recommend supporters to use Tails (The Amnesiac Incognito Live System). In a training manual for lone wolves published on IS and Al-Qaeda Twitter accounts titled "Safety and Security Guidelines for Lone Wolf Mujahideen," it states "if you need to spend more time on the Internet, we HIGHLY suggest you use Tails OS on your computer for your Jihad-related work."[102] Tails is an operating system based on the Linux kernel, which focuses on protecting the identity and privacy of online traffic. Additionally – and this is the main reasons why it is the preferred operating system of jihadists – Tails OS is built and relies on the TOR network, forcing users to always connect with TOR when using the Internet.[103] Furthermore, Tails comes with several high-end cryptography programs, with users being able to encrypt not only the USB or external hard disk but also e-mails and instant-messaging services.[104]

Smartphone Confidentiality

Smartphones are some of the key tools used in jihadi messaging, allowing them to disseminate propaganda and information with ease and reach a global audience instantly. Despite the great opportunities provided by smartphones, tech-savvy jihadists consider them a dangerous means of communication. Several

---

98 Ibid., p. 21.
99 Electronic Horizons Foundation, *Silsilat amn al-ḥāsūb. Niẓām Linux*, uploaded July 26, 2017 (https://pastethis.at/k7vo72X0) (accessed September 7, 2017).
100 Electronic Horizons Foundation, *Ṭarīqat taḥmīl wa-tathbīt niẓām Linux Mint*, uploaded August 18, 2017 (https://pastethis.at/9kzd1I6p) (accessed September 7, 2017).
101 Electronic Horizons Foundation, *Silsilat amn al-ḥāsūb. Niẓām Linux*.
102 Abdullah al-Adm, *Safety and Security Guidelines*, p. 29. [Emphasis in original]
103 Electronic Horizons Foundation, *Al-Dalīl al-shāmil li-niẓām al-tashghīl Tails*, uploaded August 18, 2017 (https://pastethis.at/P4pmvN3I) (accessed September 7, 2017).
104 Ibid.

blogs and publications by jihadi tech organizations have warned their supporters about or strictly advised against the use of smartphones.

The second edition of *Kybernetiq* features an article titled "Utopia: Security on Smartphone: Who is actually behind the attack?", which illustrates the dangers of smartphones, describing them as "our electronic ankle monitor, which we are installing ourselves voluntarily."[105] The author argues that smartphones are likely to be the main reason why several high-ranking jihadists have been targeted in the past, mentioning the assassination of a sniper instructor on a training base as precedent.[106] He warns users against the illusory feeling of being secure after strengthening the privacy features on their phone. Even if they use software hiding their GPS, he notes that there are several other ways to locate a smartphone, such as silent SMS that can track the whereabouts of users even if their phones are switched off.[107] Moreover, intelligence agencies can easily obtain the smartphone's ISMI (international mobile subscriber identity)[108] which can catch the phone-signal by using two or three MAC addresses (media access-control address).[109] Several smartphone apps also automatically send a signal and are constantly looking for nearby Wi-Fi stations. The signal is thereby obtained by tracking systems such as Google, which then forward the exact location to intelligence agencies.[110] Due to such drawbacks, several jihadi writers on operational security are convinced that the disadvantages of smartphones outweigh their benefits, and statements like the following are common: "Liberate yourself and those close to you from these chains! My dear brother, next time you are looking for a spy just look inside your pocket."[111]

However, if jihadists supporters cannot get rid of their smartphones, several applications are recommended that should help to reduce the risks mentioned above.

First, users are advised to download applications that let them control apps' permissions. Several apps have permissions to access data from smartphones, such as the contacts, photos, and the locations of users. Using apps such as APK Editor allows smartphone owners to take any downloaded apps and alter their

---

105 *Kybernetiq* 2nd edition, p. 29. Translated by the author.
106 Ibid., p. 29.
107 Silent SMS, also known as Short Message Type 0, are messages that do not appear on the receiver display or trigger any signal, but are merely sent in order to track to location of the phone user.
108 The ISMI is a unique identification associated with cellular networks, which is sent to the network and makes it possible to identify the phone user. Additionally, it can be used to acquire other details, such as the location of the user.
109 A MAC address is a unique identifier of the hardware of network adapters.
110 Ibid., p. 29.
111 Ibid., p. 29. Translated by the author.

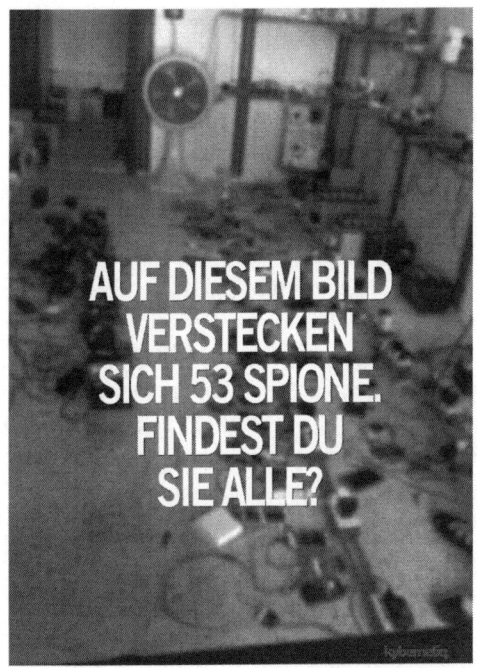

Image featured in the second edition of Kybernetiq magazine, showing numerous smartphones in the background. The caption reads: "53 spies are hidden in this picture. Can you find them all?"

coding so that they can control and limit the permissions and data obtained by the smartphone provider.[112]

Second, although jihadi tech groups view Android as a very useful smartphone operation system, one of the negative aspects is that it is owned by Google, which is claimed to be very active when it comes to invading its users' privacy and known for selling sensitive information to intelligence agencies. The EHF thus warns its followers against using any of these services, and has issued a tutorial on how to either protect one's data from the Google service or, if one has a routed phone, how to de-install Google services.[113]

Thirdly, jihadi tech experts warn about keylogging or keyboard capturing, which describes the action of recording every key stroke on a keyboard without

---

[112] Electronic Horizons Foundation, *Al-Dars al-awwal min silsilat amn al-hawātif al-dhakiyya. Ṣalāḥiyyāt al-taṭbīqāt*, uploaded August 16, 2017 (https://pastethis.at/Ahd618V2) (accessed September 3, 2017).

[113] Electronic Horizons Foundation, *Dawrat amn al-hawātif al-dhakiyya. Al-Takhalluṣ min khadamāt Google li-l-Android* (telegram.me/@HorizonsLibbot) (accessed September 7, 2017).

the writer knowing their activities are being monitored. The EHF suggests using the Hacker's Keyboard app, which it claims is protected against keylogging.[114]

Finally, as we have seen above, jihadi tech organizations call on their supporters to limit all access authorization on the IOS or Android systems, such as location tracking, the ability of apps to access one's private data, and the authority for the Wi-Fi system to continually look for new Wi-Fi connections, thereby giving away the geographical location. Additionally, they advise them to rely exclusively on encrypted messaging services.[115]

The issue of smartphones is vast and touches most other strategies applied, such as the use of TOR, VPN services, encrypted e-mail, messaging programs, and so forth. However, in recent publications, jihadists have started addressing the issue of smartphones separately, as they realize the dangers members and supporters run when constantly carrying a "spy" in their pocket. Several publications have urged supporters to get rid of smartphones altogether. This shows that in some cases jihadi tech departments advise against using new technologies if they are concerned that their drawbacks might outweigh their benefits.

Cryptocurrencies and Bitcoin

As of today, there are several cryptocurrency services available, with bitcoin leading the field. As cryptocurrencies provide a money transfer method that is hard to track and guarantees a high level of online privacy, several authors have suggested that jihadi movements will make use these technologies.[116] But so far there has been only limited evidence of jihadists' use of cryptocurrencies.

In 2014 the Twitter user @AmreekiWitness – an online supporter of IS – published an article under the pseudonym Taqi'ul Deen al-Munthir titled "Bitcoin wa-Ṣadaqāt al-Jihād" (Bitcoin and the Charity of Jihad). This was the first source connecting jihadi movements to cryptocurrencies and highlighting their benefits for their cause. It provides a general outline of how bitcoin functions, some advice on how to use it most securely and also describes the strategic

---

114 Electronic Horizons Foundation, *Al-Ḥimāya min al-Keylogger*, uploaded August 16, 2017 (https://pastethis.at/bMA947mG) (accessed September 7).
115 Electronic Horizons Foundation, *Dawrat amn al-hawātif al-dhakiyya. Ṣalāḥiyyāt al-taṭbīqāt*, uploaded March 15, 2017 (https://ln.sync.com/dl/f8869f8b0/ymcqy5v2-m9anrqt4-rejecvu3-tkgn88zd)(accessed September 5, 2017).
116 Bruno Halopeau, Terrorist use of the Internet, in Babak Akhgar/Andrew Staniforth/Francesca Bosco (Eds.), *Cyber Crime and Cyber Terrorism Investigator's Handbook*, Waltham: Syngress 2014, pp. 128 ff.

advantages of cryptocurrencies.[117] The first benefit the author highlights is the ability to circumvent other financial institutions that track money transfers, a problem which he argues had made ṣadaqa (charity) next to impossible for jihadi movements.

> "One cannot send a bank transfer to a mujahid or suspected mujahid without the kafir (unbelieving) governments ruling today immediately being aware [...] A proposed solution to this is something known as Bitcoin."[118]

Secondly, using bitcoins is also viewed as a way in which users can circumvent one of the doctrinal problems outlined by Salafi jihadist movements, who argue that by using the currencies of oppressor (ṭāghūt) states, Muslims effectively support the economies of their enemies and legitimize their rule. @Amreeki-Witnees is convinced that the use of digital money provides an alternative that enables Muslims to avoid state currencies and thus challenge the authority of all states not exclusively executing God's law.[119] He concludes by outlining the benefits that bitcoin can have for IS:

> "To set up a totally anonymous donation system that could send millions of dollars worth of Bitcoin instantly from the United States, United Kingdom, South Africa [...] or wherever else right to the pockets of the mujahideen, very little would be done [...] DawlatulIslam [The Islamic State] would simply need to set up a wallet and post their wallet address online. Then, Muslims from across the globe could simply copy the wallet address, login to their Dark Wallets, purchase whatever amount of Bitcoin they wish to send, and send them over. This system has the potential to revive the lost sunnah of donating to the mujahideen, it is simple, easy, and we ask Allah to hasten its usage for us."[120]

In January 2017, Indonesia's anti-money-laundering agency revealed the first public instance of the jihadi use of cryptocurrencies.[121] According to the report, an Indonesian national called Bahrum Naim, a foreign fighter in the ranks of IS, used online money transfer systems to fund terrorist activities of IS supporters in Indonesia. The money was reportedly used to support widows and families of

---

117 Taqi'ul-Deen al-Munthir, *Bitcoin wa-Sadaqat al-Jihad: Bitcoin and the Charity of Violent Physical Struggle*, July 2014 (https://alkhilafaharidat.files.wordpress.com/2014/07/btcedit-21.pdf) (accessed September 3, 2017).
118 Ibid.
119 Ibid.
120 Ibid.
121 Wahyudi Soeriaatmadja, Militant Bahru Naim used PayPal, bitcoin to transfer funds for terror attacks in Indonesia, in *The Straits Times*, January 9, 2017 (http://www.straitstimes.com/asia/se-asia/militant-bahrun-naim-used-paypal-bitcoin-to-transfer-funds-for-terror-attacks-in) (accessed May 05, 2018).

jihadists fallen while fighting for IS and to provide money for weapons, training, and *da'wa* (spreading of the faith).[122]

Although information about and sources on the use of cryptocurrencies is still limited, the case of Bahrun Naim and the article by @AmreekiWitnees indicate a keen interest in this and the potential that jihadists will increasingly take advantage of cryptocurrencies in the near future.

The technologies discussed in this section show that in recent years jihadists have grown more advanced in their understanding and use of privacy-enhancing technologies. However, when it comes to measures taken to mitigate government surveillance, they have not reinvented the wheel but instead are using the most popular and widespread tools available. Most of the programs employed were developed by Western privacy activists or tech-companies and have been seized for their radical agendas. Every new piece of software that aims at providing more freedom and less government scrutiny online is likely to be incorporated in their defensive arsenal. This reveals an inherent problem of privacy-enhancing technologies: while the cloak of anonymity provided can help to protect the privacy of everyday users and often even limit political oppression within authoritarian regimes, it also creates new avenues for criminal and extremist behavior. The same applies to current efforts by governments and OSNs to restrict the publicity of jihadi content online, to which jihadists supporters have responded immediately, finding new ways to return to these platforms by using some of the programs mentioned above.

Jihadists attempts to solve the online trade-off dilemma

While remaining anonymous is one of the central demands of jihadi groups, concentrating their efforts on obtaining online operational security frequently correlates with a shift towards limited-audience platforms. While Twitter used to be the most widely used platform for distributing their propaganda,[123] after being exposed to account takedowns, stricter platform policing, and large-scale spam attacks,[124] jihadi groups were forced to move to other, more secure plat-

---

122 Ibid.
123 Jytte Klausen, 'Tweeting the Jihad': Social Media Networks of Western Foreign Fighters in Syria and Iraq, in *Studies in Conflict & Terrorism* 38i (January 2, 2015) (accessed May 05, 2018).
124 Andrew Griffin, Anonymous 'Op ISIS': Online Activists spam suspected extremists with 'Rickrolls' and call them 'Daeshbags' in Revenge for Paris Attacks, in *The Independent*, November 19, 2015 (http://www.independent.co.uk/life-style/gadgets-and-tech/news/anonymous-op-isis-online-activists-spam-suspected-extremists-with-rickrolls-and-call-them-daeshbags-a6740811.html) (accessed May 05, 2018).

forms as an alternative.[125] An example of this repercussion is the increasing focus of jihadi online activities on the encrypted messaging service Telegram, which enables relatively safe online communication with little government scrutiny.[126] Since early 2016, Telegram emerged as the main hub for jihadi propaganda distribution.[127] By moving to Telegram, jihadi groups ensure that their online network remains intact, as followers are not only able to follow the links provided but download the content directly via Telegram and then re-distribute it on other platforms and channels. Yet the focus on Telegram has presented IS and Al-Qaeda with strategic problems, as it mostly works via unidirectional channels where information can be distributed but recipients cannot comment or interact or only through strictly administered chat rooms.[128] Additionally, chats and channels are not public and can only be accessed through invitation links that are shared and advertised on existing jihadi online platforms, making the content disseminated online only available for those actively following the jihadi online network.[129] Thus, despite the security provided, in the long term the limited audience of encrypted messaging services can jeopardize jihadi movements' general media strategy. Prucha (2016) has argued that "[t]he secrecy and encryption of Telegram is harmful to IS' swarming operations as the networks which are sustained on Telegram lack the outreach as well as the opportunities for projecting influence, which Twitter in particular allowed."[130]

Aware of these drawbacks, jihadi groups have found several countermeasures against the increasing isolation on Telegram that enable them to return to and compensate for the loss of publicity on social media platforms.

Campaigns to mobilize the media mujāhidīn on public OSNs

Throughout the past years, IS has launched numerous campaigns in which it urges online supporters to intensify their activities in the media jihad and stresses the importance of being active on public OSNs. These campaigns include posters, flyers, and comments as well as longer publications aimed at reversing

---

125 These platforms include Telegram, as well as WhatsApp.
126 WhatsApp has also become a popular application among jihadists. However, Telegram is still the preferred platform.
127 Mia Bloom, Hicham Tiflati and John Horgan, Navigating ISIS's Preferred Platform: Telegram, in *Terrorism and Political Violence* (July, 2017), p. 1 (accessed May 05, 2018).
128 Ibid., pp. 3 ff.
129 Ibid., p. 1.
130 Nico Prucha, IS and the Jihadist Information Highway – Projecting Influence and Religious Identity via Telegram, in *Perspectives on Terrorism* 10vi (December 2016), p. 56 (accessed May 05, 2018).

the decreased online presence of IS sympathizers on Twitter, Facebook, and YouTube.

Banner distributed by the IS affiliated Ashhaad Media organization via Telegram, urging supporters to become active in the media jihad

One example is an article published by the IS affiliated Al-Battār Media Foundation, titled "Oh Supporters (*anṣār*) – Return to the Battlefield."[131] The article states that the shift and increasing focus by IS supporters on secure platforms such as Telegram was a strategic error. It argues that as long as they are unable to join the ranks of IS, every supporter is religiously obliged to engage in the online battle by distributing IS publications, creating accounts on OSNs and defying the current policies to take down jihadi social media accounts. The author stresses the importance of platforms such as Facebook, Twitter, and YouTube in the media jihad due to their broad audience reach. He warns that by merely focusing on Telegram jihadists are running into danger of merely preaching to the choir, as the audience on Telegram is limited to those already convinced of the jihadi cause. Telegram, therefore, is not very efficient when it comes to achieving several features essential to the media jihad, such as the duty to openly refute adversaries, counter lies about jihadi movements, win over new sympathizers, and convince those hesitant to become an active supporter or join the ranks of

---

131 Mu'assasat al-Battār al-I'lāmiyya, *Aiyuhā al-anṣār 'ūdū ilā maydān al-nizāl*, August 6, 2016 (https://up.top4top.net/downloadf-42590wp43-rar.html) (accessed August 5, 2017). A similar article, warning IS supporters against isolating themselves on Telegram, was published in July, 2016 by the Al-Wafā' Foundation, a jihadi media outlet regularly publishing articles in support of the Islamic State. For a discussion of this article, see: Prucha, Jihadist Information Highway, pp. 55f.

IS.[132] He concludes by saying that forcing jihadist media outlets onto platforms such as Telegram is a deliberate policy by IS's enemies, who intended to isolate IS supporters and ban them from Twitter and Facebook. While he considers Telegram to be a secure platform for content distribution, he is convinced that returning to more public OSNs is a necessity to increase audience reach and counter the strategies of adversary governments.[133]

> "Yes, no one denies the importance of Telegram, but it is not the battlefield where the presence of the supporters (*anṣār*) is an absolute necessity. So this is a warning against the dependence on Telegram and against leaving Twitter and Facebook."[134]

This article is just one of many IS publications, posts, and statements that aim to raise awareness among sympathizers about the importance of returning to public OSNs, urge them to be persistent in their media efforts, and counter attempts to takedown jihadi content by OSN providers.

Creating Twitter and Facebook accounts by using fake phone numbers and VPNs

In addition to raising awareness among online supporters, jihadi tech organizations have focused on circulating tutorials on how to grow their presence on public OSNs by using online services that provide them with fake phone numbers. The aim of these tutorials is to teach jihadi supporters how to quickly (re-)open new Twitter and Facebook profiles or access an already established reservoir of backup accounts without compromising their privacy.

The audio, visual, and text tutorials on this issue are plentiful. Most of them suggest using the Android App Talkatone, Next Plus, Textplus and for IOS systems Sudo and Textnow, which enable users to talk and send messages online free of charge.[135] It is relatively easy to get a fake phone number for any of these services: users need to create an account and afterward receive a phone number specifically for the app that is different from their actual phone number. Registration is easy and can be done by using an encrypted e-mail service. These

---

132 Muʾassasat al-Battār al-Iʿlāmiyya, *Aiyuhā al-anṣār*.
133 Ibid.
134 Ibid., Translated by the author.
135 Electronic Horizons Foundation, *Dalīl taṭbīqāt al-arqām al-wahmiyya li-anẓimat Android* (telegram.me/@HorizonsLibbot) (accessed September 5, 2017); *Dalīl taṭbīqāt al-arqām al-wahmiyya li-anẓimat IOS (IPhone wa-IPad)*, uploaded August 24, 2017 (https://pastethis.at/u14951e8) (accessed September 1, 2017).

phone numbers can then be used to re-register on OSNs such as Facebook and Twitter.[136]

Additionally, jihadi tech organizations advise their supporters to download the App-Cloner application, which enables them to create and install multiple copies of existing apps on their mobile phones.[137] They can thereby create copies of applications such as Facebook and Twitter, which usually only allow one account per device, and use them simultaneously. An additional feature of App-Cloner is that after duplicating the application, users can change the look, name, and coding of the app, enabling them to increase the privacy measures when accessing OSNs on their smartphones.[138]

Screengrab from the EHF series on how to create social-media accounts using VPN services. The caption reads: "If they request a phone number, change the geographical location (IP Address), eliminate the tracking of the browser."

Another frequently mentioned way to register unlimited numbers of OSN profiles was presented in an EHF video tutorial in which they demonstrate and encourage an easy and efficient method of creating stocks of OSN accounts by

---

136 Ibid.
137 Electronic Horizons Foundation, *App Cloner*, uploaded August 13, 2017 (https://pastethis. at/sehHWVPX) (accessed August 20, 2017).
138 Ibid.

simply using VPN services. According to these tutorials, if OSNs demand a phone number, changing the IP address via VPN services is enough to start creating new accounts. Scores of backup accounts can thus be registered in a very short time.¹³⁹

Distributing and Hacking OSN Accounts

In addition to providing the tutorials described above, IS has tried to support its users with new OSN profiles either by trying to hack the accounts of other users or to provide donated accounts to avoid suspension. In recent years, pro-IS hacking groups such as the Caliphate Cyber Terrorism Army (CCTA) and the United Cyber Caliphate (UCC) have continuously hacked Facebook and Twitter accounts and boasted about their successes by posting pictures of their booty online.¹⁴⁰ In August 2016, the UCC claimed to have hacked more than 10,000 Twitter accounts.¹⁴¹ The latest documented report on jihadi groups hacking social-media profiles was published in April 2017,¹⁴² demonstrating that organizations such as the CCTA are very active in this field. Lately, several IS-affiliated groups have also taken to creating a reserve of social media accounts and providing other jihadists with access to OSNs. Some of these organizations

---

139 Electronic Horizons Foundation, *Sharḥ al-tasjīl fī mawqiʿ Twitter, mutaṣaffiḥ Opera*; Electronic Horizons Foundation, *Sharḥ al-tasjīl fī mawqiʿ Twitter (bidūn raqm hātif) min khilāl taṭbīq Hide.me VPN wa-mutaṣaffiḥ Firefox li-Android wa-IPhone*, uploaded March 15, 2017 (https://ln.sync.com/dl/1e1407170/vtk43cgp-m4thyjqa-zw6wjapf-a2pe9243) (accessed September 1, 2017); Electronic Horizons Foundation, *Sharḥ al-tasjīl fī Twitter min khilāl taṭbīq Vypr VPN wa-mutaṣaffiḥ Chrome li-niẓām Android*, uploaded March 15, 2017 (https://ln.sync.com/dl/f4190c780/spja3c9i-8hj84hyq-bxp8tw3s-icaywxgc) (accessed September 1, 2017).
140 The Middle East Media Research Institute, Pro-ISIS Hacking Group Shows Off Its Prowess At Hacking Facebook Accounts, Calls for Killing of German Pilot, in *MEMRI Cyber and Jihad Lab*, March 16, 2017 (http://cjlab.memri.org/lab-projects/monitoring-jihadi-and-hacktivist-activity/pro-isis-hacking-group-shows-off-its-prowess-at-hacking-facebook-accounts-calls-for-killing-of-german-pilot/) (accessed May 05, 2018).
141 The Middle East Media Research Institute, In Response to Twitter's Crackdown on Extremist Accounts Pro-ISIS Hacking Group Alleges it hacked 5000 Accounts on the Platform, in *MEMRI Cyber and Jihad Lab*, August 23, 2016 (http://cjlab.memri.org/lab-projects/tracking-jihadi-terrorist-use-of-social-media/in-response-to-twitters-crackdown-on-extremist-accounts-pro-isis-hacking-group-alleges-it-hacked-5000-accounts-on-the-platform/) (accessed May 05, 2018).
142 The Middle East Media Research Institute, Pro-ISIS Hacking Group CCTA Continues Campaign of Hacking Facebook Accounts, in *MEMRI Cyber and Jihad Lab*, April 24, 2017 (http://cjlab.memri.org/lab-projects/monitoring-jihadi-and-hacktivist-activity/pro-isis-hacking-group-ccta-continues-campaign-of-hacking-facebook-accounts/) (accessed May 05, 2018).

claim to be equipped with several thousand OSN accounts.[143] The accounts accumulated by these groups are considered as a supply that can be tapped at any time by online jihadi supporters who are experiencing difficulties in creating new OSN profiles.

Through these simple means jihadists hope to increase their presence and reestablish their strength on OSNs. Whether such strategies are successful or not can be a decisive factor and shape the future of jihadists' online activities and messaging strategies.

Conclusion and outlook

The purpose of this chapter was to explain how jihadi movements try to balance their dual interest of maintaining a presence on the Internet and OSNs while at the same time remaining anonymous when operating online. The preceding discussion contributes to our understanding of jihadists' media use by adding an in-depth analysis of the changes in and the current state of the inner-jihadist debate as well as the steps taken to improve their privacy skills and mitigate the risk of being online.

Building upon previous research on jihadists media use, it has been shown how, from the early 1990s, jihadi groups shifted their strategic focus to the online sphere and became dependent on new communication technologies for strategic and organizational purposes. Their dependency on these new online communication technologies has pushed them to find new and innovative methods, to learn about the latest technological trends, and finally adapt to the constantly changing political, social, and media environments.

However, the increase in jihadists' use of new online communication is essentially a double-edged sword, as it provides their adversaries with a significant amount of sensitive data. Jihadi groups have become increasingly aware of these new threats online and are taking the issue of operational security very seriously. To be one step ahead of intelligence agencies, they try to stay up-to-date about the latest trends and employ a variety of different measures to conceal their online activities.

At the same time, jihadists fear that relying on privacy-enhancing tools may end up hurting their overall media strategy, as withdrawing to safe and encrypted platforms often goes along with a limited audience reach. To maintain an online presence on OSNs, jihadists have urged their supporters to return to the biggest ones – Twitter and Facebook – and have used several technologies to (re)create accounts that had been taken down.

---

143 The Middle East Media Research Institute, Response to Twitter's Crackdown.

It is clear that for jihadi movements such as IS and Al-Qaeda, the opportunities provided by the Internet have become indispensable strategic assets. Going back to old recruitment patterns and means of communication seems impossible. It is therefore likely that the current cat-and-mouse game between governments and jihadi groups, in which governments constantly try to increase their reach and the data collected while jihadi movements at the same time attempt to enhance their technical skills and find new methods and strategies to avoid government scrutiny, will continue in the years to come.

Despite all of the increasing discussions and efforts taken to protect their online activities, jihadists are still convinced that when operating online, there is no strategy or tool that can absolutely guarantee online privacy. Unsurprisingly, the case of Osama Bin Laden is often mentioned in this context.[144] The documents found in his hiding place in Abbottabad, Pakistan, reveal the vigilant counter-surveillance measures he applied and how he abstained from any communication via the Internet or phones. Instead, Bin Laden exclusively relied on communication via courier-delivered letters.[145] After facing reversals on the battlefield and seeing some of their leaders targeted, IS took similar steps to reduce the online trail of their fighters. According to a leaked internal memo distributed in May 2017, IS prohibited all of its fighters from using social media, due to the threat of data leakage. Any violation of this new policy is threatened with punishment.[146] Such documents show that that jihadists' trust in online privacy-enhancing technologies is not absolute. The bigger the risk or, the more important the individual for the group, the more likely it is that he will refrain from using online communication, instead depending on couriers or physical messages that cannot be replicated, are difficult to trace, and are immediately destroyed after delivery.

With more and more high-ranking commanders and fighters keeping a low profile online, encouraging online supporters – many of which are only loosely affiliated to Al-Qaeda and IS – to engage in the media jihad has become essential for and given priority in their current online strategy. Mobilizing these dispersed and decentralized networks of media mujāhidīn and instructing them on how to avoid scrutiny when operating online is, therefore, one of the central issues that will decide about the future trajectory of jihadist movements and the durability of their media engagement.

144　See for example: *Al-Risalah* 4th edition, pp. 42f.
145　Sinai, Terrorists' counter-surveillance, p. 205.
146　The Middle East Media Research Institute, ISIS Forbids Its Fighters To Use Social Media, in *MEMRI Cyber and Jihad Lab*, May 22, 2017 (http://cjlab.memri.org/lab-projects/tracking-jihadi-terrorist-use-of-social-media/isis-forbids-its-fighters-to-use-social-media/) (accessed May 05, 2018).

Contributors

Ali Fisher

Data Analyst, Big Data and Network Analysis, Human Cognition. Recent Publications:

Ali Fisher, *Collaborative Public Diplomacy: How Transnational Networks Influenced American Studies in Europe*, Palgrave Macmillan, 2013. ISBN13: 978-0230338968.

R.S. Zaharna, Amelia Arsenault, Ali Fisher, *Relational, Networked and Collaborative Approaches to Public Diplomacy: The Connective Mindshift*, (Routledge Studies in Global Information, Politics and Society) 2013. ISBN-13: 978-0415636070.

Ali Fisher, "Swarmcast: How jihadist networks maintain a persistent online presence." *Perspectives on terrorism* 9.3 (2015).

Jamie Bartlett and Ali Fisher, "How to beat the media mujahideen", *DEMOS Quarterly*, Issue #5, Winter 2014/15.

Unmasking the Arzeshi, "Iran's Conservative Cyber-Activists and the 2013 Presidential Election", *Small Media* (2014).

Marie Gillespie et al., "Understanding the Changing Cultural Value of the BBC World Service and the British Council", Open University Cultural Value Project, July 2014.

Fisher, Ali; Prucha, Nico (2014, August): "The Call-up: The Roots of a Resilient and Persistent Jihadist Presence on Twitter". *CTX*, 4(3), 73 88.

Ali Fisher, 'A Network Perspective on Public Diplomacy in Europe: EUNIC', in Mai'a K. Davis Cross and Jan Melissen (eds.) European Public Diplomacy: Soft Power at Work (2013).

Ali Fisher and Nico Prucha, 'Tweeting for the Caliphate: Twitter as the New Frontier for Jihadist Propaganda', *CTC Sentinel*, June 2013.

Clemens Holzgruber

Studied Political Science at the University of Vienna and holds an MA in Religious Studies/Islamic Studies from the Radboud University, Nijmegen. He is currently a doctoral researcher at the Berlin Graduate School Muslim Cultures and Societies, Freie Universität Berlin, where he investigates fault lines and disputes within Jihadi-Salafism.

Rüdiger Lohlker

Professor for Islamic Studies, University of Vienna. Recent Publications:

Lohlker, Rüdiger: Die Salafisten. *Aufstand der Frommen, Saudi-Arabien und Gewalt,* München 2017 (Salafists: Revolt of the Pious, Saudi-Arabia, and Violence).

Lohlker, Rüdiger: Islambilder im Wandel, in *Österreich: Geschichte, Literatur, Geographie (ÖGL)* 1 (2018), pp. 57–68 (Changing views of Islam).

Lohlker, Rüdiger: Representation with/out Representation: Saudia Arabia as a hidden face of globalization, in *Interdisciplinary Journal for Religion and Transformation in Contemporary Society – J-RaT* 7 (2018) (i. pr.).

Lohlker, Rüdiger: Islam: Law and Violence (and Non-Violence), in Wolfgang Palaver/ Richard Schenk (eds.), *Mimetic Theory and World Religions*, East Lansing, MI: Michigan State University Press 2018, pp. 413–426.

Nico Prucha

Researcher Jihadism, esp., Online Jihadism; teaching at the University of Vienna. Recent Publications:

Prucha, Nico & Fisher, Ali: *The New Netwar: Countering Extremism Online*, Policy Exchange, September 2017.

Prucha, Nico: Tales from the Crypt – Jihadi Martyr Narratives for Online Recruitment, in Meir Hatina and Meir Litvak (eds.): *Martyrdom and Sacrifice in Islam: Theological, Political and Social Contexts*, I.B. Tauris: London, New York, 2017.

Prucha, Nico: IS and the Jihadist Information Highway – Projecting Influence and Religious Identity via Telegram, in *Perspectives on Terrorism*, Vol. 10, No. 6 (2016).

Index

'Abd al-Majiid, 'Abd al-Maajid   118f.
Abdel Haleem, Muhammad A.S.   91
Abdel Wadud, Abu Musab   31
'Abid, Makki Mahmud   139
Abu 'Ali   77f.
Abu-Hamdeh, Tamara   37
Abu Yaseer/Abu Yasir   76, 100
Ahmad, Aisha   14
Akhgar, Babak   182
al-Adm, Abu 'Ubayda 'Abdullah   164, 179
al-'Adnani, Abu Muhammad   77–81, 104f., 112f., 123f., 134f., 139
al-Almani, Abu Talha   117
al-Almani, Abu 'Umar   88
al-Amin, Hazim   125
al-'Asalī, Bassām   40
al-Assad   80, 85
al-'Ayerī, Yūsuf   40
al-Azdi, Abu 'l-Hasan   131
al-Baghdadi, Abu Bakr   59, 75, 77, 85f., 89, 96–98, 104f., 118f., 124
al-Bahhar, Abu Ziyyad   83
al-Bahraini, Abu Bara'   114
al-Bahrayni, Abu Dharr   114
al-Bin'alī, Turkī bin Mubārak   38
al-Bukhari   121, 137
al-dhubbah, Amir   122
al-Hanafī, Abū al-Hasan   37
al-'Irāqī, Abū Khattāb   34
al-Khattabi, 'Abd-el-Krim   17
al-Kosovi, Abu 'Abdallah   95f., 98, 114
al-Kurdi   137
al-Lahhām, Ahmad Bek   40
al-Libi, Abu 'l-Layth   137

al-Libi, Abu Yahya   137
al-Lubnānī, Abū Hafs   37
al-Makki, Abu Gharib   75
al-Maliki   80, 104, 125–127, 132, 139
al-Maliki, Nuri   102, 123, 129
al-Maqdisi, Abu Muhammad   75, 85, 107
al-Muqrin, 'Abd al-'Aziz   11
al-Nasa'i   110
al-Qassām, 'Izz al-dīn   37
Al-Rasheed, Madawi   126
al-Sab'awwi, Muhammad   80
al-Sabi'i, Abu Yusuf   116
Al Sa'du   116
al-Shanqiti, Abu 'l-Mundhar   108
al-Shurbshi, Osama   137
al-Suri, Abu Mus'ab   15, 130f.
al-Swaydawi, Abu Muhannad   123
al-Zarqawi, Abu Mus'ab   78f., 93, 96, 103, 122f., 125
al-Zawahiri, Ayman   85, 89f., 92
'Ali   133
Alkhouri, Laith   174
Alsheech, Eli   137
Aly, Anne   157
Arberry, A. J.   164
Ariev, Kyai Haji Hodri   117
Armstrong, Jack   125
Arquilla, John   10f., 89
Augstein, Josef   41
Awan, Imran   158
'Azzam, Abdallah   46, 94, 115, 137

Baran, Paul   147
Barr, Nathaniel   22

Berg, Nick   122
Bin 'Abd al-Latif Al Shaykh, Muhammad   112
Bin 'Abdallāh, 'Abdallāh   36
Bin al-Ashraf, Ka'b   73
Bin al-Walīd, Khālid   40
Bin Ibrahim, Muhammad   112
Bin Laden, Osama   48, 117, 136f., 191
Bin Muhammad, Abd al-'Aziz (Abu Osama al-Iraqi)   138
Bin Salul, 'Abdallah b. Ubay   116f.
Bin'alī   38
Bloom, Mia   185
Bosco, Francesca   182
Bouyeri, Muhammed   73f., 98
Brantly, Aaron   159
Breivik, Anders   16
Bunt, Gary R.   161
Bunzel, Cole   85f., 89

Callimachi, Rukmini   21
Castner, Brian   13
Castro, Fidel   17
Che Guevara, Ernesto   17
Chen, Thomas   157
Chivers, C. J.   23
Chouka, Mounir   130
Cigar, Norman   11
Cockburn, Andrew   94, 113
Conway, Maura   25, 58
Coulibaly, Amedy   75
Curtis, Alex   12, 16
Cuspert, Denis   117

Danzig, Richard   38
Davis, Mike   41
De Landa, Manuel   7
Dhu l-Bijadayn, 'Abdallāh   37f.

Er, Mevliyar   17
Eriksson, Johan   169
Ezzeldeen, Khalil   86

Fisher, Ali   8, 10f., 43f., 54f., 57–59, 62, 65, 86, 113, 143, 162, 193
Flitner, Michael   17

Forrest, Conner   178

Garoud, Alberto Bayo   17
Gartenstein-Ross, Daveed   22
Giacomella, Giampiero   169
Godin, Jake   18
Griffin, Andrew   184

Hackett, Robert   166
Hallaq, Wael   73
Halopeau, Bruno   182
Hart, Liddell   26f.
Hebdo, Charlie   75
Hegghammer, Thomas   53, 112, 160
Henry, Basil   26
Hinckle, Warren   16
Holitscher, Arthur   20
Holtmann, Philip   73, 130, 163
Holzgruber, Clemens   8, 38, 157, 193
Horgan, John   185

Ibn 'Abbas   115
Ibn al-Qayyim   110
Ibn Faris   115
Ibn Hazm   76
Ibn Kathir   138f.
Ibn Maslama   73
Ibn Taymiyya   47, 72f., 75f., 109, 116
Imam al-Sam'ani   76, 129
Ingram, Haroro J.   32, 46, 50

Jarvis, Lee   52, 157
Just, Rainer   16

Kahane, Meir   15
Kākhiyā, Tāriq Ismā'īl   36
Kassim, Rachid   21
Kassirer, Alex   174
Kippenberg, Hans G.   8
Klausen, Jytte   53, 184
Kouachi, Cherif   75
Kouachi, Said   75

Lenin, Vladimir I.   10
Lohlker, Rüdiger   7–9, 20, 22, 31, 37f., 66, 72, 160, 194

Index

Looney, Sean 25

Macdonald, Stuart 157
Mahmud, Muhammad 88
Manzoni, Andrea Zapparoli 11
Meijer, Roel 160
Menkhaus, Ken 158
Merabet, Ahmad 75
Metzger, Tom 12, 16
Mohammed, Khalid Sheikh 12
Moreng, Bridget 21f.
Muhammad 25, 73–75, 83, 90, 93, 97, 106, 109, 112, 115–117, 121, 129, 131, 135, 138
Muhaxheri, Lavdrim 84, 95, 98
Murdock, Jason 15

Naim, Bahrum 183f.
Nance, Malcolm W. 12
Normark, Magnus 159, 162
Nusayr, El Sayyid 15

Pantucci, Raffaello 12
Parker, Jodie 25, 58, 66
Parry, Richard 20
Passeri, Paolo 11
Pfahl-Traughber, Armin 16
Prucha, Nico 8, 10, 25, 43, 45, 54f., 57–59, 62, 65, 80, 86–88, 91, 93–95, 97, 105, 113, 117, 143, 162, 185f., 194
Pye, Oliver 17

Radjawali, Irendra 17
Ranstorp, Magnus 53, 159, 162, 169
Raton, Boca 12
Reader, Ian 38, 47, 71
Ronfeldt, David 10f., 89
Rudner, Martin 158
Russon, Mary Ann 15

Sageman, Marc 12
Scahill, Jeremy 113
Scarborough, Rowan 166
Schor, Gabriel Ramin 16
Seidensticker, Tilmann 8
Serr, Marcel 14
Shaghir, Mash'al Khalif 121f.
Sinai, Joshua 14, 159, 191
Sky, Emma 94
Snowden, Edward 165f., 170, 172
Soeriaatmadja, Wahyudi 183
Soriano, Manuel R. Torres 158, 167
Sosnow, R. 165, 171
Stalinsky, Steven 165, 171
Staniforth, Andrew 182
Steinberg, Guido 88, 97
Stenersen, Anne 15–17
Stewart, Frank 126

Teich, Sarah 9
Tiflati, Hicham 185
Trottier, Daniel 158
Turki, Salman 78, 84, 114, 117f.

Van Gogh, Theo 73–75, 97f.
Van Vlierden, Guy 21
Veilleux-Lepage, Yannick 162

Wagemakers, Joas 85
Wahid, Kyai Haji Abdurrahman 117
Waters, Nick 18
Weimann, Gabriel 157f., 161
Winter, Charlie 46, 58, 63f., 66, 164

Yusef, Ramzi 15

Zelin, Aron Y. 157, 161